The Making of 1916

*Studies in the
History of the Rising*

The Making of 1916

*Studies in the
History of the
Rising*

Edited by
Kevin B. Nowlan, M.A., Ph.D. (Cantab.)

1969
STATIONERY OFFICE
DUBLIN

Printed in Ireland by
Hely Thom Limited, Dublin

Contents

Contents

Foreword

This collection of essays was commissioned by Coiste Chuimhneacháin 1916. The Committee, under the chairmanship of the then Taoiseach, Seán F. Lemass, T.D., planned and organized the commemoration in 1966 of the fiftieth anniversary of the Rising of Easter Week 1916. The essays are based on published material including, in some instances, works dealing with the Rising which were issued during 1966–68.

It is appropriate that the collection should appear in print at the time when the fiftieth anniversary of the inaugural meeting of the First Dáil Éireann is being commemorated. At that historic meeting, held on the 21st January 1919, the assembled deputies confirmed the establishment of the Irish Republic with a formal Declaration of Independence in these terms:

'Whereas the Irish people is by right a free people:

'And Whereas for seven hundred years the Irish people has never ceased to repudiate and has repeatedly protested in arms against foreign usurpation:

'And Whereas English rule in this country is, and always has been, based upon force and fraud and maintained by military occupation against the declared will of the people:

'And Whereas the Irish Republic was proclaimed in Dublin on Easter Monday, 1916, by the Irish Republican Army acting on behalf of the Irish people:

'And Whereas the Irish people is resolved to secure and maintain its complete independence in order to promote the common weal, to re-establish justice, to provide for future defence, to ensure peace at home and good will with all nations, and to constitute a national policy based upon the people's will, with equal right and equal opportunity for every citizen:

'And Whereas at the threshold of a new era in history the Irish electorate has in the General Election of December, 1918,

Foreword

seized the first occasion to declare by an overwhelming majority its firm allegiance to the Irish Republic:

'Now, therefore, we, the elected Representatives of the ancient Irish people in National Parliament assembled, do, in the name of the Irish nation, ratify the establishment of the Irish Republic and pledge ourselves and our people to make this declaration effective by every means at our command:

'We ordain that the elected Representatives of the Irish people alone have power to make laws binding on the people of Ireland, and that the Irish Parliament is the only Parliament to which that people will give its allegiance:

'We solemnly declare foreign government in Ireland to be an invasion of our national right which we will never tolerate, and we demand the evacuation of our country by the English Garrison:

'We claim for our national independence the recognition and support of every free nation in the world, and we proclaim that independence to be a condition precedent to international peace hereafter:

'In the name of the Irish people we humbly commit our destiny to Almighty God Who gave our fathers the courage and determination to persevere through long centuries of a ruthless tyranny, and strong in the justice of the cause which they have handed down to us, we ask His Divine blessing on this the last stage of the struggle we have pledged ourselves to carry through to Freedom.'

These essays are presented as a series of studies in some depth of certain central aspects of that movement in Irish nationalism which resulted in the Rising of 1916. It is hoped that the work will encourage historians to advance still further the study of a phase in Ireland's history which has influenced constitutional and political developments in lands far from the shores of Ireland.

January, 1969.

Introduction

IRISH nationalism has had a long and complicated history. Geography and the pattern of early settlement played their part. It was shaped, too, by the land confiscations and plantations of the sixteenth and seventeenth centuries, by religious persecution and by the survival, in however ill-defined a way, of a certain sense of cultural individuality. Traditionally the political demand of the discontented in Ireland had been, up to the latter part of the eighteenth century, for the restoration of the liberties and rights of the Kingdom of Ireland under the British Crown. The social and religious aims were civil equality and freedom of confession. This tradition influenced much of the later thinking of constitutional nationalists.

The French Revolution, however, brought a new factor into Irish political life: republican separatism, involving the rejection of a constitutional link with Great Britain. It was not to take any deep roots in Ireland in the seventeen-nineties, but was to be rediscovered in the mid-nineteenth century by men such as John Mitchel, Fintan Lalor and, after them, the early Fenians. Though republicanism was to remain very much a minority factor for a half-century and more after 1848, it was never to be quite forgotten; and as the New Departure in 1879 was to show, the distinction between the revolutionary and the constitutional phases in Irish nationalism should not be too finely drawn.

The disastrous outcome of the risings of 1798 and 1803 brought the United Irishmen as an organisation to an end. Throughout the nineteenth century, popular political leaders sought not a republic but a lesser measure of political and legislative autonomy. They sought, too, reforms which would ease the economic and

ix

Introduction

social grievances of the ordinary people. Daniel O'Connell and his great mass movements, in demanding Catholic rights and the restoration of a reformed Irish parliament, had shown for the first time how the people of the countryside could be organised as a disciplined political force. The lesson O'Connell taught was understood by many liberals and democrats in Britain and on the continent. Later the tenant-right movement of the eighteen-fifties, again a constitutional agitation, drew attention to the problems, especially that of insecurity, of the small farmers. Still in the constitutional tradition, the Home Rule Party of the eighteen-eighties, under Parnell, succeeded in winning strong and sustained popular support for its programme of political autonomy and land reform.

The spread of the Fenian movement in America, in the wake of the post-Famine emigration, and the considerable response to the Irish Republican Brotherhood in Ireland, in the eighteen-fifties and sixties, were reminders that separatism was a political belief which could secure the loyalty of a significant minority of Irishmen. It is fair to say, however, that by the eighteen-nineties the Irish national movement, both in its constitutional and its revolutionary wings, had lost much of its earlier vigour and colour. The bitter disputes which followed the fall of Parnell had shattered the unity of the Parliamentary Party and by the late nineteenth century, too, the possibility of a fruitful union between the revolutionary and the constitutional tradition had been lost. There was no successor to the New Departure and within the republican camp there was also a drying up of the sources. The I.R.B. was almost defunct, while the failure of 1867 and the interminable disputes among the American Fenians helped to weaken the ardour of the surviving separatists in Ireland.

With the new century came important changes in the I.R.B. The Organisation attracted to its ranks a number of young men, many of them deeply influenced by the forces of cultural as well

Introduction

as of strictly political nationalism. The return from the United States, in 1907, of the veteran Fenian, Tom Clarke, further strengthened the elements of reform within the I.R.B. and by 1912 the radicals had largely secured control of the Brotherhood.

The modest revival within the I.R.B. was but one symptom of a change which was taking place in the character of Irish nationalism at the turn of the century. Social, educational and economic developments, involving a fuller participation in the life of the Victorian age, the continued decline of the Irish language and emigration to the English-speaking countries—all helped to bring the Irish people more effectively than ever before into contact with English standards and customs. Not surprisingly, there were men and women who were troubled by these developments and who saw in a cultural nationalism an answer to what they regarded as the threat of Anglicisation. Moreover, many among them found little that was attractive in the party politics of their day.

The foundation of the Gaelic Athletic Association in 1884 and the foundation of the Gaelic League in 1893 illustrate the operation of these new forces in Irish nationalism. Other factors were the Anglo-Irish literary revival and the growing preoccupation with the need for some measure of industrial and agricultural self-sufficiency. One might see, too, in the rise of Irish socialist and labour movements, in the activities of Connolly and Larkin, yet another expression of dissatisfaction with the existing character of Irish society. 'Irish-Ireland' was a complex of interests which were sometimes in conflict with one another, but they all helped to give a new and exciting quality to Irish political and intellectual life at the beginning of the twentieth century.

These developments are of considerable importance for an understanding of the political and cultural changes in Ireland between the eighteen-eighties and the outbreak of the First World War. The remarkable thing about the eighteen-nineties

Introduction

was not so much the survival of the divided Irish Party and its subsequent brittle reunification under John Redmond's leadership, as the appearance of a number of new, often apparently marginal organisations. They helped, in the long-term, to transform the Irish nationalist movement almost completely.

It would, however, be wrong to overestimate the immediate political impact of cultural nationalism and of the radical political groups. The Gaelic League sought to avoid political entanglements, while Sinn Féin, on the political side, lost rather than gained support in the years before 1914. Though the voice of dissent was there, its influence remained limited. However prosaic it might have appeared, the Irish Party was still the major political force outside the areas of Unionist influence. The Parliament Act of 1911 had opened the way for the successful passage of the third Home Rule Bill and the supporters of the Party had before them the prospect of seeing an Irish Parliament meet in Dublin for the first time since 1800.

On the eve of the World War, then, Ireland seemed destined to enjoy, at most, a limited measure of self-government within the constitutional structure of the United Kingdom. Even the prospect of this measure of political autonomy was weakened by the unresolved problem of the relations between the north-eastern counties and the rest of the country. The outbreak of war saw the postponement by an embarrassed British Government of any immediate constitutional changes in Ireland, but the war itself was to lead to even greater changes in Anglo-Irish relations than could have been anticipated in 1914.

The beginning of hostilities in Europe was quickly followed by a decision of the Supreme Council of the I.R.B. that preparations should be made for a rising to take place as soon as possible and certainly before the end of the war. In practice, the planning of the Rising was very much the work of a small group of brave and dedicated men—the members of what became the Provisional Government of the Republic in 1916. The Rising, the executions

Introduction

of the leaders, the imprisonments, and the threat of the extension
of conscription to Ireland were among the factors which contributed to the victory of the separatist republicans over the
Parliamentary Party in the General Election of 1918. That
victory, in turn, made possible the First Dáil which met for the
first time on 21 January 1919.

The character of future Anglo-Irish relations remained
dangerously uncertain in 1919. But it is now clear that the Home
Rule solution had by then become almost irrelevant to the
issue of those relations. The First Dáil and the ratification by it
of the establishment of the Republic were measures of the change
that had taken place since Easter Week. But the failure to resolve
the Ulster Question in the years that followed was a sobering
reminder of the obstacles barring the way to the effective political
unity of Ireland.

KEVIN B. NOWLAN.

The Gaelic Cultural Movements
and the New Nationalism

by
BRIAN Ó CUÍV

(I)

The Gaelic Cultural Movements
and the New Nationalism

IN a consideration of the Irish language in relation to politics
and nationalism two events in particular may well be conjoined.
On 17 June 1541 an Irish parliament met in Dublin and granted
the style of 'King of Ireland' to King Henry VIII of England.
The Lord-Deputy, Sentleger, in describing to the King the
meeting of the Lords wrote that the Bill 'ons being redde, and
declared to them, in Irisshe, all the hoole Howse moste willinglye
and joyouslye condissendid and agreid to the same'.[1] On 21
January 1919 when representatives of the Irish people, chosen in
the General Election of the previous December, met in the first
session of Dáil Éireann in the Dublin Mansion House, the
proceedings were largely conducted in Irish. It is one of the
anomalies of Irish history that these two assemblies, so different
in their purpose and separated in time by nigh on four hundred
years during which the Irish language had declined to such an
extent that it was in danger of extinction, should be linked by
the formal use of Irish in them both. For whereas in the first
instance the use of Irish was a linguistic necessity and had no
political or nationalistic overtones, in the second—since Irish was
not the native language of more than a few of those present—it
was a deliberate demonstration on the part of the conveners and
organisers of Dáil Éireann, supported by those taking part, of the
sense of separateness from England which had become so strong
in the preceding years.

It is doubtful if ever since Tudor times Irish had been the

1

official language of parliament, for the growth of the Protestant Ascendancy in the seventeenth century had brought the dominant party more and more within the English cultural sphere, and from that time we can date the serious decline of the language. To be sure, a Provost of Trinity College, Robert Huntingdon, anticipating Davis by a century and a half and Hyde by two centuries, had written:

> 'methinks the Nation should make their language triumphant also, and the rather, because their are Laws against it. For why should a free people retain any marks of Slavery'.[2]

That was in 1686, but there was little freedom for Irish-speaking Ireland after the overthrow of the Stuart line, and the colonial government had no time for Irish. Moreover we may be sure that had O'Connell achieved the Repeal of the Union his parliament would have tended to follow the 'Mother of Parliaments' in the use of the English tongue, for did he not declare:

> 'although the Irish language is connected with many recollections that twine around the hearts of Irishmen, yet the superior utility of the English tongue, as the medium of all modern communication, is so great, that I can witness without a sigh the gradual disuse of the Irish'.[3]

The utilitarian attitude among Irishmen of position was not new. As far back as 1627 Conell Ma Geoghagan, an Irish historian, had written of his fellow-chroniclers:

> 'because they cannot enjoy that respect and gaine by their said profession as heretofore they and theire auncestors receaved they set naught by the said knowledg, neglect their Bookes, and choose rather to put their children to learne English than their own native Language'.[4]

He could not know that a new Ireland, almost three centuries away, would produce another historian who would dedicate his energies to undoing the cultural and political conquest of his country and who, reversing the process of the seventeenth century, would put his children to learning Irish. He could not know that when the name of Conell Ma Geoghagan would be familiar to none but a few scholars that of Eoin MacNeill would have an honored place in our history books as a founder of an organisation which helped to save Ireland from the flowing tide of Anglicisation and out of which there came, in the fullness of time, one of the main driving forces for the political revolution.

How strange, to-day, seems the comment in *The Times,* of London, on the proposal of the Gaelic Union in 1882 to found a journal devoted to the furtherance of the Gaelic movement:

'In deprecating the artificial cultivation of Irish as the national language, we are actuated by no dread or jealousy of its power to raise up fresh obstacles to political amalgamation. Irishmen, as we have had occasion at other times to observe, inclosed within the prison of a tongue unintelligible outside, would have much less strength to agitate against the British connexion than when, as now, the agitators discourse in phrases half the world can interpret. Irish partnership in the English language has supplied Nationalists and Home Rulers and Land Leaguers and Fenians with nine-tenths of their political leverage'.[5]

No doubt there was logic in *The Times* article; yet how wide of the mark did it prove to be. The seed sown by Davis in his few short years in public life was to bear fruit in full measure in the following decades. Many of those whom the people of Ireland chose as their representatives in 1918 were competent Irish speakers, but unlike O'Connell few of them were 'native-speakers'. They had come into the political arena through the by-roads of various cultural movements, and the use of Irish as an official language in Dáil Éireann was for them by implication a declaration of faith in the 'revival' and an earnest of the place of Irish as the first language in the new state whose foundations were then being laid.

We may wonder what it was which had so conditioned Irish public opinion that in the second decade of the twentieth century the Irish language had become important as one of the 'externals' or insignia of nationhood. The answer to this is to be found, to a large extent, in the history of the Gaelic League which Hyde and MacNeill established in 1893, and in the careers of those most closely associated with it.

The Gaelic League towers so far above other Gaelic cultural movements that some people forget that there were others. In fact there were several factors which contributed in advance to the success of the Gaelic League, and it may be well to mention the most important of these here.

First of all we note the development, outside of a purely Gaelic *milieu*, of an interest in Ireland's cultural heritage, especially in relation to the Irish language, and the efforts made by learned bodies to stimulate this interest. We can trace this back to the eighteenth century both in Dublin and Belfast. It is important, if we are to understand the union of men of all creeds and diverse origins in the Gaelic League, that we bear in mind the part played by Anglo-Irish and Protestant elements in those earlier movements.

Secondly we note the recognition by scholars of standing in Europe and at home of the importance of Irish in the comparative study of the Indo-European languages, literatures and traditions. This made Irish a subject of academic importance and strengthened the hand of the advocates of introducing it into the educational system, first of all those in the Society for the Preservation of the Irish Language and later the more active body in the Gaelic League.

Thirdly we note the awakening of at least some people to a

realisation that language is to be associated with nationhood, and that, with the rapid decline in the use of Irish as a vernacular, something invaluable for the nation was in danger of being lost forever. It is here that so much is owed to Davis's fervent exposition of this theme. In this connection it may be worth adding that, if John Devoy was accurate in his recollection and assessment in old age of his Fenian colleagues, Davis's teaching was not lost on the Fenians, for Devoy wrote:

'Had the Fenian movement succeeded . . . it would have taken prompt and effective measures to restore the language',

and again

'the intention to restore the language was as strong among the Fenians as that of establishing an Irish Republic'.[6]

Certainly there were among the Fenians many, such as O'Donovan Rossa, who were native Irish speakers. Indeed we may recall that one of these, Tadhg Ó Murchadha, a tailor from Macroom who was working in Cork city in 1865, gave an account in Irish many years later of some of his recollections of the events of 1865–7, and that Terence MacSwiney helped in writing down this account and preparing it for publication at a time when he himself was busily engaged in organizing the Irish Volunteers in Cork.[7] It is possible that the Irish-speaking Fenians might have succeeded in influencing the leaders in favour of the Irish language, but it is far from certain that any effective steps to restore Irish would have been taken by a Fenian government.

Within the quarter century after O'Connell's death Irish had in fact declined abnormally as a spoken language. Among the causes, which were well known, were the Great Famine and consequent emigration, the effects of the National School system, the economic advantage of knowing English and the absence of any adequate advocacy of bilingualism—what An tAthair Peadar Ua Laoghaire so aptly described as *dhá arm aigne*. In the circumstances the remedies were less obvious, but there were men who set out to find them. It was some of these who founded the Society for the Preservation of the Irish Language in 1877. Like the later Gaelic League it was non-political and non-sectarian, and Catholics and Protestants worked well together in it. Among its early members were Dr. MacHale, Archbishop of Tuam, Dr. Croke, Archbishop of Cashel, Dr. Walsh, President of St. Patrick's College, Maynooth, who was to live to see and approve of the Sinn Féin election victory of 1918, and Isaac Butt, the parliamentary leader. No longer was Irish to be a matter of total indifference in orthodox political circles, and as a matter of fact one of the first victories for the language was won when The O'Conor Don, an Irish Party Member of Parliament, succeeded in having Irish, under the guise of the name 'Celtic', admitted as a subject under the Intermediate Board of Education. Nevertheless there was a certain sensitivity about the danger of the Society's being branded as nationalistic. In 1882, during the course of a three-day congress to consider the position of Irish as a vernacular, the Secretary concluded an address by saying:

'Let our people look to it. Let them compel some regard for their language, which, sadly neglected, still lingers amongst us, telling us more forcibly than ever, as it steadily disappears, that, while we yet may boast that proud distinction of a nation, a living language, if we lose it, we shall indeed have lost one of the grandest memorials of our race'.[8]

A mild enough appeal, one might think. Yet it drew from Michael Cusack, who is said to have been a member of the I.R.B. and who was to found a few years later the G.A.A. which would prove an even more powerful force in inculcating in

6

Irishmen a spirit of manliness in face of the pervading English influence, the criticism that the Secretary's 'concluding remark was perhaps open to misconstruction in the eyes of some, as having a political tendency, and he considered it injudicious'.[9]

The Preservation Society and the Gaelic Union, which was an off-shoot of it, lacked the dynamism necessary to convert the adult population to the gospel of an 'Irish Ireland'. Besides, during the '80s people were more seriously engaged in the Land War and more interested in the latest moves in the fight for Home Rule. Then came the Parnell split, the death of the 'Chief', and the squabbles among the members of the Parliamentary Party which to onlookers seemed so degrading. It was at this time, when political activity was at a low ebb, that the call went out for decisive action on the cultural front. In connection with this call two men played a central rôle—Douglas Hyde and Eoin MacNeill.

Hyde, who knew Irish from his childhood days in Roscommon, had been connected for many years with the Society for the Preservation of the Irish Language and with the Gaelic Union. He had equipped himself with a scholarly knowledge of the earlier language and especially of Irish literature. Through his acquaintance with John O'Leary, the Fenian, who had settled in Ireland in 1885 and who was giving his support to nationalist and Irish cultural movements of the time, he was associated with a group of litterateurs writing in English who were to play a significant part in the shaping of the resurgent Ireland. He willingly gave his help to Yeats and others of this group who were turning to Irish source-material for inspiration. This trend among writers in English was due in no small measure to the writings on Irish literature and history by O'Curry, O'Donovan, Stokes and other scholars, which had opened new cultural vistas for those who did not know the language, and which had added to the inspiration which was drawn from the writers of the Young Ireland movement of the '40s. One result was the semiromantic patriotism which was engendered through literary writings in English on Irish or 'Celtic' themes. Fundamental in this was the concept of national sovereignty which, in a strange survival of an ancient tradition, had been represented allegorically in earlier Irish literature as a woman who generally bore the name most commonly used for the country, *Éire*, but who was sometimes referred to in traditional fashion as *Banbha* or *Fódhla* or, later on, by such poetic names as *Róisín Dubh* and *Caitlín Ní hUallacháin*. There can be little doubt that the notion of Ireland as a woman in whose service Irishmen might gladly sacrifice themselves had considerable influence in the political development of our people. It is a concept which was carried over from Irish into English through which it reached a wider public, notably by means of Yeats's play 'Cathleen Ni Houlihan'. Yeats had good reason for asking in after years:

> 'Did that play of mine send out
> Certain men the English shot?'

Another product of the historico-literary movement was the cult of an ideal of heroism which was pagan in origin, centred, as it was, around Cú Chulainn. This cult and the idea that national redemption might lie in a sacrifice of life were to be important in the following years.

Despite some violent sentiments expressed by Hyde in Irish verse when he was a young student, it is unlikely that he seriously entertained any thought of a sacrifice in blood. His passionate interest was in the rich heritage of folk-tradition which still survived in the districts where Irish was spoken, and he dreaded the time when this heritage would be lost forever. He saw that in the Ireland of his day interest was slight in these things which he held dear and in the language in which they found their best expression, and when he referred to these matters in his second book, *Beside the Fire*, which he published in 1890 he did not

mince his words in his condemnation of 'the influential leaders
of the race' from whom, he thought, a lead might have been
expected:

> 'The inaction of the Parliamentarians, though perhaps dimly
> intelligible, appears, to me at least, both short-sighted and
> contradictory, for they are attempting to create a nationality
> with one hand and with the other destroying, or allowing to
> be destroyed, the very thing that would best differentiate and
> define that nationality. It is a making of bricks without straw.
> But the non-Parliamentarian Nationalists, in Ireland at least,
> appear to be thoroughly in harmony with them on this
> point'.[10]

At this time Father O'Growney had already begun the work on
which he was to expend himself during his remaining years in
Ireland, and his advice about learning Irish was being sought by
people who were becoming conscious of the national language.
Among these was a twenty-two year old clerk in the Four
Courts in Dublin, Eoin MacNeill, who became fired with
enthusiasm for the language. In 1891 MacNeill issued in *The
Ecclesiastical Record*[11] an appeal to the clergy to take up the cause
of Irish, for, he said, 'they alone practically can carry out what
the laity can only aspire to, or but weakly and partially effect'.
'The destiny of Ireland in the future, as in the past', he said,
'seems to be that of a teaching nation'. And foreseeing, as a
logical outcome, the successful evangelisation of Britain by Irish
Catholics, he went on to emphasise the importance of the
language as a barrier between different cultures:

> 'We Irish have resisted fusion for seven centuries, with the
> result that we are still a living, energetic, self-reliant nation,
> and as capable of doing a nation's work as on the day that
> Strongbow first landed in Ireland. Fusion was prevented first

by the difference of language and by physical resistance; afterwards by difference of language and religion; latterly by religion alone. Were this last difference removed, as it may yet be, most probably by our own influence, it is a mere illusion to hope that the national character could, without some other defence, withstand the forces of assimilation. Politics will not form such a defence, for politics follow the forces of the time. Physical hostility is not to be dreamt of. Clearly, unless the national character remains to attract the national aspirations and leaven the national life, Ireland must become a mere geographical expression.'

In concluding his article he extended his exhortation to the 'young men of Ireland' to 'strike a good blow for Irish' by speaking it. Those who did not know Irish should, if possible, learn it, and he added 'If we cannot learn Irish, we can at least stand up for it'. The years to come were to prove how much easier it is to stand up for Irish than to learn it. They were also to prove that physical hostility would not only be dreamed of but would become a reality and that MacNeill would play a central part in this strange course of events.

Shortly after MacNeill's appeal was published, another voice was raised in support of Irish. As if to show the injustice of Hyde's condemnation of the parliamentarians for their supposed attitude to Irish, William O'Brien, M.P., addressed the Cork National Society in 1892 and made a convincing case for restoring Irish. Not the least interesting point of his address was the statement that he had put six months spent in jail in Galway to good use in learning to speak Irish. History was to repeat itself in this respect many times in the following fifty years. O'Brien made it clear that in his view the linguistic effort should take second place to the political aim:

'I do not preach any sudden or violent diversion of our

National energies from the channels in which they are now directed, for a National Parliament is the life-giver without which no National interest can flourish, and in whóse heat all fair and seemly accessories of National life are sure to blossom forth again'.[12]

Hyde returned to the attack in November 1892 in his famous presidential address to the Irish National Literary Society when he spoke of 'the necessity for de-Anglicising the Irish Nation'. It is perhaps worth recalling that on this occasion he included games and music in his remarks against what he called 'West-Britonism', and he even urged people to wear Irish clothes. His tribute to the G.A.A. was remarkable:

'I confess that the instantaneous and extraordinary success which attended their efforts when working upon national lines has filled me with more hope for the future of Ireland than everything else put together. I consider the work of the association . . . has done more for Ireland than all the speeches of politicians for the last five years'.[13]

Hyde's appeal for de-Anglicisation, as he himself recalled years later,[14] aroused no echo among the audience. Undaunted, he delivered another address in Cork in the same strain. Then came the fateful meeting on 31 July 1893, at which the Gaelic League was founded. Hyde provided the inspiration, but it was MacNeill who took the initiative and who did much of the work in the early years. One thing on which the founders were agreed was that the organisation, whose proclaimed object was 'to keep the Irish language spoken in Ireland', should be non-political and non-denominational. This was one of its sources of strength, for it enabled it to draw supporters from all quarters, and it continued to do so for twenty fateful years during which there emerged a new Ireland, no longer satisfied with the measured concessions of British legislators but determined to have as of right a degree of independence consistent with its separate and ancient nationhood and willing to take up arms to attain it. There were other forces concerned with cultural, social, economic, industrial and political affairs, which contributed to the new spirit of independence, but the Gaelic League provided a focus where those of divergent views, interests and loyalties could associate.

In later years William O'Brien described the period after Parnell's death as 'years of hellish strife', and it is significant that it was in that time that the Gaelic League put down its roots so well. In the nationwide despondency following the political debacle, the language movement offered an outlet for the energies of those with nationalist inclinations. It already had an attraction for scholars and for the literary folk working through the medium of English, and in due course people in the Irish-speaking areas—who were fundamental to it—became aware of it. So it was that the call issued by Hyde and MacNeill from a room in O'Connell Street in Dublin in 1893 was heard and acted upon without delay, not only in Dublin but throughout the country. It has been said that 'The weakness of the League from the beginning was that it was essentially a townsmen's organization, centralised in Dublin, and never took real root in the Irish-speaking or semi-Irish-speaking districts'.[16] While it is true that in its primary aim of preserving Irish as the everyday language of the Gaeltacht areas it was not successful, it is an undoubted fact that through its activities the League was instrumental in spreading a new consciousness of national distinctiveness throughout the country. It is perhaps worth recalling that in 1908—after fifteen years growth—only 34 of the 599 League branches in existence were in Dublin. The greatest number was in Cork where there were 76, and the next in order were Kerry (52), Donegal (36), Dublin (34), Clare and Galway (each 31), Mayo (25), Antrim (22), and Monaghan, Sligo, Tipperary and Waterford (each 18). There was not a single county in which there was no branch. Moreover branches in Britain provided centres for Irish activities, and allied organisations in America through their personnel maintained a link with bodies sympathetic towards Irish political nationalism.

The earliest lists of members of the League show that bishops, priests, Protestant clergymen, members of Parliament, lawyers, journalists, teachers, students, civil servants, post-office workers, soldiers, policemen, tradesmen and labourers had joined. On the first council, along with Hyde, MacNeill and Father O'Growney, were Father William Hayden of the Society of Jesus, Patrick O'Brien, a printer on the staff of the *Irish Times*, and two men whose political views were not of the orthodox type—Michael Cusack, founder of the G.A.A., and George Sigerson, a medical man of wide interests who had been active in the Society for the Preservation of the Irish Language and who was a founder member of the National Literary Society. Sigerson had taken a keen interest in politics a quarter of a century earlier, and, anticipating Arthur Griffith's abstentionist policy by nearly forty years, had pointed out, as far back as 1868, the futility of Irish representatives going to Westminster and he had advocated the adoption of the tactics pursued so successfully against Austria by the Hungarians.[17] Sigerson's call had gone unheeded and he had turned especially to Irish literature as an expression of his national sentiments. By the time Griffith wrote *The Resurrection of Hungary* in 1904, the Gaelic League was a power to be reckoned with, and in considering the parallel that Hungary offered for Ireland Griffith wrote:

'As Deak and Kossuth realized that language alone cannot make a nation—that no nation can endure deprived of free political institutions—so the language revivalists in Ireland see that the language in itself is not an end but a means to an end'.[18]

Not all the revivalists saw eye-to-eye with Griffith in this view.

The fact that mayors, members of parliament, members of the Hierarchy, and prominent citizens, both Catholic and Protestant, associated themselves with the League from the outset did not guarantee its success. On the contrary, success was due to a small number of devoted workers who voluntarily carried the burden of organisational and secretarial work, addressed meetings, founded branches, taught classes, and did their utmost to encourage all those who showed an interest in the League's activities. These men, led by Hyde and MacNeill, had the enthusiasm of youth and the faith that moves mountains, and it was through their labours that branches were founded in cities and towns and villages throughout the land and classes were started where young people and old sat side by side learning Irish. The activities of the League were manifold. As well as classes, concerts of Irish songs and music and dances were organised. Local festivals, called *feiseanna* or *aeridheachtanna*, were held, and a national festival, *An tOireachtas*, akin to the Welsh *Eisteddfod*, was established in 1897. In the following year the centenary commemorations of the rising of 1798 quickened interest in the League, and even erstwhile critics were forced to concede that a new national spirit was being awakened.

Although the League was non-political, its widespread organisation was to prove important in the spread of new ideas. Its branches were primarily concerned with fostering the Irish language by means of classes and allied activities. But through them many young men and women became aware of something far removed from the material attitude to life so common about them. Even if they did not pursue their linguistic studies too seriously they were liable to be receptive to other ideas which would not be looked on too favourably by the British authorities. Moreover, during the first fifteen years of its existence the League pursued a policy of agitation which drew attention to it and established it as a powerful national force. The fact that the President of the League was a Protestant intellectual and a graduate of the University of Dublin gave the movement a standing which was invaluable. Hyde's friendship with Yeats, Sigerson, Rolleston, George Moore and others of the Anglo-Irish group, carried their support. Members of the Parliamentary Party saw merit in the League's objectives and some of them were wholehearted in their support. Once it became clear that an Irish Ireland was the League's aim and that its leaders really meant business, support came from other quarters, such as from Griffith in *The United Irishman*, Moran in *The Leader*, Ryan in *The Irish Peasant*, and Russell (AE) in *The Irish Homestead*.

The aims of the several nationalist elements of the time were many and varied: to counteract the low-class reading-matter and entertainment which came in steadily from Britain, to inculcate a spirit of manliness and self-reliance in the people of Ireland, to promote their social and financial betterment by co-operative and other means, to root out 'shoneenism', and so on. There was an outpouring of writing of all kinds, both in English and Irish, some of it literary, much of it purely propagandist. It would be a mistake to accept every phrase at its face value as an expression of the real sentiments of its author, for was it not the seemingly far-from-militant Douglas Hyde who wrote:

> Féach na h-airm ar ár ngualain,
> Ní'l aon phíce in ár láimh,
> M'anam d'fheicfí iad go luath linn
> Dá mbéadh Éire ina ngádh![19]

But all the writings contributed in some way to the growth of the new nationalism—the plays in Irish and English, the ballads and rallying-songs, and the journalistic writings in *An Claidheamh Soluis* and in the papers run by Griffith, Moran and the others. In the course of time there came writings with a deeper political significance from men in the Irish movement—Pearse, Mac-Donagh, MacSwiney, and others—but by then the League had succeeded in making Irish an indisputably national issue and not merely the concern of a few cranks.

At times the League appeared to some critics to hold back too much, but on the whole Hyde's judgment was fairly sound and he was by no means slow to engage in controversy with the authorities. Some of the atmosphere of those years can be got from his autobiographical works *Mise agus an Connradh* and *Mo Thurus go Americe* and from other memoirs, such as those of Seán T. Ó Ceallaigh, but the detail must be sought in the contemporary records, and especially in the annual reports, pamphlets, and journals of the League.

At an early stage 'Gaelic Organisers' were put on the road to foster interest in Irish in the Gaeltacht and elsewhere, and these men—Tomás Bán Ó Concheanainn, Fionán Mac Coluim, Peadar Ó hAnnracháin, and many others—did pioneer work. The contacts established by them in the language campaign were to prove useful later on in political and military organisation, but in the early years there was no thought of such developments.

Since the schools seemed to be the strongest single force militating against Irish, the League set out especially to tackle the problem caused by them, and for fifteen years it was constantly fighting on the educational front. The movement which the Society for the Preservation of the Irish Language had spearheaded to have Irish taught was beginning to have some slight effect, but much greater efforts were needed. The League fought not only for an extension of bilingual teaching in the Irish-speaking areas, but also for greater facilities for teaching Irish as a subject in national schools in other areas. It joined issue with the Intermediate Board, and it appealed to secondary school authorities to support its efforts. The concern of the League with the school was well founded, for Davis's dictum 'educate that you may be free' began to have added meaning with the spread of higher education. By an analysis of the 'Intermediate Results' the League showed in 1896 that it was mainly in Irish Christian

Brothers' schools that Irish was taught, and, on the motion of
Eoin MacNeill and An tAthair Peadar Ua Laoghaire, a resolution
was passed:

> 'That we cordially congratulate the Christian Brothers on their
> continued success in the teaching of Irish for the Intermediate
> Examinations, and we regret that their patriotic action has not
> been more generally followed by the other schools and
> colleges'.[20]

This resolution needs little comment. In the course of time Irish
became more general in the other schools, and fine scholars and
patriots came from them, but it is hardly a coincidence that a
high proportion of those engaged in nationalist activities passed
through Christian Brothers' Schools.

Among those learning Irish in Christian Brothers' schools in
Dublin in those early days of the Gaelic League were Patrick
Pearse and Seán T. Ó Ceallaigh. Fate was to bring them together
in the League, in the Irish Volunteers, and in the G.P.O. in 1916.

Ó Ceallaigh, inheritor of a Fenian tradition, started as an
unwilling student of Irish and came to find in the language a
motive force with a considerable potential for political ends. So
it came about that as early as 1902—long before either MacNeill
or Pearse was involved in political activity—Ó Ceallaigh was a
member of the Irish Republican Brotherhood and, as such, was
ordered to use his position in the Gaelic League to infiltrate its
Coiste Gnótha with I.R.B. members.[21] In his subsequent career as
a Sinn Féin member of Dublin Corporation he played an important part in the various moves to bring Irish into public life.
Ó Ceallaigh, then, was one of those who was deeply involved at
a young age both in political—and potentially—revolutionary
activity and in the language movement.

Pearse, on the other hand, was already a dreamer, but his
dreams were not of a free Ireland, but rather of an Ireland with

an intellectual mission. Addressing the New Ireland Literary Society in 1897 he said:

> 'I believe that the ends which, as a nation, we have hitherto striven to attain are *ignes fatui* which are fated to elude us for ever.
>
> Others have been struck before now by the fact that hundreds of noble men and true have fought and bled for the emancipation of the Gaelic race, and yet have all failed . . . May it not be that the ends they struggled for were ends never intended for the Gael? . . . To-day, after a continuous fight lasting for eight long centuries, we are, Heaven knows, farther off than ever from the goal towards which we have struggled. . . . The people are listlessly looking on—for the first time in Irish history they seem to be sunk in apathy. We are tempted to cry aloud in our despair, "O God! will the morning *never* come?" Yes, the morning *will* come, and its dawn is not far off. But it will be a morning different from the morning we have looked for. The Gael is not like other men; the spade, and the loom, and the sword are not for him. But a destiny more glorious than that of Rome, more glorious than that of Britain awaits him: to become the saviour of idealism in modern intellectual and social life, the regenerator and rejuvenator of the literature of the world, the instructor of the nations, the preacher of the gospel of nature-worship, hero-worship, God-worship—such, Mr. Chairman, is the destiny of the Gael'.[22]

It is perhaps significant that in 1897 the idea of hero-worship was in Pearse's mind, for he was to become the greatest exponent of the cult of Cú Chulainn, which for him was in no way incompatible with the full practice of Christianity, and which was to be one of the strands used in the weaving of the new nationalism. The following eighteen years, during which the promise of

Home Rule was often repeated but never fulfilled, were to see a change in the spirit of many of the Irish people. In that time, too, there was a metamorphosis in Pearse himself. For him these were to be years of labour for Irish, for education, and finally for Irish freedom, during which his dreams for Ireland changed and he came to see himself playing a central rôle in yet another sacrifice 'for the emancipation of the Gaelic race'. All that lay before him in 1897 when the League was so concerned with Irish in the schools.

In the League's struggle with the Intermediate Board matters came to a head in 1899 with the Royal Commission on Intermediate Education. Here Hyde proved to be a tower of strength, and it is greatly to his credit that when the battle over Irish brought the League into conflict with the authorities of Trinity College, he did not stand aside. Indeed, although he regretted the necessity for doing so, he gave Mahaffy and Atkinson and their colleagues more than they bargained for, and in doing so he established the claims of Irish scholarship and research to recognition in Ireland. In fact he may have thereby contributed indirectly to the revolutionary movement, for his successful campaign was followed in 1903 by the foundation of the School of Irish Learning in Dublin, and one of the most generous supporters of the School was the historian Alice Stopford Greene, who later became an equally strong supporter of Ireland's claims to political freedom. She was a friend of Casement and MacNeill, and when the Irish Volunteers were founded she gave considerable help in obtaining guns. After the Rising she was one of the the few who stood by Casement during his trial, and, indeed, she bore a substantial part of the expenses of his defence.

While campaigning on the educational front the League did not hesitate to use its influence where it saw an opportunity for some advantage for the language. Thus as early as 1896 it called on candidates in the parliamentary election for East Kerry to have speeches delivered in Irish at their meetings. In the following

year it had some success in seeking rights for Irish speakers to give evidence in Irish in courts of law. In the same year the very active Lee Branch in Cork reported that a circular issued by it 'was the means of bringing a battering-ram of resolutions at the doors of the Queen's College, Cork urging the establishment of a Celtic Lectureship, which is now as a fact established'.[23] The young man appointed to the Cork post was a prominent member of the League, Osborn Bergin, who was later to be a member of the Celtic Faculty of University College, Dublin, along with Hyde and MacNeill. As such he was on the same platform as Pearse at the monster Home Rule meeting in O'Connell Street Dublin on 31 March 1912.

By 1900 the League had made Irish such an important issue that a full debate on it took place in the House of Commons, with a large number of Irish members speaking on behalf of the language. At the same time the League succeeded in getting support in County Councils and in Dublin Corporation. With its strength growing it took up fresh issues. In 1901 it began a campaign to have St. Patrick's Day observed as a general holiday, and this was achieved in the small space of two years. By that time the National Parade, organised by the League for St. Patrick's Day, had become an important event. In 1902 an Industrial Committee was formed in the League for the promotion of Irish industries, and some League branches even succeeded in establishing new industries in their districts. Among the members of the special committee were AE, Griffith, Moran, Ryan, Count Plunkett, and Edward Martyn. Support for Irish industries brought some members of the League, including MacNeill, into violent conflict with the police when they took part in a demonstration against an 'International Exhibition' of a 'West-Britain' type, being organised to take place in Dublin in 1904. About the same time the League had succeeded in having Irish made compulsory for employment under Dublin Corporation, and within a few years the cause of Irish was re-inforced by the election to that body of a number of Sinn Féin members, including Seán T. Ó Ceallaigh and Peadar Macken, who were ardent workers in the League. Meanwhile further attention was focussed on the League in 1905 when Niall Mac Giolla Brighde, of Creeslough, in Donegal, was prosecuted for having his name on his cart in Irish only. Mac Giolla Brighde was a League member and his case was brought on appeal to Dublin where Pearse, in one of his few court appearances as a barrister, argued brilliantly, but in vain, in his defence. Even more striking was the campaign organized in the same year to force the Post Office to accept mail addressed in Irish only. In its determination to win its point the League sent two hundred supporters in a body to the Dublin G.P.O. to hand in parcels addressed in Irish, and they disrupted the normal business until the Office closed. Coming events can, indeed, cast their shadows before; yet none of those who took part in the 'Battle of the G.P.O.' in 1905 could know that the G.P.O. was to become the symbol of a resurgent Ireland.

The League's tactics in 1905 annoyed those who regarded Ireland as an English-speaking province of Britain, just as Parnell's policy of obstruction in the British parliament had infuriated his opponents in the '80s. The London *Daily Mail* commented caustically:

'It has been said that the root of the Irish problem lies in the fact of a dull people (the English) trying to govern a singularly witty people. No one will surely be so bold as to suggest that the latest agitation, by which Irishmen are induced to fill the post-boxes with letters addressed in the uncouth characters of a barbarous language, has its origins in a sense of humour',[24]

and the *Morning Post* disparagingly likened Irish to 'kitchen Kaffir'.[25] One immediate effect of the comments in the English press is told by Roger Casement who had returned to Ireland in the previous year and who had got caught up in the language movement:

'I bethought me that a people's language was a living thing, and that it was a shameful thing for an Irishman to stand by and see the soul of his country being dragged out through its lips. I accordingly gave up my club in London, and devoted the amount of the annual subscription thus saved to a training college in Munster where Irish teachers are perfected in a fuller knowledge of, and more scientific methods of imparting, "kitchen Kaffir"'.[26]

In the following year Casement left Ireland for South America where he spent over five years in the broader service of humanity; yet his interest in Irish and his belief in the usefulness of summer schools in the Gaeltacht were undiminished. On his return to Ireland in 1912 he became patron of the school on Tawin Island, in Galway, which had as its headmaster in that year, as in 1911, a young mathematics teacher named Éamon de Valera.

In the meantime the Gaelic League had won its greatest battle when it brought to a successful conclusion in 1910 the campaign to have Irish made a required subject for matriculation in the newly-founded National University of Ireland. Yet with that campaign came the first serious differences among nationalists over a policy adopted by the League. Although compulsory Irish for matriculation was supported by many of the clergy, it was opposed by the majority of the Catholic Hierarchy, and the leaders of the Parliamentary Party, John Redmond and John Dillon, found themselves aligned with the Bishops. During the campaign a manifesto, signed by Hyde and MacNeill and by other members of the Coiste Gnótha, was issued on behalf of the League. It concluded:

'If the Irish public stand by the declarations they have made, they cannot be defeated. The fears and apprehensions of the more timid will soon be dispelled. The Irish nation will achieve the most decisive victory it has ever achieved for Nationality. The power of education is the greatest power possible to men. Hitherto it has been employed against Irish nationality. Henceforth it must be employed in the service of nationality'.[27]

The day was won for Irish when the local authorities as a body decided to agree to a university scholarship scheme only if Irish were made compulsory for matriculation. This was indeed a measure of the impact which the League had made on a representative body of Irishmen. Within a few years the League followed up this victory by calling for Irish as a compulsory subject in all National Schools. Its policy in this regard was opposed strongly by John Dillon, and it is not certain what would have been the attitude of the Parliamentary Party to the Irish language in a Home Rule parliament. That the matter was never put to the test was due in large measure to a small number of members of the Gaelic League whose wish for Ireland was that she should be something more than an Irish-speaking corner of the British Empire, and whose thoughts accordingly turned to political and eventually to military action.

There had been a note of warning in Patrick Pearse's Home Rule speech made in O'Connell Street Dublin, in 1912, when he said:

'má clistear orainn de'n dul so, tá dream i nÉirinn, agus táim-se ar dhuine dhíobh, mholfas do Ghaedhealaibh gan dul i gcomhairle ná i gcaidreamh le Gallaibh go deo arís, acht iad d'fhreagairt feasta le láimh láidir agus le faobhar claidhimh. Tuigeadh Gaill má fealltar orainn arís go mbeidh ina chogadh chraorag ar fud na hÉireann'.[28]

But it was to Eoin MacNeill that it fell to send out the call to arms. Twenty eventful years had passed since he had taken the initiative which had led to the founding of the Gaelic League. Now, in the League's paper *An Claidheamh Soluis* on 1 November

1913, he published a reasoned case for action on the part of the nationalists in response to the founding of the Ulster Volunteers, and this was followed by the monster meeting in the Rotunda when the Irish Volunteers were launched under the Presidency of MacNeill. It surprised no one that members of the Gaelic League were to the fore in answering MacNeill's call, nor did it cause any surprise that it was largely supporters of the League who followed MacNeill when the split came in the Volunteers in 1914.

In fact there was in the League a number of influential members who were also members of the Irish Republican Brotherhood, and behind the scenes they were contemplating military action. Some of them considered that the time had come when the League should identify itself with the aim of political freedom, and towards this end Seán Mac Diarmada, supported by Tom Clarke and others, suggested privately that the League's constitution should be amended, and steps were taken to bring the matter up for discussion at the Árd-Fheis which was to be held in Dundalk in July 1915, despite the likelihood of the resignation of Hyde from the Presidency and a split in the League if a proposal for such an amendment were carried.[29] In the past Hyde had steered the League on a safe course, skilfully avoiding contentious political matters while being uncompromising on those things which, according to his evaluation, were fundamental to the organisation. Now, however, in the explosive situation caused by the founding of the Ulster Volunteers, the fiasco over the Home Rule Bill, and Ireland's involvement by Britain in the European War and the Parliamentary Party's attitude to it, the political issue became pre-eminent and the Árd-Fheis eventually adopted a resolution whereby Rule 2 of the League's Constitution was amended to read:

'Connradh na Gaedhilge shall be strictly non-political and

non-sectarian, and shall devote itself to realising the ideal of a
free Gaelic-speaking Ireland'.[30]

This was the parting of the ways for Hyde and MacNeill. Hyde,
convinced that a grave disservice had been done to the League,
left the Presidency which he had held for twenty-two years. The
Árd-Fheis, hoping that he would reconsider his action, elected
no one to replace him, but when he proved adamant MacNeill
was appointed to the position.

Three years earlier Pearse had said of the League that it was a
spent force:

'Tá gábhadh le Connradh Nua i nÉirinn indiu. Tá cumhacht
na sean-Chonnradh briste agus tá a mbrígh caithte. Ní bhíonn
ar aon rud acht seal. A gníomh féin ag gach líne. Connradh na
Talmhan gníomh na dara líne so do chuaidh thorainn. Connradh na Gaedhilge gníomh na líne so atá ag imtheacht'.[31]

In this judgment he was not altogether right. What had happened
was that he and others associated with him had adopted new
priorities in their plans for Ireland. The events of 1916, in which
so many members of the Gaelic League played a heroic part,
were the prelude to the eclipse of the Parliamentary Party and
the rise of a national political force which would put into practice
on 21 January 1919 the policy expounded for Ireland by Sigerson
in 1868, and would by its actions on that day show that its wish
was for an Ireland not merely free but Gaelic as well.

The rise of this new Ireland confirmed the words which Yeats
had addressed to the editor of *The Leader* on 26 August 1900:

'I myself believe that unless a great foreign war comes to
re-make everything, we must be prepared to turn from a
purely political nationalism with the land question as its lever,
to a partly intellectual and historical nationalism like that of

Norway, with the language question as its lever . . . the people of Ireland will not in our time give a full trust to any man who has not made some great spectacular sacrifice for his convictions, or that small continual sacrifice which enables a man to become himself Irish, to become himself an embodiment of some little of the national hope . . . In ten years or in fifteen years or in twenty years the new movement will be strong enough to shake governments, and, unlike previous movements that have shaken governments, it will give continuity to public life in Ireland, and make all other righteous movements the more easy.'[32]

BRIAN Ó CUÍV.

1. *Cal. S.P. Ire.*, 1538–46, p. 304.

2. *Analect. Hib.* I, p. 163.

3. O'Neill Daunt, *Personal Recollections of the late Daniel O'Connell, M.P.*, I, p. 15.

4. *A. Clonmacnoise*, p. 8.

5. *The Times*, 4 October 1882, quoted in *Gaelic Journal* I, p. 30.

6. Ó Lúing, *John Devoy* (1961), pp. 221–2.

7. *Sgéal 'Sheandúin'* (1920).

8. *S.P.I.L. Report of Proceedings of Congress held in 1882*, p. 45.

9. *ibid.*, p. 46.

10. Hyde, *Beside the Fire*, pp. xliv, xiv.

11. *Irish Ecclesiastical Record* 1891, pp. 1101, 1102, 1103–4, 1107.

12. O' Brien, *The Influence of the Irish Language on Irish National Literature and Character*, p. 25.

13. Hyde, *The Revival of Irish Literature*, pp. 156–7.

14. de hÍde, *Mise agus an Connradh* (1937), pp. 33–4.

15. O'Brien, *The Parnell of Real Life* (1926), p. 206.

16. O'Rahilly, *Irish Dialects Past and Present* (1932), p. 14.

17. This suggestion was made in an unsigned editorial published under the heading 'To your tents, O Israel!' in *The Irishman*, 29 February 1868. My authority for attributing it to Sigerson is a statement made by J. O'Leary Curtin in an address to the Celtic Literary Society which was reported in Griffith's paper *United Irishman* on 3 December 1904. I have seen no subsequent denial of Curtin's statement that Sigerson was the author. For Sigerson's connection with *The Irishman* see Hyde's obituary notice of him in *Studies* XIV (1926), p. 11.

18. A. Griffith, *The Resurrection of Hungary*, p. 80.

19. An Craoibhín Aoibhinn, *Mo Thurus go hAmerice* (1937), p. 175.

20. *Report* (1896), p. 37. For comments on the lack of national spirit and the neglect of the Irish language in some of the bigger colleges see, for example, *The Leader*, 17 August 1901, pp. 391–2.

21. Ó Ceallaigh, *Seán T.* (1963), p. 50.

22. Pearse, *Three Lectures on Gaelic Topics* (1898), pp. 47–9.

23. *Report* (1897), p. 16.

24. Quoted by Casement in 'On the Prosecution of Irish', for which see *The Crime against Europe*, ed. by Herbert O. Mackey (1958), p. 96.

25. *op. cit.*, p. 100.

26. *ibid.*, p. 101.

27. *Connradh na Gaedhilge Árd-Fheis, 1909*, pp. 5–6.

28. *Scríbhinní Phádraig Mhic Phiarais* (1919), pp. 267–8.

29. *Seán T.*, pp. 153–5.

30. *Imtheachta na hÁrd-Fheise 1915*, pp. 16–7.

31. *Scríbhinní*, p. 139.

32. *The Leader*, 1 September 1900, p. 13.

The Sinn Féin Movement

by
DONAL McCARTNEY

(II)

The Sinn Féin Movement

A FEATURE of the 1880s and 1890s in Ireland was the emergence of numerous literary circles, societies and clubs. Out of these tiny seed-beds, which were half-literary and half-political, sprang such influential movements as the Anglo-Irish literary revival, the Gaelic League and Sinn Féin. Between them these movements created and fostered the romantic nationalism of the age. Sinn Féin (variously interpreted as 'we ourselves' or 'ourselves alone') an expression of one of the forms which nationalism adopted in Ireland, had for its founder, chief philosopher and propagator Arthur Griffith (1871–1922).

Griffith, Dublin-born, began his career at fifteen, as an apprentice printer, and from then on he was to be associated with journalism, and counted the literati of the day among his friends. His political philosophy was based upon a curious mixture. One of the formative influences in Griffith's nationalism was the republican, physical force tradition of Tone, Mitchel and the Fenians. He started his first paper, the *United Irishman* in 1899, and the name itself was significant because it linked Griffith straight away with Mitchel who had a paper of the same name, and with Tone a founder of the society of United Irishmen. In the paper's first leading article Griffith wrote: 'we accept the nationalism of '98, '48 and '67 as the true nationalism'.[1]

Tone and his followers in the republican tradition despised Grattan's parliament, and indeed it might be said that Tone had given his life in an attempt to overthrow it. Griffith, however, was well-read in the political literature of the eighteenth century and his admiration for the writers and orators—especially Molyneux, Swift, Lucas, Flood and Grattan—was reflected in his great attachment to the eighteenth century brand of Irish patriotism despised by the republicans. This admiration for Grattan's Parliament and the Ascendancy patriots Griffith shared with many of the publicists in the Home Rule camp. On this point Griffith had a much closer affinity with the Home Rulers, or with Lecky, the Unionist historian and admirer of Ascendancy patriotism whom the *United Irishman* praised, than with those who had come more directly under the influence of the Gaelic revival. Like the republicans, revivalists too—Hyde, MacNeill, D. P. Moran of the *Leader*, even James Connolly—rejected the eighteenth century. For the revivalists, looking back to the remote Gaelic past, the eighteenth century was the 'via dolorosa' of the Irish nation; it was the century of the final subjection of the Gael, the time in which, to quote Moran, Irish civilisation was overthrown and a political thing miscalled the Irish nation was stuck up on a flag of green.

The two principles of separatism and the Dual Monarchy of Grattan's constitution, which in theory seemed opposed to each other, were united in Griffith's political philosophy, and account for a certain ambiguity in his political attitudes all through his career.

There were other important influences in the formation of Griffith's nationalism. Thomas Davis, the Young Ireland propagandist, whom Griffith looked upon as Ireland's greatest philosopher and thinker, was a master upon whom Griffith modelled his own career. According to Griffith, Davis was greater than any of his contemporaries and was one of the first men in the nineteenth century to resuscitate the doctrine of nationality, challenge universalism and utilitarianism, and turn faces from 'the false lights of cosmopolitanism'. Davis's insistence on national self-reliance was one of the sources of Griffith's doctrine of Sinn Féin. 'When the Irish read and reflect with Davis, their day of redemption will be at hand', wrote Griffith.[2] Parnell of the obstruction tactics, of the boycott, of the fiery speeches made at the time of the Parnellite split was another of

Griffith's heroes. Besides the influence exercised on his thought by his historical heroes Griffith's outlook was further coloured by the fact that he grew up with, and to a certain extent out of the Gaelic revival which insisted on de–Anglicisation and fostered self-reliance and national self-respect.

Essentially Griffith was more like Davis than Parnell: he was not so much the leader of a political organisation as a propagandist, a nationalist philosopher. What he attempted to provide was a political education, not a political party. In the *United Irishman* he suggested that Irish-Ireland and separatist societies scattered all over the country each in its own way 'working to uplift the mind and heart and soul of the country'[3] become loosely federated while still retaining their own individuality. This suggestion led to the establishment of Cumann na nGael in 1900 with the old Fenian, John O'Leary, as its President. Then, in 1903, Griffith called for the establishment of another body, again a loose association of individuals who were opposed to the presentation of addresses of welcome on the occasion of the royal visit. The result was that the National Council was founded with Edward Martyn as President. Cumann na nGael and the National Council, both of which had arisen out of Griffith's suggestions in the *United Irishman* had very much the same people in their membership. They were both still in existence in the first half of 1904 when Griffith began a series of articles on 'the Hungarian policy' and suggested it as a parallel for Ireland.

The Hungarian policy as outlined by Griffith argued that Hungary had won her independence from Austria by refusing to recognise the illegal abolition of the Hungarian constitution of 1848; by pursuing a policy of passive resistance and by abstention from the Imperial Diet at Vienna. Ireland should follow the Hungarian example: proceed on the basis that Grattan's constitution of 1782–3 was still legally binding; withdraw her M.P.s from Westminster and set up a Council of 300 (as O'Connell, in a moment of truth, had suggested) composed of

M.P.s and members of the County Councils and local authorities.

The great attraction of Griffith's policy was the sheer simplicity of its logic. Many Home Rulers held with Griffith—and it was all outlined in Lecky's account of the eighteenth century—that the union of Great Britain and Ireland in 1800 was illegal. But Griffith took the logical step and drew the deduction that Irish M.P.s, who since the union sat at Westminster, were thereby participating in an illegality and helping to perpetuate a crime. 'No lapse of time', he argued, 'no ignorant acquiescence, can render legal an illegal act'.[4] He wrote that he opposed the sending of Irishmen to sit in the British parliament on two grounds: firstly, because it was a recognition of a usurped authority, and secondly, because the policy of parliamentarianism had proved to be morally and materially disastrous to Ireland.

Griffith acknowledged that his policy of passive resistance was not altogether new in Ireland. John Mitchel and Fintan Lalor had preached passive resistance at the time of the Great Famine; Davitt had carried it into effect during the Land War, and Mitchel when he contested an election in 1875 had declared that he would not take his seat if elected. Griffith maintained that in fact all the great beneficial acts passed for Ireland in the nineteenth century had come not from parliamentarianism but as the result of the unconscious carrying out of a policy of passive resistance by the people, aided by occasional excursions into the domain of active resistance at strategic points. The Emancipation, Tithes, Land Acts etc., had been won in this way. What indeed Griffith was proposing, without actually naming it as such, was the adaptation to the contemporary political circumstances of the Parnellite obstruction tactics, of the boycott principle, of the G.A.A. ban on foreign games or the Gaelic League's policy of de-Anglicisation (Griffith's own National Council denied membership to anyone in the British forces). The plan of abstention from Westminster, which Griffith, a staunch Parnellite, now proposed, was to his way of thinking an extension of

Parnell's policy, something that might have been put into operation had Parnell lived.

In booklet form *The Resurrection of Hungary: a parallel for Ireland* (1904) had a wide circulation. It possessed a considerable fascination even for some of the younger intellectual Home Rulers like Tom Kettle. In an article in the *New Ireland Review* (February 1905) Kettle pointed out serious weaknesses in the parallel between Hungary and Ireland, and certain flaws in the argument. He claimed that Griffith hardly realised the magnitude of his suggestion, and that he had not developed it in sufficient detail to justify a prudent man either in accepting it or rejecting it. He criticised Griffith's 'extreme impatience' with people who were unwilling forthwith to abandon the traditions of a century in favour of Griffith's own policy; and he regarded Griffith's comments on the parliamentarians as 'so plainly false that only a disputant soaked through with prejudice could make them'. Although Kettle was not sure that the policy even after further thinking out would prove to be workable, nevertheless he described it as 'the largest idea contributed to Irish politics for a generation'.[5]

The policy, however, made an even greater impression on members of the separatist societies like Cumann na nGael, Maud Gonne's Iníní na hÉireann, the National Association and the Dungannon Clubs. Maud Gonne was a close friend of Griffith. The Dungannon Clubs had been established in 1905 in Belfast by the republicans Bulmer Hobson and Denis McCullough, and these clubs reflected even in their name, with its hint of a reference to the Volunteer Convention of 1782 at Dungannon, the inspiration of Griffith. A Dungannon Club was established among the students at University College, Dublin, with Pat McCartan as President. The people in these various groups adopted Griffith's policy and propagated it. 'The green Hungarian band' was how Moran of the *Leader*, that master inventor of nick-names described them, and they were glad to be able to

find a less foreign-sounding title for the Hungarian policy in the
words Sinn Féin.

Asked by correspondents to play in Ireland the role of the
Hungarian statesman, Deak, and lead in pursuing the policy of
passive resistance which he had outlined, Griffith, typically,
declined. He gave as his reason that he himself was a separatist,
a follower of Tone and Mitchel, and said that someone who
believed more firmly in Swift or Grattan should lead. At the
first annual convention of the National Council (28 November
1905) with Edward Martyn presiding Griffith publicly launched
the Sinn Féin programme. He was still convinced that the policy
should be propagated by individuals and only reluctantly agreed
to the formation of provincial branches. A few months later in
1906 the Dungannon Clubs and Cumann na nGael amalgamated
as the Sinn Féin League, with George Gavan Duffy in London,
Bulmer Hobson and P. S. O'Hegarty among its most active
spirits. It was not until September 1908 that the National Council
in which Griffith himself was the guiding hand, united with the
Sinn Féin League to become simply Sinn Féin. John Sweetman
became President; Griffith and Hobson were Vice-Presidents;
and other prominent members included Sean MacDermott, Seán
T. ÓCeallaigh, Wm. Cosgrave, George Gavan Duffy, P. S.
O'Hegarty, Robert Lynd, Countess Markievicz etc. By then
Sinn Féin had already fought and lost the North Leitrim by-
election. The constitution of Sinn Féin drafted by Griffith in
1908 was an attempt to reconcile the separatist demands of the
I.R.B. people in the Sinn Féin League with Griffith's own Dual
Monarchy principle. The declared objective of Sinn Féin was
now stated to be the re-establishment of the independence of
Ireland, with Grattan's constitution of the Dual Monarchy as the
minimum amount acceptable. The 1908 constitution read:

The object of Sinn Féin is the re-establishment of the independence of Ireland.

36

The aim of the Sinn Féin policy is to unite Ireland on this broad national platform:

(1st), That we are a distinct nation.

(2nd), That we will not make any voluntary compact with Great Britain until Great Britain keeps her own compact which she made by the Renunciation Act of 1783.[6]

Griffith often claimed that he was a separatist, and he was for some time a member of the I.R.B. When, therefore, he proposed a return to the constitutional position of Grattan's parliament, he said he did so because he held that in the circumstances the Dual Monarchy principle would win more widespread support. The truth was that in preaching Dual Monarchy Griffith tended to be his own best convert, and his admiration for the eighteenth-century patriots helped to make his conversion somewhat easier.

In his list of Irish patriots Griffith had a much lower opinion of Fintan Lalor than either Pearse or Connolly had. Because of Lalor's obsession with agrarianism he had failed, according to Griffith, to apprehend the truth which List in Germany or Davis in Ireland recognised, namely, that nationality was the highest value in economics. The economic doctrines which Griffith propagated through Sinn Féin and his papers owed much to the economic nationalism and protectionism of Friedrich List whose work on political economy Griffith wished to see 'in the hands of every Irishman'. And the practical application of that doctrine —support for native industry and the boycott of English goods— was borrowed to a certain extent from the writings of Swift. This side of Griffith's propaganda played a considerable part in the Irish industrial revival movement. Sinn Féin in 1908 now suggested that the proposed native government, independent of and ignoring the British government, should pursue a nationalist economic policy. It should establish an Irish consular and mercantile marine service, a national bank and stock exchange, arbitration courts, a national insurance system, a civil service, sea-fisheries, afforestation, the national control and management of transport and of waste lands, the development of natural resources etc.

However influential Sinn Féin was as a doctrine it made less impact as a political organisation. In its very best years, 1908–10, it claimed no more than something between 100–150 branches. As an organisation it never reached, before the Rising, anywhere near the degree of popularity of the Gaelic League, nor the degree of efficiency of the Irish Party's election machine. As a party its chief strength lay in Dublin, and in the Dublin municipal elections of 1908 a Sinn Féin candidate, Tom Kelly, headed the poll, and Sinn Féin received a number of votes almost equal to that of the Irish Party. In February of that same year Sinn Féin contested its only parliamentary election before the Rising. The M.P. for North Leitrim, Charles Dolan, disagreed with the policy of the parliamentarians, resigned his seat and stood as a Sinn Féin candidate in the resultant by-election. Although Griffith personally preferred a policy of educating the country to his way of thinking the situation in North Leitrim forced his hand.

With little initial organisation in the county, Sinn Féin engaged in the battle. They started their own local Sinn Féin paper the *Leitrim Guardian* which, however, only lasted the duration of the contest. Among the speakers who campaigned for Sinn Féin were Parnell's sister, Anna, George Gavan Duffy, Bulmer Hobson, Seán T. Ó Ceallaigh, Sean MacDermott and P. T. Daly. Griffith himself took part and produced election propaganda with plenty of punch to it. He claimed, for example, that the net result of Irish attendance at Westminster since 1800 was 3 rebellions, 4 major famines, 27 minor famines, 13 major industries closed down, the abolition of the Irish Exchequer and Customs, Irish taxation multiplied by 5, a 25% decrease in the population, the exile from Ireland of 5 million people, and the change over to grazing of 80% of the tillage land of Ireland.[7]

The Sinn Féin candidate was defeated: 3,103 votes for the parliamentarians' man and 1,157 for the Sinn Féin candidate. It had shown itself no match for the Irish Party, and after the election many things attested to the decline of Sinn Féin as a party. In 1907 Griffith looked for £500 to fight the North Leitrim election and received £650. A few months after Sinn Féin's defeat Griffith looked for £800 for reorganisation purposes and collected only £273. This was in some degree a measure of Sinn Féin's decline. In 1909, Griffith, against the advice of friends, launched the *Sinn Féin Daily* which lasted a few months. The financial troubles which Griffith's paper experienced may well help to explain why Griffith did not discourage the attempts made by William O'Brien to link together his All-for-Ireland League and Sinn Féin. Griffith was in favour of co-operation with O'Brien up to a point but others in Sinn Féin—including George Gavan Duffy, Hobson, McCartan, O'Hegarty and Countess Markievicz regarded any move towards co-operation with parliamentarians as a retrograde step. They got some assistance from W. P. Ryan's *Irish Nation* which provided them with a platform, and they criticised Griffith's *Sinn Féin Daily* on the grounds that Sinn Féin had no control over it; that they could not agree with everything it said; and that it had become so gentle with the parliamentarians that it was perhaps bargaining for their financial support.

The result of these differences among the Sinn Feiners was that some of Griffith's critics withdrew after the January 1910 meeting of the National Council and later established their own paper, *Irish Freedom*, the organ of a revitalised I.R.B. which by now was gathering around Tom Clarke since his return from America. But those who withdrew to *Irish Freedom* (managed by Sean MacDermott, edited by Hobson (although the nominal editor was Patrick McCartan), with P.S. O'Hegarty as one of its leading contributors) acknowledged that no matter under what name they spread their ideas, no Irish nation could be established except on the Sinn Féin principle, which, *Irish Freedom* claimed, was as strong as ever it was.

The Making of 1916

In the best days of Sinn Féin, Griffith had failed to wean from Home Rule the support of the young intellectuals like those of the brilliant Young Ireland Branch of the United Irish League associated with University College, Dublin—Tom Kettle, Cruise O'Brien, Sheehy-Skeffington, J. C. Meredith, P. J. Little, Rory O'Connor. They were strongly opposed to what they regarded as Griffith's 'injustice towards parliamentarianism'. In 1910 the prospects of Home Rule considerably brightened as a result of the general election which made the Liberal Government dependent on the support of the Irish Party. And as the hopes of Home Rule rose higher, Sinn Féin further declined.

Apart from these—from Sinn Féin's point of view—unfavourable circumstances, responsibility for the failure of the Sinn Féin party before 1916 must rest largely on the shoulders of Griffith himself. For, in the first place, he had been reluctant to turn Sinn Féin into a party, preferring to work towards the conversion of existing parties to the Sinn Féin policy. Then, having committed Sinn Féin to party politics, he still fondly clung to the Dual Monarchy idea, although his most active supporters were separatists and he claimed to be one himself. This duality in his thought restricted the development of his party, for neither separatists nor dual monarchists could give it wholehearted allegiance because of the presence of the other. Further, Griffith was reluctant to lead the very movements which he himself had originated, although he continued to exert a great deal of jealous influence over their deliberations. When he first propounded his 'Hungarian Policy' in 1904 he refused to organise and lead it as a party. When two societies united on Sinn Féin principles in 1906, a third, in which Griffith was the leading spirit, held back until 1908. Griffith was the kind of man who was always in practical politics a step or two behind his own philosophy.

In party management Griffith was no Parnell, but then in fairness, he much preferred to play the propagandist role of a Swift, Davis or Mitchel instead.

Another reason for the failure of the Sinn Féin Party is to be sought in Griffith's proud and controversial nature. Griffith, a courageous and high-principled journalist wrote many a harsh thing not only against enemies but even against potential allies. Between Griffith and that other great publicist in the Irish-Ireland movement, Moran of the *Leader*, no love was lost. Moran's paper, slightly younger than the *United Irishman*, had a wider circulation and a longer life than Griffith's. The professional rivalry between the two at times led to open journalistic warfare. Moran's facility for satire, and his description of Sinn Feiners as 'tin-pikers' did not make for friendship with Griffith, who referred to Moran as 'the very dirtiest hand we have yet seen in Irish journalism'.[8] He accused Moran of being an impostor, and accused the *Leader* of having stolen all that was neither stupid nor dishonest in its editorials from the *United Irishman*. Stephen Gwynn mediated on one occasion in what he regarded as a disedifying snarling match between two Irish-Ireland publicists who had the same objectives, and he lamented that they were dissipating their strength in being 'largely occupied with blacking each other's eye'.[9]

Griffith also got involved in controversies with Douglas Hyde. The founder of Sinn Féin was not at first very much committed to the language revival. He had noted, however, that his continental mentors, the German, List, and the Hungarian, Beust, had declared that a nation must have a language of its own, and Thomas Davis had said the same thing. The enthusiasm generated by the Gaelic League won Griffith's admiration and he strongly backed its campaign for 'essential Irish' for the new National University's matriculation. Hyde was always wary of any politicians who might try to use the language movement for their own political ends. He suspected that Griffith, during the 'essential Irish' campaign, tried to capture the League for his own political movement, and claimed (somewhat unfairly) that Griffith gave allegiance to the language only after he had seen its effectiveness for uniting the people in a popular crusade. In 1913, when a breach between Hyde and the more extreme and politically-minded 'left-wing' threatened to disrupt the League, Griffith publicly backed the 'left-wing' against Hyde. This 'left-wing' of the Gaelic League was composed of Griffith's friends—Sinn Féin and I.R.B. men—and included Eamonn Ceannt, Sean MacDermott, Thomas Ashe, Piaras Beaslai, The O'Rahilly and Seán T. Ó Ceallaigh. Hyde, who was himself no novice in public controversy, replied that Griffith had of late given up so much of *Sinn Féin's* space to Gaelic League activities that it would appear that the Sinn Féin movement was itself doing so well that it needed none of Griffith's attention. Hyde ended by quoting an Irish saying to the effect that Griffith should mind his own business and not bother with Hyde's.[10]

Griffith fought with many others including Yeats on questions concerned with the National Theatre, and with Larkin on aspects of his trade union agitation. Griffith detested Larkinism and anything that tended to disrupt the country's industry and trade. By comparison with Connolly Griffith was an old-fashioned nationalist, one who believed that the welfare of man was to be achieved through nationalism and not through any world-wide socialist fraternity. He said he would never row in 'the cosmopolitan galley'[11], that his interest was only in his own country. Because of Griffith's outspoken attacks on Larkinism, Sinn Féin won little support from the Labour movement.

The barbed qualities which Griffith displayed in all of these controversies with other public figures did not help Sinn Féin as a party. Even co-workers in Sinn Féin complained of the difficulty of co-operating with Griffith. 'He wants us to follow him blindly and sink our own minds'[12], complained P. S. O'Hegarty in 1907. In his short-lived paper, *An Barr Buadh*, Pearse in 1912 strongly expressed his opinion of Griffith's character. In an open letter to Griffith (written in Irish) Pearse welcomed signs that Sinn Féin was not yet dead, and then accused Griffith of almost killing his own brain-child. Pearse admitted that he was never very keen on the Sinn Féin child but regretted to see its own father, Griffith, strangle it. Pearse continued (I give a translation from the original Irish):

> You were too hard. You were too obstinate. You were too narrow-minded. You were too head-strong. You did not trust your friends enough. You trusted yourself too much. You over-estimated your own opinion. You distrusted people who were as loyal as yourself. You would follow no one's advice except your own. You preferred to prove to the world that no one else was right except yourself. You would do nothing yourself, but if anyone else proposed something to be done you would prove that it was not feasible. No progress was possible for an association which had that kind of man at its head. No one would remain in an association unless he had the right to speak in it. Your friends were deserting you one by one and they would all desert you if you were to continue as you were . . . You have virtues that no other Irishman has. It would be a great pity if the benefits of those virtues were lost because others were unable to work with you.[13]

Despite what Pearse regarded as evidence of the return of life to Sinn Féin, the party did not revive before the Rising. But Griffith's papers remained among the foremost nationalist organs in the country. Right from the establishment of his first paper in 1899 he had relentlessly poured out nationalist propaganda, and his preaching of political, economic, industrial and cultural self-sufficiency contributed greatly to the optimism, self-confidence and stirring of the Irish-Ireland movement. Even hostile critics acknowledged the worth of the Sinn Féin message. F. H. O'Donnell, who had once served the cause of Home Rule with Parnell wrote in 1910:

> There may be nothing new in Sinn Féin beyond its name, which is neither lofty nor lovely, but the reality of a great

reaction on behalf of higher and purer ideals of national life and national pride cannot be overlooked by any intelligent observer. There is a truer manliness and womanliness about the young adherents of Sinn Féin which, if no catastrophe occur to check the generous enterprise, must introduce a cleaner spirit and a purer air into Dublin society.[14]

When the Home Rule Bill was introduced in 1912 Griffith proclaimed: 'If this be liberty then the lexicographers have deceived us'.[15] Griffith was one of the loudest in denunciation of the later shilly-shallying that went on over Home Rule. He also voiced strong support of the Volunteers and supported the MacNeill section when the split came with Redmond. From its inception Sinn Féin had always been known for its opposition to the recruitment of Irishmen to the British forces. When the war broke out in 1914 Griffith in his paper, *Sinn Féin*, launched an intensive anti-recruitment and non-support of England campaign. He subjected the stories in the British press about German atrocities to close and critical examination, and reminded his readers of England's misdeeds in Ireland in the past. Griffith was also one of the leading advocates of the Irish Neutrality League. Not unnaturally *Sinn Féin* was classified as anti-British, pro-German and seditious and consequently suppressed. *Eire* and *Scissors and Paste* which Griffith also edited suffered a similar fate. He managed to keep their successor, *Nationality*, going down to March 1916.

Griffith had always been closely associated with the more extreme wing of the Irish nationalists. His first paper, the *United Irishman*, had received financial support from Clan-na-Gael in America and from the Fenian, Mark Ryan in London. Griffith was a member of the I.R.B. down to about 1910, and the I.R.B. now financed *Nationality* with Griffith as editor and Sean MacDermott of the I.R.B. Supreme Council as manager. Major Price, the Castle's Intelligence Officer, said that anyone who knew Ireland knew that printed matter had a great deal of influence. He added that he found that *Nationality*, which was supposed to have a circulation of 4,500 had actually 8,000 because it went from hand to hand.[16] *Nationality*, in fact, was the chief mouthpiece of the nationalists in Sinn Féin, the I.R.B. and the Irish Volunteers who had been drawn closer together as the war proceeded. In view of the position he now occupied in the nationalist ranks, it is not surprising that a poll, which was organized by *Spark*, in February 1915, to discover the nationalist whom Dublin wished most to honour, placed Griffith first, with Eoin MacNeill second, and Pearse further down the field.

Although always against force as a method to achieve his objectives, Griffith had never been against force in principle. At the January 1913 meeting of the National Council of Sinn Féin, Eamonn Ceannt fostered a resolution, which was carried, to the effect that it was the duty of Irishmen to learn the use of arms. Griffith, a rank-and-file member of the Irish Volunteers held the same views about a Rising as MacNeill. His opinion was that the Volunteers should not fight unless forced to, but should remain in existence until, like the Volunteers of 1782, they had won a constitution for Ireland. Griffith who worked in the same office as Sean MacDermott was, nevertheless, kept in the dark about the plans for the Rising. On the eve of the Rising Griffith supported MacNeill's countermanding orders. Then, on the Thursday of Easter Week he appealed to MacNeill to call out the rest of the Volunteers in support of the insurgents. MacNeill stood by his original decision against a Rising, and Griffith took no part in the fighting.

In a sense it was ironic, and especially in view of Griffith's non-participation, and of Sinn Féin's doctrine of passive resistance and its objective of a Dual Monarchy, that Chief-Secretary Birrell and the other officials examined before the Commission on the Rising should have christened it the Sinn Féin Rebellion. Griffith's old journalistic rival, D. P. Moran, saw the irony, and described it as a 'Birrellesque extension of Sinn Feinism'.[17]

In another sense, however, the sobriquet was well-merited. Long before the establishment of the Volunteers keen observers of the Irish scene, like Paul-Dubois and Erskine Childers, regarded Sinn Féiners and Separatists as the same people. 'If the Sinn Féin alternative meant anything at all', wrote Childers in 1911, 'it meant complete separation, which Ireland does not want, and a final abandonment of constitutional method'.[18] 'Sinn Féin Volunteers' was a term used not only by the British officials, but even by the general public. It was reported to the Commission investigating the Rising that Irish Volunteers in Kerry preferred to call themselves Sinn Féin Volunteers. And it is interesting to note that as early as 1915 Eoin MacNeill, chief of staff of the Volunteers, in a pamphlet entitled, *Daniel O'Connell and Sinn Féin,* regarded himself and his colleagues as Sinn Féiners.

As a party Sinn Féin had failed long before 1916, and its doctrines of a Dual Monarchy and of passive resistance had won comparatively few adherents. But Sinn Féinism had survived, and other aspects of its teaching had deeply influenced nationalists of separatist tendencies. Because it was more a gospel than a party the Castle authorities found it very difficult to state precisely what Sinn Féin meant. Under-Secretary Nathan saw it as a permeating spirit, and said that Sinn Féin opinion varied from that of the man who was simply an Irish patriot to that of the man whose hatred of England was only greater than his love of Ireland. And Chief-Secretary Birrell defined Sinn Féinism as mainly composed of the old hatred and distrust of the British connection.

Although the Sinn Féin Party was practically moribund by 1916, Sinn Féin had remained vigorously alive as a gospel and a slogan for the more advanced nationalists; and it became a label employed to describe all forms of separatist manifestations. In view of the role which Griffith had played in Irish nationalism over the years the labelling of the Rising as the Sinn Féin Rebellion was not without deep significance. And it was not surprising that when the Rising was suppressed, Griffith was among those arrested and jailed by a government that believed that this propagandist had been in a large measure responsible for creating and fostering the intellectual atmosphere which made rebellion possible.

If by his propaganda, Griffith had contributed to the Rising, the influence of his policy became even more evident in the Rising's aftermath. In the *Resurrection of Hungary* (1904), be had argued that Ireland had always benefited most from a policy of passive resistance suitably aided by occasional excursions, at strategic points, into the use of force. Now, after the Rising, the policy of passive resistance presented itself to the country for grave reconsideration. So it was that, when the Volunteers and the 1916 sympathisers, the separatists and old Sinn Féin supporters began to reorganise their forces and to create a new Sinn Féin movement in 1917, with de Valera as President and Griffith as a Vice-President, they borrowed wholesale from Griffith's earlier programme: passive resistance, abstention from Westminster, arbitration courts, the establishment of separate and independent government ministries and so on.

With the rout of the Irish Party in the 1918 General Election, the victory of Sinn Féin was assured.

DONAL McCARTNEY.

1. *United Irishman*, 4 March 1899.

2. Arthur Griffith (ed.), *Thomas Davis: the thinker and teacher*, preface.

3. *United Irishman*, 4 August 1900.

4. Arthur Griffith, *The Resurrection of Hungary* (3rd ed., 1918), p. 87.

5. T. M. Kettle, 'Would the Hungarian Policy Work', in *New Ireland Review*, February 1905.

6. P. S. O'Hegarty, *Ireland Under the Union*, p. 651.

7. *Sinn Féin*, 15 February 1908.

8. *United Irishman*, 31 January 1903.

9. *United Irishman*, 24 January 1903.

10. *Sinn Féin*, 26 July 1913.

11. *ibid.*, 25 September 1913.

12. P. S. O'Hegarty to George Gavan Duffy, 11 April 1907 (Seán Ó Lúing, *Art O Gríofa*, p. 142).

13. P. H. Pearse, *Scríbhinní*, pp. 256–7.

14. F. H. O'Donnell, *A History of the Irish Parliamentary Party*, ii. 378.

15. Arthur Griffith, 'Home Rule and the Unionists', in *Irish Review*, ii. No. 15 (May 1912), p. 113.

16. *Royal Commission on the Rebellion in Ireland. Minutes of Evidence* [cd. 8311], 57.

17. *Leader*, 27 May 1916.

18. Erskine Childers, *The Framework of Home Rule* (1911), p. 168.

Connolly, the Citizen Army
and the Rising

by
J. W. BOYLE

(III)

Connolly, the Citizen Army
and the Rising

By virtue of his rôles as a signatory of the proclamation, as leader of the Irish Citizen Army and as Commandant-General, Dublin division, Army of the Irish Republic, James Connolly symbolizes Irish labour's participation in the Easter Rising. Yet Connolly and his contingent (some 200 men) were no more representative of the labour movement at that time than were Pearse and those Irish Volunteers, who followed him, of the nation as a whole. The Irish Citizen Army when first formed was not intended as a military body designed to secure national independence, nor did Connolly himself then view it as other than a labour defence force.

When Connolly returned from the United States in the summer of 1910, he was neither a member of the Irish Republican Brotherhood nor greatly interested in the physical force movement. In 1899 he had condemned those who made a fetish of physical force and laid down principles which should govern its use, i.e., that 'the party of progress . . . is representative of the will of the majority of the nation' and that 'it has exhausted all the peaceful means at its disposal for the purpose of demonstrating to the people and their enemies that the new revolutionary ideas do possess the suffrage of the majority'.[1] In the same article he had urged the use of the ballot-box, reserving a decision on the use of moral or physical force for the day on which 'the socialist working class of Ireland will, through its elected representatives, present its demand for freedom from the yoke of a governing master class or nation'. There was no obvious cause for him to modify his views in 1910.

The reason for Connolly's return to Ireland was an invitation by the newly formed Socialist Party of Ireland to carry out a lecture tour. Shortly afterwards he was appointed a paid organiser by the party, but when it lost the financial support of some middle-class sympathisers and was unable to pay him a regular salary, he thought of finding a living in England. How this would have affected subsequent events is a matter for speculation; it is sufficient to say that Connolly was spared the necessity of further emigration by his appointment as Belfast organiser of the Irish Transport and General Workers' Union.

During the period spent by him in Ireland between 1896 and 1903, Connolly's activities had been almost wholly political. Now, within a year of his return he found himself plunged in trade union work. There had been a general upsurge of unrest in the labour world during the preceding years: the growth of industrial unionism, represented in the United States by the Industrial Workers of the World (for which Connolly had acted as an organiser); the spread of syndicalist theories in France and other countries; increasing militancy on the part of British and Irish workers as the gap between static wages and rising prices widened. The rise in union membership was accompanied by demands for higher wages and better working conditions on the part of group after group of workers. In Ireland the I.T.G.W.U., founded in December 1908 by James Larkin, took the lead, organising dockers, carters and general workers in other occupations. By the spring of 1911 the union, which had survived a succession of crises, including the imprisonment of Larkin, was established as the most militant organisation of its kind.

The year 1911 was marked in Great Britain by a succession of strikes, the biggest being the seamen's and the dockers' in June and July and the railways workers' in August. Irish workers were drawn into both. Among the Irish ports affected was Belfast, where Connolly had settled his family when the S.P.I.'s funds began to run low. Connolly, who had joined the moribund Belfast branch of the I.T.G.W.U., saw the possibility of strengthening it and uniting the port workers, hitherto divided by their religious and political affiliations between the I.T.G.W.U. and the National Union of Dock Labourers. Larkin, after some promptings, made him the Belfast organiser. By skilful tactics Connolly succeeded in gaining higher wages for his members, who worked in the deep-sea docks, and improving relations with the cross-channel dockers in the N.U.D.L. He then set about organising the sweated mill-girls in the spinning section of the linen trade. The sectarian rivalries that divided the Belfast working class handicapped trade union officials, especially those dealing with general as opposed to craft workers, but Connolly persevered in his difficult task.

The industrial unrest that was so marked in 1911 continued until the outbreak of war in 1914, interrupted only by short intervals of uneasy peace. Connolly's activities were not confined to Belfast; he was frequently called upon when disputes broke out in other centres even as far away as Wexford. During the eight-month Dublin lock-out and strike that began in August 1913 Connolly was much of the time in Dublin, at times in charge of what was an industrial war, at times addressing meetings in Great Britain, so that he was able to pay only flying visits to Belfast. Though he addressed meetings for the S.P.I. and its successor the Independent Labour Party of Ireland, and though he wrote political articles, much of his energy was of necessity absorbed by trade union struggles.

The Irish Citizen Army arose directly out of the industrial clash. Its origins have been described by Seán O'Casey, its first secretary, by R. M. Fox and incidentally by Captain Jack White and others. It was formed with a twofold purpose, to enable the locked-out men to protect themselves in their clashes with the police over blackleg labour and, by drilling, to keep them fit and give them a sense of cohesion at a time when enforced idleness was demoralising. The suggestion of a 'citizen army' was not totally novel. During a Dublin carters' strike in 1908 when he was still an official of the N.U.D.L. (though suspended shortly afterwards), Larkin had defied the employers, telling them to get the British Army out as they had done in Belfast, but adding that he hoped 'the day would arrive when these men would have to face a citizen army'.[2] However, he took his suggestion no further after a settlement was reached. At one stage of the Wexford struggle, which involved foundry workers and dock labourer members of the I.T.G.W.U. in the second half of 1911, P. T. Daly had enrolled a 'workers' police' after one of the locked-out men had been killed in a police baton charge; once again the successful conclusion of the dispute put an end to the scheme. In 1913 violence was the keynote from the beginning. One man was killed by a police baton on Saturday, 20 August (the tram strike had begun on Tuesday) and the next day hundreds were injured when police in O'Connell Street clubbed and kicked indiscriminately both passers-by and those waiting to hear Larkin speak. It was the introduction in November of large numbers of blacklegs from Great Britain to clear the glutted Dublin quays that brought matters to a head, as police and soldiers safeguarding the imported 'free labour' clashed with the pickets.

In the early days of the strike and lock-out an Industrial Peace Committee, composed of such men as George Russell (AE), Padraic Colum, Rev. R. M. Gwynn of Trinity College, Dublin, Professor Houston of the Royal College of Science and Francis Sheehy Skeffington, had tried unsuccessfully to bring about a settlement. In a further effort they turned themselves into a Civic League, and it was at a meeting of this body held in 40 Trinity College on 12 November that Captain J. R. ('Jack') White, if the account given in his autobiography, *Misfit*, is correct, suggested the formation of the Irish Citizen Army.

White, an ex-Sandhurst and regular army officer who had fought in the South African war, but had in the intervening years abandoned imperialism and the ascendancy ethos for a passing affair with Tolstoyan anarchism before espousing Home Rule and labour sympathies, approached Connolly with his proposal. Connolly accepted it (he had referred to the need to provide workers with means of defence some days earlier) and at a victory meeting to celebrate Larkin's release from prison on 13 November announced its formation in these words: 'I am going to talk sedition. The next time we are out for a march I want to be accompanied by four battalions of trained men with their corporals and sergeants. Why should we not drill and train men as they are doing in Ulster?'[3] It should be noted, however, that Connolly's call was for volunteers for the 'Labour Army' and that, despite his reference to Carson's Ulster Volunteers, he saw it as a reply to the use of police and soldiers on the employers' side in industrial disputes, a reply endorsed by Larkin.

Captain White was the commander of the new army. He entered enthusiastically on his task, drilling the men at Croydon Park, the house and three acres of ground in Clontarf leased by the I.T.G.W.U. as a recreational centre, and leading them on marches. He had difficulties. Men were called away to meetings and strike duties, so that numbers fluctuated and continuity was broken. As the abler-bodied found employment those of poorer physique were left, men who were ill-clothed and badly under-nourished if not literally starving. Though they checked the worst excesses of the police and helped to maintain morale they were not an impressive body, armed with staves and hurley sticks, lacking uniforms. In addition, the Irish Volunteer force, which had grown with astonishing speed since its beginning in November 1913, drew into its ranks many who were attracted by its success and the facilities it could command. By March 1914 the labour army was on the point of dissolution.

It was at this stage that Seán O'Casey suggested its reorgan-

isation to Captain White. At a preliminary meeting, attended by
Connolly, Countess Markievicz, P. T. Daly, W. Partridge and
Seán O'Casey, with Captain White in the chair, a draft constitution was drawn up. Connolly and Daly then proposed that
a public meeting should be held on 22 March, and that Larkin
be asked to preside. Larkin agreed and the public meeting, held
in Liberty Hall, approved the constitution and appointed an
army council with O'Casey as its first secretary. The constitution
was as follows:

1. That the first and last principle of the Irish Citizen Army is
the avowal that the ownership of Ireland, moral and material, is
vested of right in the people of Ireland.

2. That its principal objects shall be:—

a. To arm and train all Irishmen capable of bearing arms to
enforce and defend its first principle.

b. To sink all differences of birth, privilege and creed under
the common name of the Irish people.

3. That the Citizen Army shall stand for the absolute unity of
Irish nationhood and recognition of the rights and liberties of
the world's democracies.

4. That the Citizen Army shall be open to all who are prepared
to accept the principles of equal rights and opportunities for the
people of Ireland and to work in harmony with organized labour
towards that end.

5. Every enrolled member must be, if possible, a member of a
trade union recognised by the Irish Trades Union Congress.

GOD SAVE THE PEOPLE[4]

Clause 5 was an addition, on the initiative of Larkin, to the
original draft. The first Army Council's officers were: Chairman,
Captain White; vice-chairmen, Jim Larkin, P. T. Daly, W.
Partridge, Thomas Foran, F. Sheehy Skeffington; secretary, Seán
O'Casey; treasurers, Countess Markievicz, Richard Brannigan.

Studies in the History of the Rising

It is significant that the constitution, apart from clause 5, laid stress less on the working-class nature of the army than on its broadly democratic objectives and, in particular, on the 'absolute unity of Irish nationhood'. This phrase was aimed at Asquith's partition proposal, made on 9 March 1914 when he was moving for the third time the second reading of the Home Rule Bill, that any Irish county could vote itself out of Home Rule for six years. The prevailing tone, however, with the echo of Fintan Lalor in clause 1, indicated some shifting from a purely labour standpoint to one which might attract trade unionists in general and the more radically-minded nationalists, thus offsetting the appeal of the Irish Volunteers.

Despite the abnormal demands made on him in trade union matters, abnormal because of the militant nature of the Irish Transport and General Workers' Union and of the degree of industrial unrest during the years 1910–14, Connolly found time for political work. He started branches of the Socialist Party of Ireland, which in 1912 he converted into the Independent Labour Party of Ireland, carried to a successful conclusion (also in 1912) a campaign to induce the Irish Trades Union Congress to form an Irish Labour Party, wrote many articles on political subjects and even contested a municipal election in Belfast. In all these activities his main concern was to further the political education of the Irish working class, to make it conscious of its separate identity and interests and to persuade it to prepare, politically and industrially, for the day when it would itself take power and establish a classless society in Ireland. While he did not at any time deny the claims of Ireland to an independent nationhood, his immediate preoccupation was with social rather than national revolution.

Several factors were responsible for Connolly's diminished interest in Irish national demands during these years. The most important was his absorption in trade union struggles, but there were others. In common with Larkin and the leaders of the Irish T.U.C. he bitterly resented the Irish Parliamentary Party's rôle in excluding Ireland from a series of measures that would benefit the working class directly—the medical sections of the National Health Insurance Act (1911), the Feeding of Necessitous School Children Act (1906) and the House and Town Planning Act (1909). The enmity displayed towards organized labour by the ward officials of the United Irish League and the Ancient Order of Hibernians, and their sectarian activities, strengthened his determination that labour should establish itself as a separate force. If further disenchantment with bourgeois nationalist politicians of various hues was needed, it was furnished during the 1913 struggle by the hostility, or at least indifference, of the vast majority of Irish M.P.s, and by the denunciations of Arthur Griffith in his Sinn Féin rôle as protector of Irish enterprise against the wrecking tactics of the I.T.G.W.U. and its leaders. Finally, though Connolly welcomed the Home Rule Bill despite its limitations, he, together with the Irish T.U.C., complained that the constituency divisions set out in the schedule accompanying this Bill would ensure the supremacy of middle-class parties in the expected Home Rule parliament by favouring the rural areas at the expense of the urban centres.

Connolly had little time to devote to the Irish Citizen Army during the bitter aftermath of the lock-out, even though he had welcomed its formation and took part in its re-organisation. He criticised those British trade union officials who, though they had supported the strike fund generously, had refused to use the sympathetic strike as a last weapon against the Dublin employers and ordered seamen and dockers to return to work in Irish and cross-channel ports. His bitterness of spirit found expression in an article in *Forward* (9 February 1914), which concluded with the following paragraph:

'And so we Irish workers must go down into Hell, bow our backs to the lash of the slave driver, let our hearts be seared by the iron of his hatred, and instead of the sacramental wafer of brotherhood and common sacrifice, eat the dust of defeat and betrayal.'

Studies in the History of the Rising

The feeling that the Irish labour movement had been betrayed by British labour industrially was soon extended to politics. The British Labour Party had already shown coolness in 1913 to the proposal that the new Irish Labour Party should be an independent organisation and should receive part of the political levy payable to the British party by Irish members of British unions. When Asquith made his partition concession to Ulster Unionists in March 1914, the Irish T.U.C. protested immediately to a number of organisations, including the British Labour Party. The labour M.P. George N. Barnes defended Asquith in the columns of *Forward*, saying that the compromise was put forward as the price of peace and emphasizing that he and his colleagues took their line from the Irish nationalists since Ireland had not returned any labour M.P.s—a defence much employed by British labour speakers.

The partition proposal aroused the deepest feelings in Connolly, who urged that it be resisted—by force if necessary. It would be worse than the partition of Poland, for there at least no national leaders gave even an unwilling consent as Redmond and Devlin were prepared to do in Ireland. It would be a betrayal of 'the national democracy of Ulster' to a bigoted enemy, it would mean 'a carnival of reaction both north and south', it would disrupt the labour movement, perpetuating 'in a form aggravated in evil the discords now prevalent, and help the Home Rule and Orange capitalists and clerics to keep their rallying cries before the public as the political watchwords of the day'.[5] When the Liberal government backed down before the opposition of the officers in the 'Curragh mutiny' and abandoned its plan to move troops to Ulster to counter Unionist opposition to Home Rule, Connolly's militancy and indignation grew even greater.

The crowded events of March 1914 evoked from the parliamentary committee of the Irish T.U.C. a manifesto calling upon Irish workers to take a stand against partition; citing the examples of the Curragh officers and the Ulster Volunteers, it urged the Irish working class to vindicate its right to arm and fight in defence of economic freedom. The manifesto stimulated recruiting for the Irish Citizen Army, which gradually assumed the appearance of a regular military force as dark-green uniforms and slouch hats were acquired. The army had its own flag, the Starry Plough, consisting of a plough picked out by stars on a blue background. Captain White organised parades, though it was difficult to secure constant attendance from men whose hours of work were irregular. Facilities, too, were limited to Croydon Park and a Fianna hall, as the Irish Volunteers refused to share drill halls with the Citizen Army.

Relations between the Citizen Army and the Volunteers, at least at top level, were cool. The constitution of the Citizen Army with its stress on equal rights and opportunities for all and on its connection with organised labour, differed markedly from the generalisations of the Volunteer manifesto. Friction developed in the competition for recruits. Both Captain White and Constance Markievicz tried to induce the two bodies to co-operate, but the Volunteer executive rejected an offer from Captain White, who, feeling that he was making little headway, resigned as chairman soon afterwards and was replaced by Larkin. Both organisations were represented in the Wolfe Tone demonstration on 26 June at Bodenstown, where the Citizen Army contingent led by Larkin was welcomed by Tom Clarke, the chairman of the Wolfe Tone Commemoration Committee. The improved relations were only temporary and deteriorated when in the same month Redmond forced the Volunteer executive to accept his nominees, who represented all that labour had fought against during the 1913 lock-out. Shortly afterwards O'Casey resigned as secretary when the Citizen Army council refused to pass a motion requesting Constance Markievicz, who was also connected with the Volunteers, to choose between the two organisations.

Apart from occasional visits to Dublin, Connolly during these months was still living in Belfast, struggling with union problems but following events closely. He welcomed the Howth gun-running of 26 July in an article published in *Forward* on 1 August. In it he denounced the 'hired assassins'—the soldiers who had fired on a hostile crowd in Bachelor's Walk, killing three; he concluded significantly with a verse quotation to the effect that behind governments stood armed men and that therefore 'liberty has ne'er been won except by deeds of war'. War indeed was inevitable, for ultimatums and orders for mobilization of troops were actually being issued on the European mainland. According to Cathal O'Shannon, Connolly writing in his Belfast office declared, on hearing the orders, that a blow for Irish independence must be struck and asked to be put in touch with the I.R.B. From that time onwards he was determined that the chance of revolution should not be missed.

It is abundantly clear that Connolly envisaged more than Irish independence as the outcome of such action. In the first article he wrote for the *Irish Worker* (8 August) after the outbreak of war and Redmond's assurance to the British government of Irish support, he dealt with the duty of the 'working-class democracy in face of the present crisis'. He declared that it would be perfectly justified in joining forces with a German army in Ireland if by so doing it could break the connection with the empire that had dragged it into war; if the European working class were to erect barricades and disrupt transport services to put an end to war the Irish working class had a duty to follow suit. Its immediate task was to prevent food leaving the country until provision was made for Irish workers, otherwise the urban population would starve when high prices sucked food out of the country to feed British armed forces. To accomplish this might mean armed battling in the street. But—and here Connolly's social revolutionary aim is openly stated—by starting thus, 'Ireland may yet set the torch to a European conflagration that will not burn out until the last throne and the last capitalist bond and debenture will be shrivelled on the funeral pyre of the last war lord'.

The departure of Larkin for the United States on 24 October brought Connolly to Dublin as acting secretary of the I.T.G. W.U. The lock-out had left the union in a disorganised state, with a shrunken membership, numerous debts and an insurance section so chaotic and insolvent that the authorities threatened to remove it from the list of approved societies. Connolly set about its reconstruction, a task unfinished at his death and completed only towards the end of the First World War. It should not be forgotten that Connolly's union activities, which included several strikes and hard but successful negotiations, continued right up to Easter 1916; they were conducted together with, and not merely parallel to, his other work.

Not only did Connolly become acting general secretary of the I.T.G.W.U., he also took over the editorship of the *Irish Worker* and the command of the Irish Citizen Army, using these two key posts to advocate co-operation with the Irish Volunteers. The developments of September had made co-operation easier. Redmond, whose first proposal to the British government in August had been that the Volunteers should take over the defence of Ireland from British troops, enlarged his offer in his Wooden-bridge speech of 20 September to include service 'wherever the firing line extends'. When the original members of the committee repudiated Redmond and his followers, two groups were left in the Irish Volunteers. The first favoured a wait-and-see policy, i.e. that action should be taken only at the end of the war in support of Ireland's claim to independence, or during it if a German landing in force occurred or if the authorities attempted to suppress the Volunteers or enforce conscription. The second group, in the main I.R.B. members, urged an active course, that a blow should be struck at an opportune moment during the war. Connolly, while uncertain of the relative strength of the two groups, wished to make common cause with the second.

As he was not admitted to the counsels of its leaders until January 1916, he concentrated on urging a forward policy for the entire body. He was determined to start a rising with the Irish Citizen Army, if necessary alone, in the hope that it would draw in others; the I.R.B. leaders, adopting similar tactics, hoped their own example would be followed by the mass of the Volunteers.

Pursuing his objectives, Connolly worked to improve the organisation and efficiency of the I.C.A. He appointed as his chief of staff Michael Mallin, who was secretary of a silk-weavers' union and had British Army experience. Guns were acquired by a variety of means; some dated from the Howth gun-running, some were sent by Fred Bower (an English stone-mason friend of Larkin and Connolly) who hid them between marble slabs, others were British army rifles with which their owners had parted willingly or unwillingly. Through the unwitting assistance of a British officer, a Citizen Army man (James O'Neill) learned to make bombs from pieces of lead piping; other bombs were made from copper pipe and tin cans. In his efforts to equip his army Connolly, on a visit to the north in 1915, approached Robert McClung (a Belfast ironmoulder prominent in I.L.P. activities) and asked his help, but McClung declined.[6] An attempt to make a machine gun failed only because a cartridge belt could not be made to function perfectly in the short time left before Easter Monday.

The efficiency of Michael Mallin's training was demonstrated in June 1915 at an all-Ireland drilling competition for Irish Volunteer units held in Tullow, Co. Carlow. The Citizen Army was allowed to enter and to the delight of its leaders it took first place for drill and handling of arms. A large contingent also took part in the parade at O'Donovan Rossa's funeral (1 August 1915) and sixteen men formed part of the guard of honour.

Connolly supplemented the active work of the drill instructors by his writings and speeches. In the columns of the *Irish Worker* until its suppression in December 1914, and in its illegal successors, especially the *Workers' Republic* which appeared in May 1915, he called unceasingly for opposition to British army recruiting and economic conscription (as well as to threatened military conscription), and for support for the Irish Citizen Army. He made little attempt to hide his desire for immediate action. He published regular articles in the *Workers' Republic* on insurrectionary tactics (the first on the Moscow 1905 rising) and analyses of street fighting.

The final conjunction of the Irish Citizen Army and the militant section of the Irish Volunteers took place in January 1916. When Connolly had failed to find a printer willing to produce the *Workers' Republic* he installed an old printing press in Liberty Hall and provided an armed guard to protect it; from this comparative security he published inflammatory articles that caused the military committee of the I.R.B. considerable uneasiness. Fearing correctly that he might start a rising with the Citizen Army alone, they arranged a meeting with him lasting several days (19–22 January). Though full details are not available it is clear that he accepted a date for the Rising rather later than he would have wished, and agreed to cease criticising the Volunteer leaders publicly. He was co-opted a member of the military committee, which consisted, in addition to Connolly, of Clarke, Pearse, MacDermott, Plunkett and Ceannt (MacDonagh joined subsequently), and was shown the military plans. The agreement meant that the Rising was to be the joint work of the I.R.B., those of the Irish Volunteers who would follow the I.R.B.'s lead, and the Irish Citizen Army.

Assured that the Rising would now take place, Connolly increased the speed of preparation. As part of his new duties he lectured on military tactics, drawing on his youthful experience in the British Army, to Volunteer as well as Citizen Army units. Finally, as if to give visible evidence that the cause of Ireland was the cause, if not of labour as a whole, at least of the Citizen

Army, he had an Irish flag (bearing the harp without a crown on a green background) hoisted over Liberty Hall a week before Easter. The subsequent course of events, the part played by Connolly and the Irish Citizen Army are described elsewhere in this volume.

Some matters arising out of the participation of Connolly and his followers in the Rising may briefly be considered. Whatever changes in sentiment took place after the event, it is obvious that during it Connolly and the Irish Citizen Army did not embody majority opinion in the Irish labour movement. The Irish T.U.C. represented nearly 100,000 trade unionists. While there was substantial agreement among them on such matters as the improvement of pay and working conditions, there was no unanimity in politics. The decision to add a political wing to the industrial body was reached in 1912 by an unimpressive majority, and was not supported with any great enthusiasm during the remaining years of peace. Congress did not commit itself on Home Rule. Many Irish trade unionists were content with Redmond's party and policy and were opposed to militant separatism. A substantial number in Belfast and other northern towns were Unionists politically, even if their delegates to the Irish T.U.C. were not; the strength of anti-Home Rule feelings among the rank-and-file was shown by the meeting (29 April 1914) of several thousand trade unionists in the Ulster Hall, where resolutions were carried pledging devotion to Sir Edward Carson as their leader. Support for the War against the Central Powers was not confined to such workers; the president of the Belfast Trades Council, which was prepared to accept Home Rule, had a son killed in France early in the War. When the Irish T.U.C. met in August 1916 its president, Tom Johnson, could go no further than to pay tribute to 'all our comrades who have been brave enough to give their lives for the cause they belived in',[7] whether in the War or the Rising. Any other course would have disrupted the organisation.

6

I.T.G.W.U. members were themselves not unanimous in their approval of Connolly and his actions. Some had objected to the installation of the printing press for the *Workers' Republic* and to the Citizen Army's use of Liberty Hall on the grounds that they formed no part of a trade union's activities and would lead to the suppression of the union. The executive of the union was initially opposed to the hoisting of the green flag over the building, and agreed reluctantly after Foran, the president, and Connolly had exerted great pressure. It should be added that only half of the Citizen Army contingent in the Rising were members of the union. On the other hand there were trade unionists who had joined the Irish Volunteers. Richard O'Carroll (of the Guild of Brick and Stonelayers) and Peadar Macken (painter), ex-president and vice-president respectively of the Dublin Trades Council, both killed in Easter Week, were merely two of the most prominent. But the majority of Dublin trade unionists, like their fellow citizens, held aloof; approval came later.

More debatable are the reasons that may have impelled Connolly to take part in what is often considered a purely nationalist rising. The events of 1914 may provide an explanation. As the months passed the cause of Ireland loomed ever larger in the speeches and articles of Connolly, and for that matter, of Larkin too, a development that reflected the various stages of the Home Rule crisis. The Dublin lock-out had left an aftermath of bitterness directed against the majority of British trade union leaders as well as against Irish capitalists and parliamentarians, and a feeling that the Dublin working class was isolated. The partition proposals aroused violent sentiments in both men, and if Connolly was the more coherent of the two, it was because he believed that partition would ensure the continuance of the Orange (and Green) bigotry that had bedevilled his labours in Belfast. His hope that a modest instalment of national freedom was forthcoming, and that with it the Irish working class would emerge as a distinctive political force capable of gaining what remained and reaching its own social objectives, was fading swiftly. Constitutional methods seemed increasingly futile in the face of Carson's threats, the Curragh mutiny and Redmond's concessions.

For Connolly the outbreak of war was conclusive. The failure of European social democracy to halt it, and thereby overthrow capitalism and imperialism, left him with the Irish (or more accurately the Dublin) working class as his only immediate resource. But it, in turn, failed him as the British recruiting campaign backed by Redmond got into its stride. To the large numbers of trade unionists who were called up or joined up (evidence for which can be found in the Dublin Trades Council's minutes of the early months of the war) were added many workers sacked by firms applying economic conscription. As the war progressed it seemed to Connolly that the working class might be lost permanently both to the cause of labour and the cause of Ireland. In an article of great bitterness, published in the *Workers' Republic* of 5 February 1916, he wrote: 'For the sake of a few paltry shillings Irish workers have sold their country in the hour of their country's greatest need and greatest hope'. In Irish society only the militant labour leaders had not apostatized. The sense of degradation was so deep that 'no agency less powerful than the red tide of war on Irish soil' could remove it. The shedding of blood could bring social as well as national redemption. If that happened, Connolly may have hoped, as he had hoped at the outbreak of war that Ireland, in seeking to recover her national freedom, might yet set a torch to a European social conflagration.

J. W. BOYLE.

1. *Workers' Republic*, 22 July 1899.

2. *Freeman's Journal*, 30 November 1908, quoted in E. J. Larkin, *James Larkin*, p. 58.

The Making of 1916

3. C. D. Greaves, *The Life and times of James Connolly*, p. 263.

4. P. (*sic*) O'Cathasaigh, *The story of the Irish Citizen Army*, p. 14 and appendix.

5. James Connolly, *Socialism and Nationalism*. (ed. Desmond Ryan), pp. 109–11.

6. Personal interview with Robert McClung. McClung was later an official of the Workers' Union, and of the A.T.G.W.U. In 1915 many Belfast engineering firms were engaged in manufacturing the iron castings and aluminium liners of hand grenades, which the ordnance department of the British Army completed by adding gunpowder and fuses.

7. *Annual Report, I.T.U.C. & L.P. (1916)*, p. 23.

Ulster Unionism
and the new Nationalism

by
DAVID KENNEDY

(IV)

Ulster Unionism
and the new Nationalism

ON 8 February 1912 Winston Churchill, then a cabinet minister
in a Liberal administration pledged to give Ireland Home Rule,
arrived in Belfast to address a Home Rule meeting. He was
denied the use of the Ulster Hall and agreed to speak at a football
ground in the nationalist quarter of the city. He was boohed on
arrival at Larne and mobbed in the streets of Belfast. Along with
John Redmond and Joe Devlin he spoke in Celtic Park. All
this is well-known. But the fact that the meeting ended with
50,000 Home Rulers singing *God Save the King* has been
forgotten.

This fact illuminates the Home Rule movement. It was
essentially a constitutional movement and its leader, John
Redmond, insisted that it was a loyal one. Physical force had
been discredited. The *Annual Register* for 1910 noted with a
shudder that two obscure members of the Dublin Corporation
had attended the funeral of Fitzharris ('Skin the goat') who had
driven the Invincibles to the Phoenix Park. In 1911 the Primate,
Cardinal Logue, welcomed the King and Queen at Maynooth.
There were murmurs of protest but they were drowned in the
loyal cheers of the mob.

Ranged against Home Rule were the Unionists. Like the
Nationalists they also claimed to be supporters of king and
constitution. Home Rule, they argued, would overthrow the
constitution, deprive them of civil and religious liberty, and, as
it had not been submitted to the electors for their approval, the

Government had no mandate for it and resistance to it was a patriotic duty.

At the time of Gladstone's first Home Rule Bill Lord Randolph Churchill had drummed up support for the Conservative opposition by banging the Orange drum in Belfast. The Bill was defeated because of the defection of the Liberal Unionists. Many Ulster Liberals followed Joseph Chamberlain into the Unionist camp. They found there not just a negative anti-Home Rule policy but a positive imperialism which fitted the brash exploding city of Belfast as neatly as it lay on Birmingham. Belfast's major industries were trading in the same markets as those of Great Britain and drawing cheap food for their poorly paid workers from the same overseas sources. The Irish landed interest which might have opposed this policy had been bought out and had invested the purchase money in British industry. The former tenant farmers were too unorganised to protest effectively, though there were a few pockets of resistance. In North Antrim a Presbyterian minister, Rev. J. B. Armour, won the applause of the farmers of the Route when he told them that Belfast was the implacable foe of agricultural Ulster.

While the Conservatives were eager to exploit the Belfast attitude they did not create it. It had its origin in the seventeenth-century plantation, the most successful of all attempts to replace the native Gaelic stock by English and Scottish planters. In the intervening centuries there had been much fusion of races and tongues and some interpenetration of religious beliefs, but the Catholic revival of the nineteenth century threw up a formidable barrier between native and planter. The magnitude of this revival, mainly the work of Paul Cullen, appointed Archbishop of Armagh in 1849, the methods by which it was achieved, and the self-sufficient image of the Church which it created, aroused the apprehensions of Ulster Protestants who had known the more ecumenical regime of his predecessor, the Ulsterman, Archbishop Crolly.

The barriers erected by Cullen were protective in origin, called into being by two centuries of Protestant Ascendancy. Now the economic and social bases of that Ascendancy had been undermined, by the disestablishment of the Church of Ireland, by the Land Purchase Acts, by the extension of the franchise and the secret ballot, and by the payment of parliamentary representatives. It was feared that Home Rule would complete the work, overthrowing not only Ascendancy but Protestantism as well. These fears were crystallized in the slogan 'Home Rule is Rome Rule'.

The Ulster Unionist Council made skilful use of these fears to build a united Protestant front against Home Rule. Incidents were magnified by publicity to exacerbate feelings between Catholics and Protestants. A domestic squabble arising from a mixed-marriage, the McCann case, became an act of papal aggression solemnly debated in the House of Lords. A clash between rival processions at Castledawson became a Catholic attack on a children's Sunday School procession.

The Protestant front showed a definite line of strain right down the middle. In Irish eighteenth-century usage Protestant meant Episcopalian. Presbyterians were outside the ruling circle and suffered many of the disabilities under which their Catholic fellow-countrymen laboured. The landlords, mill-owners and artisans were, in the main, Episcopalians: the small farmers were Presbyterians. Many of the latter remembered ancestors who had fled to America to escape landlord tyranny at home or who had been goaded into revolt in 1798. This tradition had not wholly died out. There were several people born in it whose lives spanned much of the nineteenth century. John Mitchel's daughter, Henrietta, met Dr. Mark Ryan, Fenian and I.R.B. member, in Dublin in 1904. The daughters of Samuel Neilson and Luke Teeling joined in welcoming Daniel O'Connell on his visit to Belfast in 1841. Mary Ann McCracken who had seen her brother hanged in Belfast's Corn Market in 1798 survived him by 68 years and, had she lived one year longer, would have seen the birth of her grand-nephew, Henry Harrison, who became Parnell's secretary.

But it was round the venerable figure of Robert Johnston, born in Crebilly in 1840, Fenian and member of the Supreme Council of the I.R.B., that republican activity in Belfast centred at the end of the nineteenth century. His daughter Anna, under the pen-name of Ethna Carbery, along with her friend Alice Milligan, published a nationalist periodical, the *Shan Van Vocht*, from her home, Lios na bhFian. Her propaganda drew into the movement younger men who thought that much of the Fenian plotting was divorced from reality. In his life of W. B. Yeats Joseph Hone tells how the young poet, a member of the I.R.B. at this time, was taken by Maud Gonne to a republican household in Belfast. 'The old man kept explaining at great length how this man or that would break up the British Empire and his homely wife would say at intervals: "Robert is so hopeful".' The young men saw that the force of public opinion was needed to give a new momentum to nationalism and one of them, Bulmer Hobson, with the support of Maud Gonne organised a '98 centenary commemoration in Belfast. This led to a performance of Yeats's *Cathleen ni Houlihan* in Belfast and to the decision to use the theatre for nationalist propaganda. With his friend David Parkhill and other members of the Protestant National Association Hobson went on to found the Ulster Literary Theatre. He also founded in 1904 a quarterly magazine, *Uladh*, with the aim of 'building a citadel in Ulster for Irish thought and art'. In its pages and in the theatre was presented the work of the most talented Ulstermen and women of that generation. Among them were Robert Lynd, Rutherford Mayne, Helen Waddell, Lynn Doyle, Joseph Campbell, the Morrow brothers, Stephen Gwynn and Herbert Hughes. Although the original nationalist impulse grew weaker with the years the Theatre developed a rich vein of comedy which helped to sweeten relations between

Unionist and Nationalist in a period of bitter political strife.

The Ulster Literary Theatre was an offshoot of the Irish literary movement which in turn was stimulated by the Gaelic League. The League came to Belfast about 1895 and had among its patrons the Church of Ireland bishop and the Moderator of the General Assembly. It influenced the Rev. Dr. R. R. Kane to declare that although a Protestant and an Orangeman he gloried in the name of O'Cahan. The League, though avowedly non-political, was the most potent instrument of political change in Ireland. Much of its success was due to the organising ability of its secretary, Eoin MacNeill. A similar ability to put ideals into practice is shown in the work of George Russell (born in Portadown) for the Irish Agricultural Organisation Society. This too had its converts in Protestant Ulster. All three streams, Gaelic League, Ulster Theatre and the I.A.O.S., converged in Eoin Mac Neill's native glens when Bulmer Hobson, organising co-operatives around Cushendall, joined with other members of the Ulster Theatre and with Glens of Antrim residents, Miss Margaret Dobbs, Miss Ada McNeill and Sir Roger Casement, to found Feis na nGleann in 1904.

These movements were breaking down barriers between Catholic and Protestant, between Unionist and Nationalist. But their appeal was limited to an elite and their action was slow. A more explosive instrument of change was the labour unrest which erupted in the Belfast docks in 1907. In that year Jim Larkin, a man of Ulster stock, (his father was from Co. Armagh, his mother from Co. Down) arrived from Liverpool as organiser of the English-based National Union of Dock Labourers. He was soon in head-on collision with the political and industrial City bosses. He led a dockers' strike for better conditions—6d an hour and a 60 hour week. The strike spread to the engineering works of Messrs. Coombe, Barbour, to Gallaher's tobacco factory and to the police. Catholic and Protestant workers joined to defend their rights. On the twelfth of July Orange and

Green bands marched, not to the 'Field' but to a labour meeting addressed by Larkin, Joe Devlin and Lindsay Crawford, head of the Independent Orange Order. Larkin was denounced in the Unionist Press as a socialist and, more significantly, as a Catholic. The *Belfast Newsletter* threatened: 'If workmen listen to him then Belfastmen, steady Unionists and Protestants, will suffer.' Seven thousand soldiers were drafted into the city and provocatively concentrated in the Falls Road area, far from the docks. Here, during a riot on 12 August, they fired on a crowd, killing two young workers, both Catholics.

Bulmer Hobson's Dungannon Club came out on the side of the strikers with a militant handbill which preached Arthur Griffith's economic nationalism with forthright Ulster vigour. It was addressed to the 'Men of Belfast' and it said:

The English Government have sent English regiments to Belfast to do the work that the Irish police have refused to do. Where the baton of the R.I.C. has failed to break our ranks they think the bayonet of an English soldier may daunt an Irishman's heart . . . The R.I.C. are finding out this truth at last, that they are the sons of Ireland before they are the servants of the English Government, and that if they strike it won't be the heads of their brother Irishmen they'll hit. The English carrying companies who desire to control all the transit and carrying trade of Ireland on their own terms, and for the profit of England, think they will compel Irishmen to work for them and dump their shoddy on Irish shores for less than a living wage. So they are fighting the Belfast man, because Belfast is in Ireland, and they think that Ireland must always pay the bill when England calls the tune.

The strike was settled in September during Larkin's absence in Liverpool at his mother's funeral. On his return Larkin repudiated the settlement and was dismissed from his post as organiser. In 1908 he went to Dublin to found the Irish Transport & General Workers' Union. When a branch of this union was founded in Belfast in 1909 a breach was created between two sections of the dockers. The Catholics on the deep-sea docks joined Larkin's union; the Protestants on the cross-channel docks remained with the N.U.D.L. The success of James Connolly in organising and extending the Belfast branch of the I.T.G.W.U. in 1911 did nothing to heal the breach. The founding of the Ulster Labour Unionist Association made the breach permanent. At the inaugural meeting of this body Sir Edward Carson appeared on the platform flanked by a ship-builder and an Irish peer whose income was derived largely from mining royalties. The *Times* commented: 'By disciplining the Ulster democracy and by leading it to look up to them as its natural leaders, the clergy and gentry are providing against the spread of revolutionary doctrine and free thought.'

The Irish Party tried to ignore the workers' struggle, pleading that it was distracting the people from their primary task, the winning of Home Rule. With the introduction of Asquith's Home Rule Bill in 1912 the stage was set for the final contest.

Ulster Unionists met the challenge by reviving the lines of action laid down for them by the Loyalist Anti-Repeal Union in the 1880's—the emphasis on Protestantism, the arming and drilling of Orangemen, the alliance with the English ruling caste, the proposal of a solemn covenant to declare Ulster's implacable hostility to Home Rule. Working-class Orangemen supplied the emotional impetus behind the movement, Belfast's industrialists directed and financed it, and the *colons* of Tyrone and Fermanagh, Abercorns, Montgomerys, Coles, Archdales and Brookes, formed the necessary link with the English ruling caste and with senior army officers.

For titular head they chose a Dublin barrister, Sir Edward Carson, Conservative M.P. for Dublin University. Carson's rugged appearance, his force, his sense of drama, his histrionic ability, his emotional fervour, his brogue—in a word, his Irishness—endeared him to the Ulster crowds. This man spoke their language and could command their loyalty. Few were as clear-sighted as young St. John Ervine who discerned the actor's mask: the 'last stage Irishman' he called him. The real Carson hid behind several masks. There was the hypochondriac who lived to be eighty; there was the barrister who while vehemently denouncing the Liberal administration defended two Liberal cabinet ministers in the Marconi case; there was 'the uncrowned king of Ulster' who later refused to accept office in the first Government of Northern Ireland.

But most great political leaders are complex personalities and Carson proved to be a great leader. He had to operate on several planes at once. He had to present Ulster to the timid British public as trembling on the brink of civil war. He had to convince the House of Commons that in arming to resist an act of parliament Ulster was actuated by the most devoted loyalty. He had to keep in touch with influential men and women of the Tory Party and relay their orders to his followers in Belfast. Among the avowed partisans of Ulster in England were politicians like Lord Hugh Cecil and F. E. Smith; the poets Rudyard Kipling and Sir William Watson; and in the army Field Marshal Lord Roberts and Sir Henry Wilson. There were others, even more influential, behind the scenes who were able to bring psychological pressure to bear on the new king, George V.

A public campaign was carefully prepared and adroitly publicised. It began with a monster meeting at Craigavon, James Craig's house near Belfast, in September 1911. This was followed by one in the Belfast suburb of Balmoral. The Primate of the Church of Ireland and the Moderator of the General Assembly opened the meeting with prayer and the ninetieth psalm was sung. The new leader of the Conservative Party, Bonar Law, a man of Ulster Presbyterian stock, told the assembled thousands that help would come to them in their struggle to save the Empire.

Studies in the History of the Rising

The rapprochement between Presbyterian and Episcopalian was completed with the signing of the Solemn League and Covenant on 28 September 1912. By it 470,000 Ulstermen and women pledged themselves to use 'all means which may be found necessary to defeat the present conspiracy to set up a Home Rule parliament in Ireland.' The signing of this pledge produced such a state of spiritual exaltation that a writer in the *Times* could say that from this day on 'Ulster seemed to enter into an offensive and defensive alliance with the Deity.' Very few Protestants could withstand the social and economic pressures compelling people to sign, but there were some who held aloof.

A year earlier Carson had pointed out that something more than words was needed. 'We must prepare', he said, 'the morning Home Rule passes ourselves to become responsible for the government of the Protestant Province of Ulster.' In 1913 the Ulster Unionist Council, without the formality of an election, nominated a provisional government. Carson was to be head of the executive, and committees were set up to take control of finance, military affairs, education, law, customs and the Post Office. It will be noted that Ulster was prepared to take upon herself more extensive powers than those conferred on the Dublin parliament by the Home Rule Bill. In effect, on the day Home Rule came into force there was to be a unilateral declaration of independence in Belfast.

A government must have an army. Various semi-secret bodies were now amalgamated to form the Ulster Volunteer Force. Training was in charge of Colonel Wallace, a Boer War veteran. Recruiting was stimulated by pressure from employers and 56,651 men had been enrolled by September 1913. By 31 March 1914 the number had risen to 84,540. It is impossible to say how many of these were effective. An officer of the army reserve, F. P. Crozier, organised a Special Service Section of 300 attested men in Belfast, and it has been stated that there were 13,000 such men in Ulster.

The Making of 1916

Fred Crawford has told how in the 1890's he smuggled in rifles, opened a rifle range in Lord Ranfurly's desmesne in Dungannon and drilled armed men there. He formed a secret society called 'Young Ulster', a necessary qualification for membership being the possession of either a rifle or revolver with 100 rounds of ammunition. In 1905 he had advertised in a continental paper for 10,000 rifles and 2,000,000 rounds of ammunition, giving the Ulster Reform Club as his address. He admitted that this was a publicity stunt, but for the next five or six years he and others were quietly importing arms. He claimed that by 1913 some 10,000 rifles had been distributed mainly in areas 'where the Nationalists were strong and the Unionists weak'. Among his customers were Lord Leitrim who ordered 1,000 revolvers for his tenants in Donegal, while in Belfast the Queen's Island Club took 2,000 and Coombe, Barbour's works, 1,000.

Crawford's most spectacular operation was the successful landing at Larne on 24 April 1913 of a shipload of rifles and ammunition bought at Hamburg. The Ulster Unionist Council financed the venture, and although Bonar Law's biographer, Robert Blake, states that the Conservative leader had no advance knowledge of the plan this is contradicted by Crawford. The arms[1] were distributed throughout Ulster in the motor cars of the aristocracy, with the connivance of naval, military, police and revenue officials, and in the presence of an 'unofficial observer' from Buckingham Palace.

Redmond professed to regard Ulster's arming and drilling as bluff and no doubt many Belfast business-men had no stomach for civil disorder. But there were other Irishmen who thought the Unionists had set a headline which they might copy. The first to express this opinion publicly was Captain Jack White, son of Field-Marshal Sir George White. When some of his contemporaries tried to enroll him in the U.V.F. he said he could never feel happy running guns in a Rolls Royce. His rebellious nature found its outlet in the help he gave Larkin's union in its struggle with the Dublin Employers' Federation. The brutal conduct of the police prompted him to suggest that the strikers should drill to protect themselves.

At a meeting in Beresford Place Larkin commended the idea to the workers. Sean O'Casey recorded his speech.

"'If Carson had permission to train his braves of the North to fight against the aspirations of the Irish people, then it was legitimate and fair for labour to organise in the same militant way to preserve their rights . . .

They were going to give members of their union a military training. Captain White would speak to them now and tell them of the plans he had to create from among the members of the labour unions a great Citizen Army . . ."

Captain White told them that . . . the Irish Citizen Army would fight for labour and for Ireland.'

On 1 November 1913 *An Claidheamh Soluis*, the official organ of the Gaelic League, carried an article by Eoin MacNeill entitled 'The North Began' which praised the example set by the U.V.F. and pointed out that the British Army could not now be used to prevent the enrolment of Volunteers in Ireland. A few days later MacNeill took the chair at a meeting in Dublin at which it was decided to form the Irish Volunteers 'to ensure and maintain the rights and liberties common to all the people of Ireland without distinction of creed, class or politics.' Among Ulster names mentioned in the preliminary moves were those of Bulmer Hobson, Joseph Campbell, R. M. Henry and Roger Casement, but of these only Hobson's and Casement's names appeared on the committee.

The Parliamentary Party stood aloof from or actively opposed the formation of the Volunteers at first, and Bishop O'Donnell of Raphoe described them as 'a vulgar and late imitation of

Carsonism.' But the I.R.B. saw the importance of this move and got twelve of their number elected on the Provisional Committee. The founding of the Volunteers marks a point of inflexion on the curve of Irish nationalism, a turning away from the methods of parliamentary agitation towards the policy that Arthur Griffith had been advocating for ten years or more, the policy of self help, Sinn Féin.

The I.R.B. was interested in this new movement as it had been interested in so many national movements since the abortive Fenian rising of 1867. The work of one I.R.B. man, Bulmer Hobson, in various cultural activities in Ulster has already been mentioned. In the I.R.B. organisation itself he was supported by Denis McCullough, head of the Belfast centre, by Sean MacDermott who was working in Belfast at this time, and by Patrick McCartan in Co. Tyrone. In 1905 these young men founded the Dungannon Clubs which looked to Mitchel's and Lalor's idea of a moral insurrection. In 1907 the Dungannon Clubs amalgamated with John O'Leary's Cumann na nGael which had Robert Johnston as a vice-president and Griffith's National Council to form a new organization, Sinn Féin.

Griffith, although a member of the I.R.B., realized that it was useless to preach separatism and the use of physical force to the Irish people at the time. He advocated a return to the constitution of 1782 with the Irish nation linked to Great Britain under an arrangement similar to the dual monarchy of Austria-Hungary. He urged the Irish Party to emulate the Hungarian deputies and withdraw from Westminster. In his weekly paper, *Sinn Féin*, he discussed with pungent candour the Gaelic League, the literary revival, the G.A.A., even the Catholic Church in Ireland, and assessed them all on the basis of their ultimate contribution to Irish nationhood. The Ibsenesque realism of his paper, its discussion of industrial resources and economic problems, appealed to the young men and women. But the movement suffered a set-back when its nominee prematurely challenged an

Irish Party candidate at a bye-election in 1908 and was soundly beaten. With the introduction of the Home Rule Bill in 1912 enthusiasm for Sinn Féin waned still further. To the electorate the Party seemed on the eve of victory: to abandon it now would be suicidal.

The founding of the U.V.F. brought Sinn Féin into the arena again. Ulstermen were practising what Griffith preached—self-help. Ulstermen had taken up arms 'against the usurped authority of the Parliament of Great Britain' and Sinn Féin promised that Ulster would have 'the sympathy and support of Nationalists' in its struggle. Patrick Pearse wrote: 'You are creating a Provisional Government of Ulster—make it a Provisional Government of Ireland and we will recognize and obey it.'

But these protestations of accord cut no ice in the North, either with the Unionists who ignored them, or with the older Nationalists who regarded them as mere word-spinning. For-tunately they were not put to the proof; at least, not yet. If the British Government intended to use force against Ulster—and there is evidence that Churchill planned a military and naval coup against Belfast in March 1914—the plan did not come to fruition, and after the Curragh 'mutiny' the Provisional Govern-ment knew that it was safe from direct assault. It is unnecessary to go into the details of the Curragh incident here. Through the bungling of the Commander-in-Chief, Ireland, Sir Arthur Paget, the stupidity of the War Minister, Seely, and the machinations of Sir Henry Wilson at the War Office, the leader of the 'mutineers', Brigadier Hubert Gough, emerged with a statement signed by Seely declaring that the army would not be used to enforce Home Rule in Ulster. From its now impregnable position the Ulster Unionist Council gave Crawford the order to land his cargo of arms.

The Conservative Party may now have thought that it had overplayed its hand. Asquith expressed the opinion that the Curragh affair had weakened the Tories with the electorate. Men were asking why officers should be allowed to opt out from active service against their friends when the same privilege was denied to other ranks engaged in industrial disputes. The King spoke of 'this disastrous and irreparable catastrophe which has befallen my army'. By this time too the shadow of war was falling over Europe. These considerations lent urgency to the conversations which Asquith had begun with Bonar Law during the previous winter for an agreed settlement of the Home Rule question.

In August 1913 Asquith had written to the King to say that if the Conservatives would accept the principle of Home Rule the Government would consider any reasonable suggestion about Ulster. He followed up this line of approach in a series of talks with Bonar Law and found that agreement could probably be reached on the basis of 'exclusion of Ulster'. The difficulty was to define the words 'exclusion' and 'Ulster'.

In November 1913 Churchill carried the proposals a stage further in talks with Austen Chamberlain. In a memorandum to Bonar Law, Chamberlain reported:

> I said the bare exclusion of Ulster was worst and most humiliating solution for them and did not satisfy us. The bill without Ulster was only one degree worse than the bill with Ulster. So we must change the issue. They would say we always wanted Home Rule all round . . .
>
> He suggested that it would be well to find out what delegation of powers we had in mind; whether my federalism was or was not equivalent to what they had in mind.
>
> If Asquith were to go to Bonar Law and offer as part of a federal settlement by consent: 1. to reserve all powers not specifically delegated; 2. to reserve customs and excise; 3. to reserve the post office; 4. to reserve the judiciary or at least the High Court; 5. to give Ulster its own parliament; I believe Bonar Law could not refuse such an offer.

W.S.C. did not raise any objection to 1 & 4; Asquith had already agreed to 2 & 3; 5 followed from our whole conversation.

A separate parliament for Ulster had already been mooted in private among Irish Unionists but had been denounced as giving away the case against Home Rule. Asquith and Redmond were prepared to give Ulster a large measure of autonomy under the Dublin parliament—Home Rule within Home Rule—but Bonar Law still maintained in public that the people of Ulster were determined 'to be governed by the British and not by a Dublin parliament'. Carson, unlike the right-wing Tories, was not prepared to wreck Home Rule for the rest of Ireland if he could have a satisfactory solution for Ulster.

Carson explored the position cautiously and in all secrecy with the Irish Unionists. Those in the south and west told him in October 1913 that they saw Home Rule was inevitable and were prepared to accept it. In putting the case for exclusion to his friends in Ulster he told them they must ensure that while remaining under Westminster they would have complete control of local government within their own area. But what was this area? In the debates on the Bill he had at one time moved an amendment demanding the exclusion of all nine counties, but this was admittedly a wrecking tactic. Bonar Law thought that if the Government would agree to exclude four counties and allow two to decide by plebiscite whether to come in or not this 'would be so reasonable that I think we should be in a hopeless position if we had to refuse it' yet 'I don't believe Carson could possibly accept this solution'. Under great pressure and to save the principle of Home Rule Redmond agreed to the temporary exclusion of part of Ulster.

By May 1914 the Home Rule Bill had become law and the Government had undertaken to deal with Ulster in an amending bill. In July the King invited the leaders of both sides to a conference in Buckingham Palace in an effort to reach agreement. Asquith, Lloyd George, Redmond and Dillon met Bonar Law, Lansdowne, Carson and Craig under the chairmanship of the Speaker of the House of Commons. For three days they wrangled over the area to be excluded. The Nationalists were willing to allow each Ulster county to vote as a unit for or against exclusion. The Unionists held out for six counties. All efforts by the Speaker and by the English members at mediation having proved useless the conference broke up.

Before the members left the King received each one in separate audience. To Craig he pointed out the difficulties of his position and asked if Craig would advise him to sign the Home Rule Bill. Craig replied that as a constitutional monarch His Majesty should act on the advice of his ministers and sign. But His Majesty would understand that he, Craig, would resist the Bill by every means in his power and would advise Ulstermen to do the same. A further glimpse of Craig on this occasion comes from Asquith's pen. 'Captain Craig who had never spoken to Dillon in his life came up to him and said: "Mr. Dillon, will you shake my hand? I should be glad to think that I had been able to give as many years to Ulster as you have to the service of Ireland."'.

On the day the conference broke up Austria's ultimatum to Serbia was delivered. In his final interview with Redmond the King said that 'he knew Ireland would be the greatest recruiting ground in the whole Empire.'

Ulster Nationalists strongly opposed the exclusion of any part of their Province from the scope of the Home Rule Bill. They formed a substantial majority in each of three of the nine Ulster counties; they had a small majority in two more; and there were compact Nationalist enclaves in each of the other four. They held seventeen of the thirty-three Ulster seats. As Irishmen they rejected the partitioning of their country, and as Catholics they bitterly resented Carson's talk of 'the Protestant Province of Ulster'.

Hints that the Government was moving towards special treat-ment for Ulster reached Redmond's supporters here in the autumn of 1913. Bishop O'Donnell of Raphoe, a trustee of the Irish Parliamentary Party funds, wrote to Redmond on 9 October of the growing apprehension on the part of many Catholics and Nationalists. 'There is a good deal of feeling,' he said, 'that the Nationalists of Ulster should form a special com-mittee, organize, and speak out . . . If anything special is attempted for Ulster by the Government you will have a most troublesome business on hand'. In January 1914, he reminded him of the self-control being exercised by Nationalists, and in February he wrote that they would strain at Lloyd George's scheme of temporary exclusion. The growing restlessness of the rank and file found expression in the decision to stage a public meeting of Ulster Nationalists at Derry on 14 March. Although the plan had the support of the Bishops of Raphoe and Derry it was abandoned at Redmond's insistence. He had, in fact, just then secured the reluctant agreement of the Ulster bishops to the plan for the temporary exclusion of part of Ulster. Cardinal Logue wrote: 'I find it a bitter thought that I have to consider becoming a foreigner in my own cathedral city'. The Party machine was strong enough to prevent an open rupture and for the moment 'the worst danger of an explosion seemed past' but events were moving rapidly in that direction.

The young men showed their attitude by joining the Irish Volunteers in large numbers. By the end of May 1914 more than 40,000 had been enrolled in Ulster. Captain Jack White organised a brigade in Derry, then moved to Tyrone and initiated a summer camp for training officers. Among those who applied for admission was a young man called Eamonn de Valera. Devlin alerted Redmond to the danger in allowing such a vigorous organisation to develop outside Party control. It will be necessary to smash the Volunteers, Devlin told Herbert Moore Pim. Redmond demanded twenty-five seats on the

Volunteer Executive Council for his nominees. MacNeill and Hobson persuaded their colleagues to accept the Party's representatives in spite of grave doubts about Redmond's motives and in order to avoid an open split in the organisation.

On 26 July 1914 a cargo of arms for the Irish Volunteers was landed at Howth. The Crown forces made an ineffective attempt the seize the arms and on their way back to barracks fired on a jeering crowd killing three people. Irishmen angrily contrasted this action with the tacit acquiescence of the Government in the Larne gun-running. On the outbreak of war, a week later, the Derry Volunteers sent a telegram to Redmond: 'Army and Naval Reserve met. Decided refuse join colours until assured that King will sign Home Rule Bill.' But Redmond did not support this attitude and in a short time 25,000 reservists, members of the Irish Volunteers, were called up. Such indications of the temper of the Irish people may have made Redmond cautious about recruiting and at first he merely offered to join the Irish Volunteers with the U.V.F. in the defence of Ireland.

Carson, too, was slow to commit the U.V.F. to anything more than home defence duties. Arms for the U.V.F. were landed in Belfast even after the outbreak of war. Recruiting was discouraged while Craig and Carson 'were arranging the best terms for the U.V.F. to offer its services'. On 1 September Carson arrived unheralded in Belfast and spent three days in secret negotiations with the Unionist Council. He admitted afterwards: 'When we got a distinct promise from the Prime Minister and the House of Commons that Home Rule should stand over until the war ended then we got up our splendid Ulster Division.' In offering the U.V.F. to the army he laid down conditions which the War Office accepted: the men were to form a separate unit and were to serve under their own officers.

The Government brought in a bill suspending Home Rule until the end of the war and on 18 September both the Home

Studies in the History of the Rising

Rule Bill and the Suspensory Bill received the royal assent. This was regarded by some Unionists as a betrayal and the police reported: 'There was a very bitter feeling on the part of the Unionists against the Government for passing the Bill and against His Majesty for signing it. This was shown by the disrespect with which His Majesty's picture was greeted at Picture Houses, and by the action of members of the congregations at several Protestant churches in walking out during Divine Service when the National Anthem was being sung.'

Redmond, however, professed to be satisfied and two days later he made a recruiting speech to a detachment of Irish Volunteers in Co. Wicklow. The speech was immediately repudiated by MacNeill and by the I.R.B. men on the Volunteer Executive. The split went right through the organisation. The majority took Redmond's side and formed the National Volunteers. Only about five per cent of the total remained with MacNeill in the Irish Volunteers. At the end of 1914 the figures for Ulster were: Nat. Vol. 53,560; Ir. Vol. 2,282. About one man in ten had a rifle.

Devlin personally took control of the new Volunteer Executive Committee in Belfast during the transition period from October 1914. New trustees were appointed and most of the former ones, among them Denis McCullough, were ousted. Application was made to the bank for the transfer of funds standing in the name of the Irish Volunteers. Representatives of public bodies who could be depended on to follow the Party line were co-opted on the Committee. Recruiting for the army was carried on at Volunteer H.Q. Gradually the enthusiasm of the members waned; there was a falling off in parades; committee time was largely taken up with trivialities; rifles were handed over to Dublin and seen no more; and Devlin sat back and allowed the movement to talk itself to extinction. The police were able to report: 'The United Irish League and the A.O.H. . . . have exercised an influence for good, and they have assisted in recruiting and subscribed to war charities. The National Volunteers are members of these two bodies. The Sinn Féin section includes the Irish Volunteers and the National Fianna . . . They do not exercise any influence save with their immediate followers and sympathisers.'

Yet even among loyal supporters of the Party there was growing uneasiness about recruiting and about political developments. Several young priests openly advised young men not to join the British army. Ernest Blythe, a member of the I.R.B., travelled through the North recruiting for the Irish Volunteers and organising republican centres. Both he and McCullough were arrested in 1915 and the MacNeill party was harassed not only by the police but by Devlin's supporters. In Co. Tyrone a concert in aid of the Irish Volunteers was attacked by the A.O.H., and MacNeill accused the police of fomenting trouble between his followers and the A.O.H. at a Volunteer parade near Pomeroy. But the slumbering animosity between the Parliamentary Party and Sinn Féin needed little encouragement to awaken it. Redmond had labelled the MacNeill Volunteers 'Sinn Féiners'. He had used the term pejoratively, as a label for faction and failure. It was to recoil on the Party, after the Rising, for it identified those who died with Sinn Féin though few, if any, of them were followers of Griffith.

A Belfast Unionist paper made the blunt comment: 'If Nationalists will not enlist because the war is just they should not do so because they have got Home Rule; for they have not got it.' MacNeill had organised the Volunteers to defend the rights of Irishmen and he now declared that they would 'resist any attempt to force the men of Ireland into military service under any Government until a free National Government of Ireland is empowered by the Irish people themselves to deal with it.' At Liberty Hall James Connolly's defiant banner expressed the same attitude more concisely: 'We serve neither King nor Kaiser but Ireland.'

Studies in the History of the Rising

Both Connolly and the I.R.B. were preparing not only to defend their rights but also to strike a blow for freedom. Connolly had the Citizen Army: the I.R.B. intended to use the Irish Volunteers. A military committee of the I.R.B. drew up plans for a rising which they concealed from MacNeill, although one of them, Patrick Pearse, was Volunteer Director of Organisation. Casement, though not a member of the I.R.B., shared their aims. In the pre-war months he had alerted them to the coming European War. He had gone via the United States to Germany to enlist German aid for an Irish rising. In his absence the I.R.B. distributed his pamphlet *Ireland, Germany and the Freedom of the Seas* throughout Ireland by post. To avoid the attentions of the censor the young lady who afterwards became Mrs. Denis McCullough posted a batch in Belfast in envelopes bearing the name of a well-known firm of Unionist sympathies.

In the pre-war negotiations Asquith had warned the King that if Home Rule were not granted 'Ireland would become ungovernable unless by the application of forces and methods which would offend the conscience of Great Britain.' But the necessities of war meant that men were in power in England and in Ireland who represented the worst spirit of Ascendancy, the mentality pilloried by Churchill in a famous speech at Bradford in March 1914. He recalled there that Asquith had asked the Ulster Unionist Craig: 'If Home Rule were to fail now how would you govern the rest of Ireland?' Craig replied: 'We have done it before.' Churchill commented: 'There you get a true insight into the Tory mind—coercion for four-fifths of Ireland is a healthful, exhilarating and salutary exercise—but lay a finger on the Tory one-fifth—sacrilege, tyranny, murder!' Lord Kitchener, an Irishman by birth, now in charge of the War Office, was of this mentality. He told Captain White that 'he would not trust a single Irishman with a rifle in his hand one single yard.' He blocked Redmond's efforts to have his National

Volunteers given the same privileges as Carson's on joining the British army.

In 1915 Bonar Law and Carson became cabinet ministers in a coalition government. An Ulster Unionist, J. H. Campbell, became Irish Attorney-General. Brigadier-General Hackett Pain, formerly Chief of Staff of the U.V.F. became O/C Northern District, Irish Command. Fred Crawford was made a colonel and retained in Belfast. Mrs. A. S. Green commented: 'The Larne gun-running won as many titles, honours and offices for its organizers as if it had been an incident in the battle of Ypres.' At the same time Redmond was refused a post in the Irish administration. 'Home Rule', said Bishop Fogarty, 'is dead and buried'. Kitchener's recruiting posters calling on Irishmen to fight for the rights of small nations and for the sanctity of treaties evoked cynical laughter. The R.I.C. recorded a marked falling-off in the number of recruits coming forward for the Crown forces. But in spite of snubs and frustrations Redmond continued loyally to support the war, and thousands of Irishmen died in the 1915 landings at Suvla Bay and Gallipoli.

Only two thousand men came out in arms to proclaim the Republic at Easter 1916. In Ulster McCullough and McCartan with 130 Volunteers assembled at Coalisland and dispersed again without a shot having been fired. In general, public opinion was apathetic if not actively hostile to what seemed to be at best an act of sublime folly. On 26 April 1916 the Executive Committee of the Belfast National Volunteers passed unanimously a resolution condemning 'in the strongest possible manner the action of the Sinn Féin party in Dublin in bringing about a reign of terror and playing into the hands of the enemies of our country.' But as the Ascendancy machine ground into action and the leaders were taken out and shot in groups of twos and threes until fourteen had died the spirit of nationhood awakened again in Irish hearts. From the pen of a young priest in Belfast, Father Charles O'Neill, came a ballad that was sung in every Irish town and village.

'Twas England bade our wild geese go
That small nations might be free,
But their lonely graves are by Suvla's waves
And the fringe of the grey North Sea.
O! had they died by Pearse's side
Or fought with Valera too
Their graves we'd keep where the Fenians sleep
'Neath the hills of the Foggy Dew.

Copies of the Belfast Unionist press denouncing the Rising reached the men of the Ulster Division in Flanders as they prepared for a major offensive. One of their officers recorded his astonishment at their calm acceptance of the news. A few weeks later many hundreds of them found their last resting-place on the Somme. They were Ulster's version of Pearse's blood sacrifice, and to their relatives at home their deaths in the service of Britain were a pledge of loyalty to which every tie of sentiment and affection would bind them for life.

Pearse and his comrades were shot after summary courts-martial. A few months later another execution was carried out with all the solemn panoply of the law. Roger Casement had landed on the Kerry coast from a German submarine on Good Friday 1916, was arrested a few hours later, charged with treason under a statute almost as old as the Norman invasion, tried in London with Carson's former 'Galloper', F. E. Smith, as Crown counsel, and sentenced to death. This was the public process. It was accompanied by a private process of defamation also carried out by agents of the Crown. Yet it was the prisoner in the dock, humiliated, alone, his past services to suffering humanity ignored, who indicted his accusers at the bar of world opinion. He reminded Smith that he too had engaged in seditious practices but 'the difference between us was that the Unionist champions chose a path they felt would lead to the woolsack; while I went a road I knew must lead to the dock.'

The Making of 1916

In 1905 Casement had contributed an article to *Uladh*, the journal of the Ulster Literary Theatre. It began by drawing attention to the fact that a Donegal man had been charged before a magistrate with the crime of painting his name in Irish on his cart. It continued:

> I have said that the *Morning Post* likened Irish to 'kitchen kaffir' . . . I bethought me that a people's language was a living thing, and that it was a shameful thing for an Irishman to stand by and see the soul of his country being dragged out through its lips. I accordingly gave up my club in London and devoted the amount of the annual subscription thus saved to a training college in Munster where Irish teachers are perfected in a fuller knowledge of and more scientific methods of imparting 'kitchen Kaffir'.

The word 'Kaffir', like a searchlight, throws its probing beam backward upon Ireland's past and forward on the future of the British Commonwealth.

DAVID KENNEDY.

1. These rifles remained in Ulster throughout World War I. They were used to arm the Special Constabulary in 1920. The Belgian Government tried to buy them in 1940 after the fall of France. They were subsequently issued to the Ulster Home Guard.

BIBLIOGRAPHY

Adgey, R. J., *Arming the Ulster Volunteers*. Belfast.
Armour, W. S., *Ulster, Ireland, Britain*. London.
Armour, W. S., *Armour of Ballymoney*. London.
Blake, R., *The Unknown Prime Minister*. London.
Churchill, R., *Winston S. Churchill*, vol. 2. London.
Crawford, F., *Guns for Ulster*. Belfast.
Crozier, F. P., *Ireland for Ever*. London.

Studies in the History of the Rising

Ervine, St. J., *Craigavon Ulsterman*. London.
Ervine, St. J., *Sir Edward Carson and the Ulster Movement*. Dublin.
Fergusson, Sir J., *The Curragh Incident*. London.
Fox, R. M., *Jim Larkin*. London.
Fox, R. M., *The History of the Irish Citizen Army*. Dublin.
Good, J. W., *Irish Unionism*. Dublin.
Good, J. W., *Ulster and Ireland*. Dublin.
Green, Mrs. A. S., *Ourselves Alone in Ulster*. Dublin.
Gwynn, D., *The Life of John Redmond*. London.
Gwynn, D., *The History of Partition*. Dublin.
Henry, R. M., *The Evolution of Sinn Féin*. Dublin.
Hyde, H. M., *Carson*. London.
Jenkins, R., *Asquith*. London.
Lynch, D., *The I.R.B. and the 1916 Rising*. Cork.
Macardle, D., *The Irish Republic*. Dublin.
Mac Giolla Choille, B., *Intelligence Notes 1913–16*. Dublin.
Macready, Sir C. F. N., *Annals of an Active Life*. 2 vols. London.
McNeill, R., *Ulster's Stand for Union*. London.
Martin, F. X., *The Irish Volunteers*. Dublin.
Martin, F. X., *Leaders and Men of the Easter Rising*. London.
Martin, F. X., *Eoin MacNeill on the 1916 Rising*. In *Irish Historical Studies*, March 1961.
O'Hegarty, P. S., *A History of Ireland under the Union*. London.
Pim, H. M., *Sinn Féin*. Belfast.
Ryan, D., *The Rising*. Dublin.
Savage, D. C., *The Origins of the Ulster Unionist Party*. In *Irish Historical Studies*, March 1961.
Strauss, E., *Irish Nationalism and British Democracy*. London.
White, J., *Misfit*. London.
Various contributors, *Fifty Years of Liberty Hall*. Dublin.
Various contributors, *1913 Jim Larkin and the Dublin Lock-out*. Dublin.

The Two Faces of Home Rule

by
F. S. L. LYONS

(V)

The Two Faces of Home Rule

'Anyone who studies the history of the Irish revolution during the nineteenth century finds himself faced with a double struggle—the struggle of the Irish nation against the English government, and the struggle, perhaps no less bitter, between the moderate patriots and the so-called party of physical force'.

(James Joyce, 'Fenianism', in E. Mason and R. Ellman (ed.) *The Critical Writings of James Joyce*)

HOWEVER dangerous the temptation may be to make patterns in history, it is a temptation which most historians find irresistible. Those who have written about modern Ireland, certainly, have shown no disposition to avoid it. On the contrary, they seem to have embraced it enthusiastically, charting with almost mathematical precision the swing of the pendulum back and forth from 'constitutionalism' to 'extremism'.

Superficially, of course, there is much to be said for this kind of pattern-making. If we look at the history of Ireland in the nineteenth and early twentieth centuries we can indeed see what appears to be a steady oscillation between peaceful and violent ways of asserting the national demand. Thus, in the first fifty years of the period, the uprisings of 1798 and 1803 give place to movements for Catholic Emancipation and for the Repeal of the Union, movements which gain their most striking successes within the framework of law and order by the use of the parliamentary weapon which membership of the British House of Commons had placed in the hands of the Irish representatives. But these agitations fail in their ultimate objective of Repeal and the pendulum swings again towards force, the Young Ireland 'insurrection' of 1848. The collapse of that attempt and the aftermath of the Famine create the conditions for another phase of moderate and ineffectual politics—the period of the 'fifties, when the would-be 'independent Irish party' addresses itself to the grievances of the peasants. When this 'independent' party is seen to be not only incompetent but also corrupt, the mood changes yet again to violence, mobilised this time by the Fenians. After the fiasco of their rebellion in 1867 the country turns once more to the paths of peace—first the rather genteel Home Rule movement led by Isaac Butt, then the much more purposeful and emphatic pressures of Parnell. With the Parnell Split, so runs the familiar argument, disillusion with the parliamentarians once more sets in and the young men begin to find other means of expressing their nationalism—the language revival, Sinn Féin, the whole trend towards 'Irish Ireland'. But constitutionalism is not yet quite finished. On the contrary, the vagaries of British politics give John Redmond a position of balance at Westminster between 1910 and 1914 even more advantageous, so it seems, than Parnell had exploited in 1886. This position, however, is gradually and painfully eroded— eroded by Liberal weakness, by Tory bellicosity, above all by the steely resistance of Ulster Unionists to any form of Home Rule. From this frustration the spiritual heirs of Wolfe Tone turn away in disgust and the result is 1916. Government repression, Irish repugnance to the World War, and the threat of conscription do the rest. In 1918 the parliamentary party are decisively rejected; Sinn Féin and Republicanism (linked together institutionally since 1917 as they had been in many people's minds much earlier) at last dominate the scene.

Such, or something like it, is the sequence of events still faithfully described in our text-books. Set out in such stark simplicity, it is, it must be said, a very inadequate rendering of a highly complex period of Irish history. It is inadequate chiefly because it tends to assume, rather as Joyce's remark at the head of this essay assumes, that while two distinct interpretations of Irish nationality undoubtedly exist, these two interpretations are totally different and mutually antipathetic. On the one hand, we are to understand, are the devotees of the Republic, never relinquishing the separate ideal, however long they may have to wait or however far underground they may be driven; and on the other hand are the moderates, the practical men, content to win by peaceable means whatever self-government may be wrested by cunning and discipline from the superior power of the enemy.

But surely such a straightforward division of nationalists into two camps is quite unrealistic, because it ignores a fact which is central to any true understanding of modern Irish history. This is that nationalists have not generally been born 'extremists' or 'constitutionalists'. There will no doubt be some who are fanatically of the left, or rigidly of the right, throughout their careers, yet the biographies of most of the leaders, and the histories of most of the movements, exhibit no clearly-defined contours but rather a fascinating confusion. Men may change their ideas, parties may change their policies; events and accidents will have all sorts of unforeseen consequences; the mere passage of time will bring its own modulations. This is hardly surprising. Mutability is, after all, one of the commonest features of the human condition. Consistency, said Emerson, is the hobgoblin of little minds. One might go further and suggest that in politics it is as often as not a recipe for disaster.

Of course there is a danger here. Is not such a view of history, it may be asked, too cynical? Does it not reduce politics to mere opportunism? And if so, what becomes of the idealism and the patriotism which have led so many men on so many different occasions to die for Ireland? Yet even to phrase these questions in such terms seems to me to imply misunderstanding of the issue involved. Just because a man changes his mind need that be due to any loss of idealism, or excess of cynicism? May it not just as well be due to a sober assessment of the possibilities of any given situation? Take, for example, the cause of a young nationalist growing up in the shadow of the Fenian fiasco of 1867. He could have two quite different reactions to that failure; each of them could be perfectly sincere and he could even himself experience both of them at different times. He could either allow himself to be dazzled by the republican mythology, join the I.R.B., and have no truck with anything short of 'the full national demand'. Or, he could look dispassionately at the recklessness and incompetence which had marked so much of the history of insurgent Ireland and ask the potent question—was it desirable, indeed even justifiable, to inflame young men with hopes that could never be realised, to lead them out in so woefully unprepared and disorganised a fashion to death in the streets or on the scaffold? Such a man might be torn between recognition of the *right* to rebel and realisation of the *inexpediency* of rebellion. He might well hesitate to repeat once more a chapter which could have, as it would seem to him, but one end. Rather than write that chapter he might feel with the utmost conviction that the path of patriotism lay in constitutional agitation rather than in hopeless violence.

This is no imaginary situation. It is, in fact, a fair description of the choice that faced many individuals of the Parnellite generation, of whom John Dillon may perhaps serve as the archetype. Brought up in the traditions of Young Ireland, in youth an extremist by temperament, his later career is the record of a gradual evolution towards constitutional nationalism. But—and this is surely the point—the distinction in his mind was not a simple distinction between right and wrong, or even between left and right. It was a distinction between the ideal and the real, between the unattainable vision and the practicality that had to be worked for and grasped when the moment was ripe. He did not regard physical force as immoral, rather as unfeasible; and even at that, as his record in 1916 reveals, he could not withhold

either his sympathy or his respect from those who were prepared
to die for their beliefs.[1]

For the generation that has grown up since the Treaty and
which has only recently been celebrating the fiftieth anniversary
of the Easter Rising, it requires a great effort of the historical
imagination even to comprehend the kind of mental processes
I have been describing. After all, it may be argued, it is the
republican tradition which triumphed in the end; the constitutionalists were wrong and that is the end of the story. But this
reasoning (apart altogether from the fact that Pearse might have
some reservations about the nature of the triumph) is the crudest
kind of historical fallacy. There is no surer way of going wrong
about the past than to interpret it in terms of the present. The
past has to be looked at in its own terms, through the eyes of the
men who were actually living at the time and faced with burden-
some decisions of which they could not see the outcome. The
most we can do is to take these complexities into account and
extend to the men caught up in that past our compassion as well
as all the objectivity we can muster.

But part of our historical misunderstanding may come simply
from a misuse of terms, and particularly from our tendency to
equate extremism and constitutionalism with left and right. If
there is any single generalisation that is valid for the whole
period 1798 to 1921 it is surely this—that no substantial gains
were made by Irish nationalism without powerful and sustained
pressure. It is, however, a very inadequate definition which
identifies pressure with violence and reserves a monopoly of it to
the exponents of physical force. On the contrary, those constitutional movements which have been most formidable in our
history are precisely the movements which have combined action
in parliament with the mobilisation of extra-parliamentary
agitation. Such movements, in short, have been Janus-faced, one
face looking towards Westminster, the other looking towards
Ireland. Whether one considers Catholic Emancipation, or

Repeal, or Home Rule, it is the ability to look both ways that marks the difference between success and failure. And since of these three it was the Home Rule movement which had the longest, and in many ways the most distinguished, record, it is from the history of Home Rule that I shall try to develop this theme in the remainder of my essay.

Circumstances were, outwardly at least, propitious when in 1870 Isaac Butt launched the Home Government Association. The memory of the Fenian collapse of 1867 was only three years in the past and men were ready to sail for the time being upon a different tack, the winning of beneficial, if limited, reforms from the British government. Gladstone, indeed, had already encouraged this new development by disestablishing the Irish Church in 1869, following this the next year by his first fumbling attempt to solve the Irish land question. To Butt, conservative in temperament to the end of his days as in his earlier career he had been conservative in politics, this moderate, piece-meal approach to the country's problems was entirely congenial. Although by defending Fenian prisoners in court in the previous decade he had gained considerable respect from the physical force section, his own views, which looked towards a federal solution for the problem of governing Ireland, were a world away from those of the revolutionaries who had risen in arms for the republic. Moreover, although in 1873 he was able to transform his original organisation into the rather more broadly based Home Rule League, and also to launch in England a Home Rule Confederation in which the Fenians took a close interest from the start, his notion of how best to extract even partial concessions from parliament was totally inadequate. The House of Commons, he felt, must first be impressed by the moderation and sweet reasonableness with which the Home Rulers presented their case. When this evidence of political maturity had been sufficiently paraded at Westminster the walls of prejudice would collapse and Ireland would be granted her modicum of self-government.[2]

Studies in the History of the Rising

Alas, no walls collapsed at the shrill piping of Butt's penny-whistle. His policy was futile, and soon seen to be futile by Irishmen at home and abroad. The story of what followed is familiar and need not be told in detail. A handful of the members returned to parliament in 1874, most notably the Belfast provision-merchant, J. G. Biggar, began to experiment with a more positive policy. Or, strictly, a more negative policy—the policy of deliberately obstructing the debates of the House of Commons so that English business could not proceed until Irish grievances had at least been ventilated, if not remedied. This policy, however, was not carried out with full intensity until after Parnell had entered the House in 1875. He was only 29 and utterly inexperienced. And since he was also the scion of a Protestant landlord family he seemed a most unlikely leader for a Catholic middle-class movement. Yet, though he was indeed an aristocrat to his finger-tips, that was not the key to his character or his politics. The driving force of his life was a cold, profound hatred for England. The only way to treat an English-man, he once told his brother, was to stand up to him, and this remained his constant rule of conduct. He and his small group of fellow-obstructionists rapidly perfected their technique, to the fury of English M.P.s, the chagrin of Butt and the delight of a growing number of Irishmen.[3] Soon Parnell began to reap the harvest of his audacity, replacing Butt as president of the Home Rule Confederation of Great Britain in 1877 and, as an almost inevitable consequence, attracting to himself the speculative gaze of Fenians in general and Irish-American Fenians in particular.

It was, in fact, from the United States that the next initiative was to come. The Irish-Americans, chief among them John Devoy, were beginning to turn over in their minds some way of marking the approaching centenary of Grattan's 'constitution of 1782' by achieving a significant advance in the cause of Ireland's nationality. If, for example, the Irish representatives at West-minster could be persuaded to leave the House of Commons in a body at some well-chosen moment and recreate the 1782 parliament in Ireland what a celebration of the centenary that would be! Unfortunately, such a plan involved not only winning the support of the parliamentarians, but also persuading Irish Republicans to lay aside their deep-seated distrust of constitutionalism and work with Parnell and his friends. Dr. William Carroll, an emissary from the Irish-American organization, the Clan na Gael, visited London in March 1878 to bring about this alliance, but met only with failure. Parnell indeed was impressive in his firmness—even more so perhaps in his capacity for silence and caution—but the leaders of the Irish Republican Brotherhood would have nothing to do with the contaminating influences of an alliance with the parliamentarians.[4]

There was, however, another possibility. On either side of the Atlantic awareness of a new agrarian crisis in Ireland was growing. In both Britain and Ireland food prices had been falling under the stress of American competition and in Ireland, especially in the west, two bad summers in 1877 and 1878 had seriously damaged the potato crop, with the result that the poverty-stricken peasants, never much above the level of mere subsistence, were threatened with starvation. There was no novelty in this, indeed, but one would have had to go back to the dreaded 'forties to find a graver situation. And just as in the 'forties James Fintan Lalor had pointed to the fact that the plight of the tenant-farmers might lead to a national explosion of incalculable force, so in the late 'seventies some were beginning to wonder if the real dynamic of Irish nationalism in the immediate future might not be in a land war rather than in a highly problematical withdrawal of Irish M.P.s from Westminster.

What form the explosion might take—if there was to be an explosion—was still a mystery when the Fenian, Michael Davitt, was released at the end of 1877 from a long, harsh term of imprisonment in Dartmoor. Visiting America the following year he soon became committed, with Devoy and his friends, to what Devoy called a 'new departure' in Irish politics. As this new departure was formulated by Devoy in October 1878 it had two points. First, that the parliamentarians should drop Butt's vague federalism and come out clearly for a general declaration demanding Irish self-government. Secondly, that they should devote themselves to a vigorous agitation to achieve peasant ownership of the land of Ireland, while not disdaining along the way any concessions that would give the tenant greater security in his holding. At the end of 1878 Davitt and Devoy sailed for Europe with two objectives resembling those that Carroll had set himself earlier that year—to involve Parnell in this pro-gramme and to convince the stalwarts of the I.R.B. that no adulteration of the pure milk of revolutionary gospel was thereby intended.

There is no doubt that they failed in their second aim—that was predictable. But over their meetings with Parnell hang several large question-marks which the surviving evidence has never been enough to dispel. When they first met him in March 1879 he seemed extreme enough to satisfy Devoy's exacting standards, though no positive results emerged from their con-versations. But when they met again in June the situation had radically changed. The sputtering agrarian disturbances in Mayo had burst into flame and Davitt—himself a Mayo man—had already begun to be irresistibly attracted towards this peasant movement. Could he commit Parnell to what might well turn out to be a social revolution? Subsequent events suggest that at the Dublin meeting he succeeded in this—at any rate Parnell addressed his first big meeting of Mayo tenants only a week later and in October agreed to become president of the organ-isation which had been set up to conduct the agitation, the Land League, not just of Mayo, but of Ireland.

Yet did that Dublin meeting lead to anything more than Parnell's adherence to the agrarian aspect of the 'new departure'?

Devoy maintained subsequently that a definite alliance had been entered into between Parnell, Davitt and himself to promote the 'new departure' in the full sense of the term, not excluding the possibility of an armed uprising in the future. Both Parnell and Davitt later denied the existence of any such alliance and the weight of evidence, though it is inconclusive, supports their view of what happened, or did not happen. Indeed, on any reasonable estimate of probabilities it is unlikely that Parnell would have abandoned his freedom of manoeuvre in any such fashion. On the other hand, American help was valuable to him—financially, it was soon to become indispensable—and no doubt he did not go out of his way to disillusion these influential, if somewhat embarrassing, friends.[5]

It has seemed worthwhile to dwell in some detail upon this famous episode because it illustrates so well the dilemma of a parliamentary leader conscious that at Westminster he still had no more than nuisance value, anxious to broaden the base of his movement, but at the same time chary of committing himself to what in 1879 must have seemed the exceedingly visionary aims of Clan na Gael. Devoy and the Clan could be good friends or formidable enemies. It was certainly desirable not to alienate them, but equally necessary not to hand the constitutional move-ment over to them bound hand and foot. Moreover, although they could offer him much, they could not offer him what he most needed—the impetus of a mass-movement in Ireland.

In 1879 that impetus could only come from one direction— the Land War. Identifying himself with it as closely as he did during the next two years, Parnell was able not only to extract from the government a great step forward in land reform (the Act of 1881), but also to establish himself as something he had not succeeded in being up to that time, a genuinely national leader. Since the Land War often boiled over into actual violence, and since the government felt compelled to bring in exceptional legislation for the punishment of crime, he had the chance to combine agrarian agitation with vigorous parliamentary opposition. The immediate results were his personal triumph at the election of 1880 (he was returned for three seats), the increase in his parliamentary following to 24 members—with the likelihood of further reinforcement if he played his cards correctly—and his emergence as chairman of the parliamentary party.

From then until his arrest in October 1881 he continued to double his parliamentary and agrarian roles. He did this with quite extraordinary skill and nerve, fighting coercion but not jeopardising reform, and at the same time resisting the pressure of extremists in his own camp to abandon the parliamentary struggle without, however, losing touch with the Irish-Americans who were still hopefully expecting the new departure to be put into effect. How he contrived to remain a constitutional leader while at the same time dominating the Land War has been told many times elsewhere. Here is it only necessary to stress the point that these crucial years established a pattern of nationalist activity which, though it was never to be repeated in similar circumstances or in the same form again, was to cast a long shadow over the Home Rule movement. What Parnell had really succeeded in doing was to bring both faces of Irish nationalism into focus simultaneously by demonstrating that parliamentary policies were never so effective as when backed by a formidable agitation at home. His strength—apart from the great personal qualities of coolness, tenacity and prudence he brought to his task—came precisely from the fact that he had, however briefly and precariously, managed to fuse into one a constitutional and extra-constitutional pressure.[6]

Of course, in order to keep his heterogeneous movement together he had to resort to all sorts of ambiguous stratagems and it is not surprising that both his Land League associates and the government were alike baffled by him. The former were disappointed by his refusal to withdraw his forces from parliament and initiate a general strike against rent in Ireland, but such was his ascendancy over them that they loyally accepted his decision to stay where he was and see the Land Act through. However, once the Act was through it was Gladstone's turn to be disappointed by Parnell's apparent intention to prevent it from coming into actual operation. In fact Parnell had no intention of destroying this undoubtedly major reform—though he was prepared to test it by holding the tenants back until certain selected cases had been brought before the land courts—and his extravagant abuse of the measure was perhaps intended more for the benefit of Irish-America than directed at the government. Gladstone, naturally, understood only what he read in print, and what he read in print was enough to put Parnell behind bars in Kilmainham in October 1881.

Yet in reality Gladstone, by shutting him up, was doing Parnell a service. The land agitation, under the combined pressures of coercion and reform, was beginning to run down and the long-awaited No Rent Manifesto, issued just after Parnell's arrest, was, significantly, a failure. It suited Parnell very well to be out of the way while this was happening, and if a spell in prison would earn him the sympathy of his friends on the left that was a bonus not to be despised either. Moreover, if—as actually turned out to be the case—crime and outrage *increased* in the country while he was in Kilmainham, this might help to drive it into the heads of ministers that the Irish leader was potentially a constructive, not a destructive, force. On the other hand there were good reasons why he should not wish to be shut up too long. A serious deterioration in public order might damage his authority as much as the government's and he had no desire to allow the initiative in Ireland to slip into the hands of secret societies. Apart from this, he was after all a political leader first and foremost. His ultimate objective was not just land reform, it was as much self-government as he could win for Ireland, and the sooner he was in a position to drive on towards this the better.

Studies in the History of the Rising

By the end of April 1882, after tortuous and largely subterranean negotiations, the main lines of a bargain, the Kilmainham
'treaty', had been struck. Parnell agreed to 'use his influence'
against intimidation and outrage and 'to co-operate cordially for
the future with the Liberal party in forwarding Liberal principles
and measures of general reform', in return for which the Liberals
undertook to drop coercion and to amend the Land Act in
certain particulars, notably by extending its benefits to lease-
holders. Since there was no longer any reason for keeping
Parnell in prison he and his principal associates were released
early in May.

Irish historians have generally seen in this 'treaty'—as many
contemporaries thought they saw—a decisive move by Parnell
to the right. A recent and acute English critic suggests that the
word 'right' in the context is inappropriate. If there was a move
to the right, he argues, it was tactical, not strategic. The strategy
remained the same—to win the maximum possible self-government for Ireland.[7] Yet, while there may be some truth in this
contention the fact remains that, in 'new departure' terms, a
shift to the right had occurred. Parnell was before all things a
possibilist in politics. He would push unflinchingly for his
objective, but it had to be a realisable objective. Irish-American
fantasies had not so far shown themselves to be realisable, nor
did it look as if they would be in the future. For that matter,
Land League fantasies had very little future either. If Parnell were
really to achieve something positive he had after 1882 to do two
things. First, he had to broaden the basis of his organisation. Not
only had the Land League been effectively destroyed while he
was in Kilmainham, but it had always been a sectional organisation and he needed something more than this. Secondly, with
a broader movement supporting him in Ireland, he had to
explore how far English parties were prepared to go in granting
Irish self-government and how precisely Home Rule was to be
defined.

The Making of 1916

The history of the period between 1882 and 1885 is largely the history of the achievement of these two objectives. Within six months of his release Parnell had replaced the Land League by an 'open' organisation, the Irish National League which, while giving him the support in the country that he needed, was firmly under the control of the parliamentary party. Partly because it was an open organisation, and partly also perhaps because the situation in Ireland had become so much less tense since the Land War had died away, conservative nationalists, including ultimately even the Roman Catholic Hierarchy, began to find Parnell's movement more and more to their liking. And when in 1884 the extension of the franchise practically guaranteed that at the next election he would have a Home Rule party of over 80 members behind him it became quite clear that he would be more formidable than ever before, though he could scarcely have foreseen that when the election came at last in 1885 it was to allow him for a brief moment to hold the balance of power at Westminster.

Even before that happened, however, there were signs that both great English parties had awoken to the significance of what he stood for. With the bidding that ensued and the gradual raising of the price until Gladstone finally declared for Home Rule we are not here concerned. The real significance of these middle years of Parnell's career lies not in the details of political bargaining with English parties nor even in the high drama of the introduction of a Home Rule Bill in 1886, but rather in the fact that the Irish leader owed his dominant position to the fact that not only had he created a compact and disciplined party capable of operating efficiently in the House of Commons, but that this party rested upon a truly impressive body of support at home. This harmony between the national organisation and the parliamentary party, it cannot be too often stressed, was the real source of Parnell's strength.

Yet there were items on the debit side. Once English Liberals had opted firmly for Home Rule and English Conservatives (and Liberal Unionists) had opted as firmly against it, Parnell had in effect lost his position of balance. Henceforth the Liberal alliance was essential to him, and because it was essential his freedom of manoeuvre was correspondingly limited. Moreover, the *rapport* that existed between party and national organisation was largely due to his own personal ascendancy over both; after 1886 that ascendancy became increasingly erratic, partly because of genuinely bad health, but partly also because of the O'Shea entanglement. Accordingly, when the Land War once more flared up in the winter of 1886-7, the nationalist strategy—the Plan of Campaign—was devised not by him but by John Dillon, William O'Brien and Timothy Harrington. As the struggle developed, it was carried on very much against his wishes and received only the most grudging support from him after the agitation had reached the verge of collapse through lack of funds. True, there were compensations. The very harshness with which the government attempted to repress this tenant movement, represented by its organizers as being closely akin to English trade unionism, helped to enlist Liberal sympathies for this new phase of Irish distress. Simultaneously, the clumsy attempt by *The Times* to implicate Parnell in the Phoenix Park murders of 1882 only led, through its well-merited failure, to an actual increase in his prestige, which reached such heights that in 1889 he visited Gladstone at Hawarden to hold with him apparently satisfactory conversations about the kind of Home Rule settlement the Liberals would propose when, as they expected, they were returned to power at the next election.

All these high hopes were brought to nothing by Parnell's involvement in the O'Shea divorce suit; by the split in the parliamentary party and the national organisation; by his bitter and totally irreconcilable quarrel with the Liberals after Gladstone had declared that for the Irish leader to remain in power would render his own leadership of the Liberal party 'almost a nullity'; and, finally, by the mobilisation against the discredited leader of conservative opinion in Ireland, taking its tone, as was only to be expected, from an outraged Hierarchy. The struggle between Parnell and his opponents, though intense and savage, was mercifully brief. It lasted only eleven months, until his death in October 1891, but short and concentrated as it was, it marked the Home Rule movement indelibly.[9]

The most immediate and damaging consequence of the tragedy was that the parliamentarians were split for nine years (until reunited under Redmond in 1900) into not two but three sections Redmondite, Dillonite and Healyite—which pursued their squalid vendettas oblivious, it seemed, of the mounting tide of disgust and disillusionment in the country.[10] But from this disgust and disillusionment sprang also a long-term consequence of profound significance. We can see now what was hidden to most contemporaries—that the years between the death of Parnell and the Easter Rising, outwardly so sterile, carried within them the seeds of a revivified nationalism. This expressed itself in a variety of ways, but all had this in common—they were independent of, and largely ignored by, the representatives of 'official', i.e. constitutional, nationalism. This was true of the Gaelic League, of Sinn Féin, of the whole movement towards self-reliance in culture, economics and politics which was coming to be known as 'Irish Ireland'. Even more, of course, was it true of that stirring of old bones that followed the return of the veteran Fenian, Tom Clarke, from exile in 1907, when the I.R.B. began a reorganisation destined before long to attract into its ranks the most ardent spirits of the rising generation.[11]

This was largely hidden to contemporaries because the Irish Ireland movement in all its aspects was the work of a minority which, however articulate, was numerically very small. So far as public manifestations of nationalism went, the parliamentarians remained in control. And it would be foolish to underestimate their strength in that period of new births. Even during the years of the split, when Home Rule had gone down a second time to defeat in 1893, the idea of Irish self-government still had enough vitality behind it for its Unionist opponents to want to exorcise it by the policy of 'killing Home Rule with kindness'. That policy did not achieve its main objective, but from it there certainly accrued to Ireland solid benefits in the way of further instalments of land reform, a measure of local (in effect, county) government and the setting up of a Department of Agriculture and Technical Instruction.

Even these gifts, however, did not by any means remove Irish grievances nor still the restless urge towards agrarian agitation. In the last years of the nineteenth century William O'Brien launched yet another organization, the United Irish League, dedicated initially to breaking up the great grazing ranches of the west and providing larger farms for the land-starved peasants. After a slow start, the League gradually spread over much of the country and its use of the old weapon of the boycott brought the government to reply with its old weapon of coercion. Many arrests were made, whole counties were 'proclaimed' and it seemed as if a third act of the Land War was about to unroll. But in reality this was not so. It was not so because both the leader of the agitation, William O'Brien, and the Chief Secretary charged with keeping it in check, George Wyndham, were much more anxious to achieve a peaceful and permanent settlement of the land question than to engage in outright conflict. And when in 1902 an Irish landlord, Captain John Shawe-Taylor, issued an invitation to representatives of tenants and landlords to meet round the table and negotiate such a settlement, the outcome (to the astonishment of both sides) was agreement on a scheme of land purchase which Wyndham successfully embodied in a major Land Act the following year. The Wyndham Act was far from perfect—it shrank from compulsion, it was tender—too tender said many nationalists—to landlords, and its finances were so ill-conceived that they had to be thoroughly overhauled six years later. Nevertheless, the tradition that sees in this legislation a turning-point in the agrarian struggle is well-founded, for the evidence is clear that purchase was rapidly accelerated and that the great principle of the land of Ireland for the people of Ireland was in a fair way to being realised.

Yet the way this reform had come about was disquieting to those who believed that nationalism could fulfil its destiny only by steering resolutely clear of entangling alliances with the hereditary enemy, the Irish Protestant ascendancy class. Amongst parliamentarians the most consistent exponent of this doctrine was John Dillon and it was his viewpoint which in the end prevailed. There were no more joint exercises with the Irish Unionists and William O'Brien, who had looked forward to a steadily widening horizon of 'conference plus business' with landlords, or anyone else ready to deal with him on these lines, left the party in disgust. In reality, of course, landlords who co-operated with nationalists were almost as suspect to their own more exclusive brethren as were nationalists who co-operated with landlords to *their* irreconcilables, and before long Wyndham had been driven out of office on the ground of having given some encouragement to moderate Unionists working for the 'devolution' to Ireland of a small and innocuous measure of self-government.

Irish nationalists could afford to look on unconcerned while Irish Unionists cut each others' throats. The parliamentarians, indeed, seemed to have recovered ground very fast after their reunion in 1900. They had taken over the United Irish League as the national organisation and retained control of this even after O'Brien had broken with them. In addition, through the medium of the Ancient Order of Hibernians they had a powerful means of mobilising the Catholic vote, especially in the Ulster constituencies. True, the sectarian character of the A.O.H. caused considerable uneasiness to some of the younger supporters of the party, but this did not take from its effectiveness. Indeed, since both the U.I.L. and the A.O.H. were dominated by an organiser of genius, Joseph Devlin, it could be said that in the early years of the new century the two faces of Home Rule were more in accord than they had been since Parnell's prime.

There remained, however, Parnell's legacy—the Liberal alliance. When the Liberals swept back to power in 1906 it was essential for the Irish parliamentary party to be able to show that Home Rule was once more an imminent reality. But in fact it was nothing of the sort. Not only was the Liberal majority much too large to be influenced by Irish votes at Westminster, but the Liberal leaders themselves were deeply divided about what they meant by Home Rule and when they would attempt to pass it into law. Their own freedom of manoeuvre was limited in any event. Apart from the fact that the House of Lords was certain to reject a Home Rule Bill, Home Rule had not been an issue at the general election of 1906 and Liberals in general, after nearly twenty years in the wilderness, were hungry for social reform. What the Irish party actually got, therefore, was something suspiciously like what the Conservatives had just been offering them. There was some remedial legislation, certainly (including the long-awaited establishment of a National University), but the nearest the Liberals came to Home Rule was the totally inadequate Irish Council Bill put forward in 1907. This—which was in effect another version of the despised 'devolution'—has rightly been described by James Joyce as 'a wavering scarecrow' and it was indignantly rejected at a national convention of the U.I.L. But, as Joyce also shrewdly appreciated, one consequence of this fiasco was a weakening of the standing of constitutionalism in Ireland.[12] Even within the ranks of the party there was discontent—one member resigned his seat in order to contest it as a Sinn Féin candidate, and though he was beaten the incident was a significant straw in the wind. Outside the party signs of restiveness were multiplying, as may be seen from the constant stream of criticism directed against the parliamentarians in newspapers like the *Irish Independent* or weeklies like *The Leader*, and of course in the organs of the Gaelic League and Sinn Féin.

This unhappy experience underlined the two chief weaknesses in the constitutional position. On the one hand, English parties, it seemed, could only be coerced, not persuaded, and the Irish parliamentary party were in no condition to coerce either of them. But on the other hand, shifty and unhelpful as the Liberals had hitherto shown themselves to be, Redmond and his followers were wedded to them whether they liked it or not, since they represented the only hope of Home Rule in the future, however distant and problematical that future might be. Fortunately, the crisis of 1909–11, arising out of Lloyd George's budget and the subsequent struggle with the House of Lords, transformed the situation. It was transformed in three ways. First, the two elections of 1910 wiped out the huge Liberal majority and allowed Redmond to resume that position of balance which alone could enable the Irish party to bring their influence to bear at Westminster. Secondly, the Parliament Act of 1911 so limited the veto power of the House of Lords that a Home Rule Bill, once passed by the House of Commons, could become law on its third presentation to the Lords. And finally, Redmond had been able to exploit the pivotal position he had achieved in 1910 by making the speedy introduction of Home Rule the condition for his continued support of the Liberals.[13]

There was, however, another side to the coin. While it was true that Redmond could turn Asquith out of office he could only do this at a heavy cost—the postponement of Home Rule indefinitely. Parliamentary politics therefore resolved themselves largely into a game of bluff, and at this game, it must be said, Redmond did not shine. One reason why he did not shine—and it may perhaps be counted to his credit—was that he assumed that the game would be played by the constitutional rules to which he was accustomed. As he saw it, a Home Rule Bill would be introduced into the House of Commons and there passed by the combined votes of Liberal, Labour and nationalist votes; it would then be ceremonially rejected by the House of Lords. When this had happened three times Home Rule would automatically become law and the Irish question would at last be solved. Nothing could have been further from the truth. Such an agreeable theory underestimated the strength of Ulster Unionist resistance and the lengths to which, under the dynamic leadership of Sir Edward Carson, it was prepared to go; it overlooked the readiness of English Conservatives to compensate for the loss of their last bastion of constitutional opposition, the House of Lords, by encouraging the Ulster Unionists in their intransigence and promising them all possible aid; and finally, the theory of the inevitability of Home Rule was based on the assumption that as much time as was needed would be available, whereas time was precisely what was most lacking. The Home Rule Bill introduced in 1912 only reached its critical stage in July 1914, and by then the world had other things than Ireland to occupy its attention.[14]

Thus, although Redmond and his party fought hard to hold the Liberals to their pledges they fought a losing battle. Even their agonised acceptance of the need for some kind of special treatment for 'Ulster'—which would result in a form of opting out from Home Rule and would therefore be a grave concession by nationalists who were committed to the ideal of Ireland one and indivisible—availed them nothing. Ulster resistance hardened and became steadily more formidable. In fact, the northern Unionists not only laid their plans for setting up a provisional government should Home Rule come into force, but in 1913 created their own private army, the Ulster Volunteers, which the following year was equipped by a daring coup with arms run from Germany to Larne and thence distributed with formidable efficiency all over the province.

The truth was that the Ulster Unionists had learnt too well the Parnellite lesson that Redmond seemed to have forgotten.

The Making of 1916

The only way to deal with an Englishman is to stand up to him, Parnell had said, and Asquith, as he swayed and dithered and temporised, seemed bent upon illustrating the truth of the maxim. But Redmond had no effective means of applying the only sort of pressure to which the Prime Minister appeared capable of responding. The national organisation, the U.I.L. had grown old, flabby and complacent; still adept at getting out the vote, it had few other functions and had been for too long content to trust everything to the manoeuvres of the parliamentary leaders in London.

However, there were others in Ireland who understood very well what lesson the Ulster Volunteers were busy applying. The formation of the Irish Volunteers in 1913 was the answer of the south to the intransigence of the north, and since that year saw also the creation of the Citizen Army, a small force based upon organised labour, Ireland now had three separate para-military organisations. Such a situation confronted Redmond with a challenge he dared not ignore. In June 1914 he moved to take over control of the Irish Volunteers who without doubt contained, as well as an important republican element, many of his own supporters. Ostensibly he succeeded, though it does not in fact appear that those who were preparing to use the Volunteers for ends which would have horrified Redmond were significantly hindered in their work. What Parnell would have done with such a body we can only speculate. What Redmond actually did with it can be summed up in one word—nothing. Indeed, even his nominal control lasted only for a few months, for when at the outbreak of war he grandiloquently proclaimed Ireland's support for the Allies, the extreme element in the Volunteers broke away from the main body. The latter remained with Redmond as the National Volunteers, but the minority, retaining the name of Irish Volunteers, passed increasingly under the influence of the I.R.B. and were to provide the main striking-force for the Rising in 1916.[15]

Thus Redmond's belated move to link the Irish party to resurgent nationalism in Ireland was frustrated by his commitment to the war effort, though even without that commitment it is difficult to feel that one who was apparently so oblivious of the second of the two faces of Home Rule—the necessity of a strong organisation at home— would have been able to control the Volunteer movement for long. As he became more and more a recruiting-sergeant for the British army he drifted further and further away from the realities of Irish politics. And since the war was intensely unpopular in Ireland, both Sinn Féin and the revolutionaries began to gain ground at the expense of the constitutionalists. The I.R.B., indeed, had early determined that the war should not pass without a demonstration in arms. Patrick Pearse and the little group around him grew steadily more exalted, contemplating with an almost sublime enthusiasm a blood-sacrifice which would, even if snuffed our by superior force, lead to an enhancement of the separatist ideal. And at Easter 1916 they achieved precisely this.

Even so, the hostility initially shown to the Rising by many in Dublin and in the country at large is well-known. How this attitude was transformed by the executions and the military rule that followed is an oft-told tale. What is perhaps less familiar is the story of the prolonged and desperate bid the parliamentarians made to snatch a settlement from the aftermath of the Rising. In their efforts they went dangerously far—to the extent of accepting what they took to be a temporary exclusion of the six north-eastern counties from Home Rule. Even here, however, they were dogged by disaster. Although Carson brought the Ulster Unionists to agree to this scheme for partition (*they*, however, believed it was to be permanent) the English Tories in the Coalition government succeeded in wrecking a settlement. Although Redmond made one further effort a year later in the Irish Convention the forces of dissension had strengthened in the interval and the last reserves of his failing strength were used up in a struggle which appears in retrospect to have been entirely futile. In the absence of a peaceful solution the clash between the government and the heirs of 1916 came steadily closer. The excesses of a coercionist regime combined with the growing threat of conscription worked only to the advantage of the separatist elements welded in 1917 into a single formidable movement which constituted as great a threat to the old parliamentary party as it did to British rule in Ireland.[16]

Against advancing doom the constitutional leaders had nothing to offer. Dillon, indeed, who had for years argued that the only way to hold their own against the extremists was to vie with them in opposition to official policy in Ireland, fought hard to restore some semblance of vigour to the party. But he only became chairman on Redmond's death in March 1918 and by then it was too late. The parliamentarians had staked their all upon negotiation—indeed upon conciliation—and in doing so lost the all-essential contact with public opinion in Ireland. When in the end negotiation failed them, they had no resources left. Disregarded in England, despised in Ireland, they drifted from defeat to defeat, from expedient to expedient, until when death came at last in the General Election of 1918 it came almost as a happy release. Fittingly enough, it was John Dillon who pronounced the epitaph of the once great Irish party when, writing to his friend T. P. O'Connor after that fatal election, he listed the reasons for their downfall. Some of these reasons—the Parnellite split, the dislike of many of the clergy for an independent lay party, and the hostility of newspapers like the *Irish Independent*, went far back into history. Others—such as the attitude of the government after 1916 and Redmond's support for the war—were more recent. But a large part of the fault Dillon laid upon the parliamentarians themselves. They were to blame, he wrote, 'in not realizing what was going on, digging a gulf between the party and the younger generation, making absolutely no effort to counteract the poisonous propaganda or to maintain our organisation and our movement'. And he added: 'After the Rebellion . . . the Irish party came to the parting of the ways. If we had then attacked the government and warned them of the results of their policy, we could have rallied a particularly united Ireland behind us'.[17] It was not to be, however, and the Irish party stands in history as a monument to the danger and futility of a constitutional movement facing only in the direction of Westminster and unmindful of the subterranean but powerful forces stirring behind it at home.

F. S. L. LYONS.

1. For his career see F. S. L. Lyons, *John Dillon: a Biography* (London, 1968).

2. Butt's career has recently been the subject of two monographs— Lawrence J. McCaffrey, 'Irish Federalism in the 1870's: a Study of Conservative Nationalism', in *Transactions of the American Philosophical Society*, new series, vol. 52, part 6 (Philadelphia, 1962); and David Thornley, *Isaac Butt and Home Rule* (London, 1964).

3. See especially, David Thornley, 'The Irish Home Rule Party and Parliamentary Obstruction, 1874–87', in *Irish Historical Studies*, vol. xii, no. 45, March 1960.

4. Thomas N. Brown, *Irish-American Nationalism* (Philadelphia and New York, 1966), chap. 4.

5 *Ibid.*, chap. 5. See also T. W. Moody, 'Irish-American Nationalism', in *Irish Historical Studies*, vol. xv, no. 60, September 1967.

6. C. Cruise O'Brien, *Parnell and his Party, 1880–90* (Oxford, 1957), especially chap. 2.

7. The point is very persuasively made in Michael Hurst, *Parnell and Irish Nationalism* (London, 1968), chap. 5.

8. C. Cruise O'Brien, *Parnell and his Party*, chap. 6; M. Hurst, *op. cit.*, chap. 6.

9. For the history of this episode, see F. S. L. Lyons, *The Fall of Parnell* (London, 1960).

10. See F. S. L. Lyons, *The Irish Parliamentary Party, 1890–1910* (London, 1951), especially chaps. 1 and 7.

11. The new movements in Ireland are well described in C. Cruise O'Brien (ed.), *The Shaping of Modern Ireland* (London, 1960).

12. James Joyce, 'Home Rule Comes of Age' in E. Mason and R. Ellman (ed.), *The Critical Writings of James Joyce*, pp. 193–6. For the Irish Council Bill and its consequences, see F. S. L. Lyons, *John Dillon*, pp. 293–9.

13. D. R. Gwynn, *The Life of John Redmond* (London, 1932), chaps. 4 and 5.

14. *Ibid.*, chaps. 6 to 9; A. T. Q. Stewart, *The Ulster Crisis* (London, 1967); F. S. L. Lyons, *John Dillon*, chaps. 11 and 12.

15. See F. X. Martin (ed.), *The Irish Volunteers, 1913–1915* (Dublin, 1963).

16. For the transformation of the situation after 1916, see T. Desmond Williams (ed.), *The Irish Struggle, 1916–1926* (London, 1966); F. X. Martin (ed.), *Leaders and Men of the Easter Rising: Dublin 1916* (London, 1967); F. S. L. Lyons, *John Dillon*, chaps. 13 to 16.

17. F. S. L. Lyons, *John Dillon* p. 455.

The Decline and Fall of the
Irish Nationalists at Westminster

by
R. DUDLEY EDWARDS

VI

The Decline and Fall of the
Irish Nationalists at Westminster

In 1911, John Redmond and the other Irish nationalist members of parliament at Westminster had good reason to believe that they were about to secure self-government for Ireland. The first Irish Home Rule Bill had been defeated in 1886. In 1893, they had been baulked by the veto of the House of Lords on the Second Home Rule Bill but now by the Parliament Act this privilege had been reduced from an absolute to a temporary one which could not preclude the setting-up in Dublin of an Irish parliament in some three years time—if all went well.

It is true that the English ascendancy resented Liberal rule and that Irish Unionist resistance had again re-established itself under the new energetic leadership of Sir Edward Carson. Under his influence on 3 January 1912, the Ulster Unionist Council resolved not to submit to an Irish parliament and commenced to organise and drill a volunteer force. The new leader of the British Unionist party, Andrew Bonar Law, sensing a weakness in the Liberal Prime Minister, Herbert Henry Asquith, but conscious that they no longer had in the House of Lords an unassailable defence weapon, pledged the organization's support to the resistance movement in Ulster. A quailing Asquith might be driven to a general election, and lose. On 16 March 1912, the more extreme Irish national party, Sinn Féin, proclaimed that if the measure of Home Rule conceded was not adequate it would set out to get self-government by other means. A fortnight later a great Dublin Home Rule demonstration was addressed by, among others, John Redmond, the leader of the United Irish League, and by P. H. Pearse. It was followed, on 9 April, by a great Belfast demonstration against Home Rule, which was addressed by Bonar Law and Carson. Civil war did not seem far off.

Such was the prelude to the introduction by the Prime Minister, on 11 April, in the House of Commons of the third Home Rule Bill which slowly but inevitably moved towards the statute book. On 19 July, Asquith in Dublin spoke at another great rally for Home Rule, and the diminutive Sinn Féin party used the opportunity to demand that the projected Irish parliament should have the right to collect all taxes. Two months later, on 28 September, there commenced in Belfast, with much of the atmosphere of a revived reformation movement, the signing of the Ulster Covenant to resist Home Rule. Half a million Protestants gave adherence to it.

Early in 1913, the Home Rule Bill passed its third reading in the House of Commons and was sent to the House of Lords. Interest in the unique constitutional development did not preclude Sinn Féin from stressing the limited powers of the proposed legislature by declaring that only independence of England would be satisfactory. It was the Unionist extra-parliamentary movement which attracted most attention and before the end of the year, on 17 October, Sir Edward Grey, as one member of the cabinet, was arguing on 'Home Rule within Home Rule' for Ulster. Outside of Ireland, hardly anyone noticed the establishment on 25 November in Dublin of another Volunteer force which to many was simply the nationalist counter-organisation to the Belfast Unionist movement.

For Redmond and his fellow Irish parliamentarians, 1914 seemed certain to bring Home Rule. A disturbing compromise temporarily excluding the north-eastern counties became increasingly of interest to British Liberal politicians, anxious to avoid another election. Redmond at first contented himself with stiffening Asquith's resistance, being shocked to learn, on 9 March, that he had offered, though Carson had refused, a six year exclusion for some Ulster counties.

Redmond was too much caught up in Westminster politics to deviate far from the Liberal leader.He was obliged, on St. Patrick's Day, to restrict himself to condemning as outrageous any more permanent partition of Ireland than this. To the rest of the Irish nationalist world even temporary exclusion was unthinkable treason. T. M. Healy and William O'Brien, leaders of minor Irish nationalist groups in parliament, appeared to regard this as something to which they would not have agreed had they been in Redmond's place. Like Asquith, Redmond seemed weak. Sinn Féin, because of its opposition to the parliamentary machine, made direct approaches to the northern Unionists, only to be ignored. Redmond, however, took the matter so seriously that he determined to consolidate the Home Rule struggle by bringing the Dublin-centred Volunteer movement under his own control. For this purpose, with his chief lieutenant John Dillon, he discussed the enlargement of the Volunteer Executive with two outstanding Volunteer personalities, Sir Roger Casement and Professor John MacNeill, on 26 April. Accordingly in the following month the party became identified with the Irish Volunteers as they called themselves to assert themselves against those of Ulster. Redmond's association coincided with the involvement of a small group of English and Anglo-Irish Liberals interested in securing equipment for the Irish Volunteers, much as the Tories had done for the Ulster Unionists.

Meantime, at Westminster on 23 June, the Asquith government introduced a Home Rule Amendment Bill into the House of Lords providing for the temporary exclusion of the Ulster counties from the jurisdiction of the proposed Irish legislature under the Home Rule Bill which had recently been passed and only required the royal assent to become law. The House of Lords, on 8 July, altered this to permanent exclusion which led

Carson four days later to endorse it by saying 'Give us a clean cut', thus finally dropping the Ulster Unionists' opposition to Home Rule for the rest of Ireland. This was no comfort to the 'Southern Unionist' group—as the small aristocratic and capitalist element in the rest of the country came to be called. In the last days of July, to those 'in the know', it seemed likely that Redmond was about to become the prime minister in an Irish legislature but that four or six Ulster counties would still remain under the jurisdiction of the Westminster parliament; on this Asquith's Liberals believed they would have sufficient endorsement from British public opinion to neutralize Ulster Unionist threats of armed resistance to Home Rule.

Suddenly the Austro-German crisis leading to the Great War loomed up and, on 31 July, the Home Rule Amendment Bill was postponed. On the day before the United Kingdom entered the first World War, Sir Edward Grey, describing the adverse scene to the Commons, was able to take some small comfort from the private assurances of Carson that, in the face of the German menace, the Ulster agitation would be called off.

It was to equal Carson's gesture that Redmond announced nationalist Ireland's support. With a conscious recollection of the Volunteers of 1782 in another British crisis, he went on to picture the new Volunteers 'north and south', meaning Protestant and Catholic, united in holding Ireland against the enemies of her British ally.

On the day after England declared war a proposal for such joint action was made to the Ulster Volunteers on behalf of the nationalists, only to be ignored. Simultaneously Redmond told Asquith that, at least nominally, Home Rule would have to become law, if only to quieten the more extreme nationalists whose Irish-American revolutionary connections might seek to make of England's difficulty an Irish opportunity; this Home Rule could obviate.

Asquith's reaction was to **enact Home Rule, on 18 September,** but suspend it for the year or for the war's duration—it was expected to be a very short war. Even this did not preclude Carson from making a scene in the Commons which the Prime Minister had hoped to avoid. If Redmond was disappointed he did not fail to behave like a gentleman. Looking forward to the end of the war, anxious to improve on the Home Rule position and avoid partition, he was very susceptible to the argument that Ireland should help England and come to the defence of gallant Belgium and other small nations under attack from Germany and the central powers. Accordingly at Wooden-bridge, on 20 September, as the leading Irish nationalist, Redmond at a Volunteer review urged enlisting for service in Flanders, and he followed this up at Wexford, on 4 October, with an appeal to go to Europe.

The immediate result was that MacNeill and some other founders of the Volunteers, concerned to keep them in Ireland, seceded with about ten or twelve thousand men. Some of those had already established contact with persons anxious to secure equipment for the Volunteers as a defence force and Sir Roger Casement was led further afield, travelling from America to Germany and reaching Berlin on 31 October. While Redmond and the majority were led to see the position of England and her allies as fighting for civilization and religion against the new barbarians, the *Irish Volunteer* contained romantic articles, as on 21 November, depicting a possible alliance of America, Germany and France against Britain. It was a condition of cold war within the nationalist camp, all the more bitter for being a fratricidal one. While this was troublesome to Redmond it was only marginal. More serious to him was the gradual conviction that the War Office was determined not to co-operate with him in his idea of organising a separate Irish force or special Irish units within the British army. While the Ulster Volunteers' officers were favoured with army commissions, the Irish nation-alists at Westminster were made to feel that the British army was still the army of the governing class, the class from which there came the Curragh Camp officers who had risked being tried as mutineers rather than be involved against the Ulster Volunteers. It was in these circumstances that Redmond was led, on 25 March, to criticize the War Office publicly though, for some considerable time, quite unavailingly.

In the following months, Berlin was visited by Joseph Plunkett on behalf of a small Irish and American-Irish group interested in winning support for a possible Irish rising. Their importance was to grow when the opponents of Irish nationalism became members of a British coalition government on 27 May 1915.

The fact that Redmond refused to join the cabinet should not be overlooked in estimating the extent to which he was in touch with Irish opinion. Perhaps in this his very nobility of character led him astray as his quondam opponents, Carson and Bonar Law, thereafter exercised a growing influence on government policy in regard to Ireland. From this time increasing attention was directed to the number of recruits for the war. To Redmond, the decline in the number of recruits was due to the Irish reaction to the coalition government and to the policy of the War Office. The decline, however, was becoming a political fact as the Unionists in the cabinet saw in conscription a useful diversion from Home Rule which became the subject of renewed agitation as the statutory suspension for twelve months came closer. On 14 July, the Dublin Corporation resolved that parliament should be asked to end the suspension on 17 September without awaiting the end of the war. In the meantime, the MacNeill Volunteers' Executive had secretly resolved, on 30 May, to resist conscription, if enacted, and this fact had been duly published on 12 June. To the nationalists generally this question became linked to Home Rule.

As the British dominions determined for themselves individually the extent of their committment to the war, it was argued that Ireland should be in the same position. Such thinking was all the more understandable as the government in the first months of the war made a show of consulting Redmond about Irish affairs. After the formation of the coalition government, however, Redmond felt that a change was taking place and that Unionist and Orange influences were creeping back into Dublin Castle. One proof of this appeared to be the growing favour of the Dublin administration towards conscription and this inevitably strengthened the opposition to conscription among nationalists. Within a week of advocating Home Rule and on the very day, 20 July, when Redmond disclaimed all intention of putting pressure on the cabinet to implement Home Rule as long as the war effort had to command top priorities, the Dublin Corporation condemned conscription. Four days later John Dillon announced that the United Irish League was against conscription although theoretically it was in favour of recruiting. By 2 November, Captain Stephen Gwynn, M.P., was clear that thousands of Volunteers had been lost to the war effort by the failure of the British government to listen to Redmond. Undoubtedly the anti-recruiting movement was gathering force and influencing people by calling into question the nationalism of those who followed Redmond's advice. On 22 May 1915, F. S. Skeffington warned Thomas MacDonagh that the Irish Volunteers were militaristic and no longer defensive. So general among nationalists was the objection to conscription that Sir Mathew Nathan, the Under-Secretary, a week before Christmas 1915, expressed fears of 'an outbreak' should the government give way to Unionist pressure and impose conscription on Ireland. It would appear that while he made little of the small group of revolutionaries he wisely discerned in conscription an excuse to be used by the nationalists to get public opinion generally on their side as a justification for a possible rising.

A social factor was also involved in the question. Early in 1916 the Irish Citizen Army, organized by James Connolly after the defeat of the Dublin workers in the great 1913 lock-out, had begun to fraternize with the more extreme Volunteers, and, on 8 January, announced a common policy against the recruited Volunteers 'wearing the livery of England', as those in khaki were described. Nathan had the discernment to advise action against the militant group but his superior, Augustine Birrell, Chief Secretary, was influenced by the parliamentary party leaders to leave this small group to their drill and their route marches. It was one indication, however, of how remote the national constitutional leaders were from government that they seem never to have been told of the discovery of John Devoy's negotiations for German aid, the code message dealing with which was intercepted by the British and American authorities apparently on 18 February 1916. Concerned as he was for the success of the recruiting campaign and for the victory of Britain and her allies, Redmond was very gratified to be able to note, on 15 March, the opinion of Bonar Law that post-war Ireland would never be the same as pre-war Ireland and, by implication, the common sacrifices against Germany would lead to a united Home-Rule Ireland in the glorious future.

Such was the situation when unexpectedly the news of the rebellion in Ireland reached London early in Easter Week. Not surprisingly, on 27 April, the rebels were denounced by the leader of the United Irish League as enemies of the best interests of Ireland and allies of the 'barbarous' central powers. To Redmond their action was a stab in the back when he was encouraging the Irish sacrifices in the holocaust of Flanders that north and south might be brought together in a home-rule parliament for all Ireland at the conclusion of the war. Because he denounced Pearse and his fellow leaders of the insurrection as traitors, Redmond was subsequently condemned by many Irish nationalists to whom the name of Parnell was sacred. But they forgot that Parnell denounced the Invincibles whose assassination of Lord Frederick Cavendish and the Under-Secretary, T. H. Burke, on 6 May 1882, imperilled the understanding with

Gladstone known as the Kilmainham Treaty. Just as Parnell, departing from his custom, panicked into denunciation, as if Gladstone in the moment of highest confidence expected it of him, so did Redmond who had guaranteed the fidelity of the Volunteers on 3 August 1914. Inevitably the mood communicated itself to others among the national parliamentarians in the early days of May, though T. M. Healy on 2 May, was quick enough to sense the reaction of Bonar Law that the Rising was not to be condemned absolutely as it would bring about another attempted Home Rule settlement. Again, Redmond, on 3 May, denounced the Rising as unpatriotic, overstressing the German connection. On the following day, after the news of the first executions, however, he expressed himself as against undue severity and made reference to the action of Louis Botha, the Boer leader who extinguished a rebellion with but one capital sentence. The harm, however, had already been done. Not only was Redmond credited with having called for the executions but his followers were stated to have cheered the news that the sentences had been carried out. Healy has put it on record that Laurence Ginnell, M.P. claimed that he had witnessed this though Healy insisted that his statement was a mistaken one. Perhaps he confused vocal condemnations of the rebellion with Unionist applause of the first executions. Whatever the explanation, as the executions went on changes in attitude began to manifest themselves among more orthodox nationalists. It is true that, on 10 May, the Redmondite party collectively condemned the Rising, that on the following day William Martin Murphy allegedly called for the blood of Connolly in a leading article in the *Irish Independent*; but on 11 May, Dillon denounced the severity of Sir John Maxwell and declared the executions had washed out the work of a generation of parliamentarians.

From this point, Irish public opinion began to change and Major Price, head of intelligence in Dublin Castle, blamed the Party's denunciation of the government as having stimulated this change. Before 12 May, Redmond had begun to express things differently. C. P. Scott had already speculated on the chances of an imposed Home Rule settlement being acceptable to Carson and Redmond. Concurrently the nationalist leader had come to the point of stating that if Home Rule had been in operation 'recent events' would never have happened. Asquith came over to Ireland, stopped the executions, and had talks with many people including some of the prisoners. Meanwhile in London his most outstanding colleague, David Lloyd George, got into conversations with Carson and with Redmond in an effort to explore the effect of the Rising on Anglo-Irish relations. And on his return Asquith proposed to Lloyd George that he should investigate the chances of imposing a Home Rule settlement upon Carson and Redmond to be put into operation when the war ended. More formally, the Prime Minister, on 21 May, proposed at the cabinet that Lloyd George should be deputed to negotiate on Home Rule and administer Ireland. It appeared to be Asquith's answer to the problem—he had reported on returning from Dublin that the government of Ireland had broken down. There was more than an implication that Lloyd George was expected to take on the role of Chief Secretary and terminate the absolute military control of Sir John Maxwell.

It was ironical, reflected Redmond, on 25 May, that the revolutionary group and not the constitutional party had stimulated the government to settle the Irish question. Four days later the Lloyd George plan emerged: there was to be instant Home Rule imposed by the government, accepted by Carson and Redmond, providing for the setting up of a twenty-six county legislature consisting of the existing members of parliament elected in 1910, supplemented by government nominees representing the minority. The six north-eastern counties were to remain part of the United Kingdom outside the Home Rule area for the duration of the war, there being some ambiguity as to what would happen then. The existing representation was to be

maintained at Westminster. It was understood that the negotiat-
ing minister relied upon Carson to deal with the Unionists
(whose leader Bonar Law was favourable) as Redmond was to
do with the nationalists. The immediate advantage of the plan
was that it would freeze the existing political situation, putting
Redmond into power as Irish Prime Minister and terminate the
political dangers that could follow the increasing resentment
towards the Maxwell regime at the number of persons punished
over the Easter Rising. On this latter point there was a serious
report on the last day of the month from the Inspector General
of the Royal Irish Constabulary. To facilitate the smooth transition, the Prime Minister and the leader of the Unionist Party
hoped that Lloyd George would undertake the office of Chief
Secretary of Ireland. In these circumstances, it was hoped that
recruiting would begin again quickly if only to replenish the
vacancies created in many regiments by the increasing number
of casualties in France. The plan miscarried, as Lloyd George's
interest was diverted to the War Ministry, on the drowning of
Kitchener, and because there was a revival of the Unionist Whig
magnates' determination to prevent Home Rule. Whether
Redmond in office in Ireland could have discharged the rôle for
which he was cast is very doubtful. All this, however, was nearly
two months ahead on 29 May.

As early as 1 June, the Unionist effort, apart from Ulster,
against instant Home Rule commenced privately. It was not easy
to get it off the ground as Carson, once convinced, could not be
moved and moreover after Lloyd George appealed to him on
3 June that their common plans on a more effective war effort
depended on getting the Irish difficulty out of the way, Carson
went to Belfast and put it in such a form to the Ulster Unionists
that while the responsibility was theirs he had himself endorsed
the proposal for the good of the empire. They were led to believe
that the exclusion of the northern counties was permanent. The
loss of Kitchener whose ship was mined on the way to Russia,

gave startling point to Carson's argument though it changed the priorities in the mind of Lloyd George anxious, as soon as possible, to get the conduct of the war out of the hands of the generals.

On 10 June under the influence of Redmond and of his Ulster lieutenant Joe Devlin, but subject to some reservations of Dillon's, the United Irish League endorsed the plan, though it was only with the greatest amount of reluctance that the northern nationalists agreed to partition which they were assured was temporary.

Concurrently one non-Ulster Unionist leader, Walter Long, had made sufficient progress against the plan to declare it would split the Unionist Party. By 19 June it was clear that some cabinet members would resign. A manifesto by Unionist lords—including Balfour of Burleigh, Cromer, Halsbury, Midleton and Salisbury—remonstrated against 'trafficking in the sacred principles of self-determination', on 23 June. The very success of Redmond at Belfast with the northern nationalists led critics like Healy to forecast that it would provoke Lord Lansdowne and other Unionists, particularly those connected with the twenty-six counties. On 25 June, Lord Selborne resigned from the cabinet. Bonar Law, two days later, began to wonder how rejection would react on the Irish Party. This was followed, on 30 June, by a speech in the House of Lords by Lansdowne in which he queried how the Defence of the Realm Act (D.O.R.A.), under which Maxwell's military governorship operated, would be preserved under Redmond. The matter dragged on through July, Asquith becoming more and more fearful under the shower of Unionist protests. Then it was decided to whittle down the offer. On two points the cabinet tried to meet the critics, on 19 July. It was decided to maintain D.O.R.A. and Maxwell; and the Irish representation at Westminster was to be cut to 43. But this was too much for Redmond and he rejected the changes whereupon Asquith abandoned the plan on 24 July. From this date Redmond's followers became alienated from Asquith, and, as Bonar Law predicted, the Party suffered in public estimation. It even went to the length of issuing a statement under the title 'The Broken Treaty' impliedly blaming the Prime Minister, though it kept only to the text of the Irish nationalists' speeches in parliament on the issue.

The withdrawal of the plan for instant Home Rule showed the strength and the weakness of John Redmond. By employing the tactics of Parnell, resorting to the extra-parliamentary influence of a party leader, he secured his vote of confidence but at a frightful cost. By a threat to resign he had secured acceptance from Ulster nationalists of the principle of temporary exclusion. But he had put his trust in three other men without his degree of power over their colleagues. Bonar Law could lead the Unionists in defiance of Asquith and Lloyd George, but not in agreement with the latter. Carson could persuade the Ulster Unionists to follow his lead but not the great individualists of the remaining three provinces. Lloyd George could charm Law and Carson but was distrusted by the Unionist magnates and was too ambitious to replace Asquith as Prime Minister and to risk a controversy with such a weak man at the wrong moment. Thus Asquith got the blame except in Ireland where Redmond shared his loss of prestige.

As Healy pertinently remarked, on 25 July, the six-county concession had worsened the Party's situation. In any future negotiations Redmond would be kept to this condition. It was only to be hoped that this did not apply to others. Not that the Party saw it in this way; their loyalty to Redmond, if only because of the recollection of the Parnellite split kept them closer together than was the case with the great English parties. More immediately, the six-county concession led Redmond to take up a more critical attitude than hitherto. In particular, he lent himself to a public policy of securing the restoration of civil government in Ireland. Early in August, H. E. Duke was appointed Chief Secretary and, before the end of the month, Wimborne returned as Lord Lieutenant, but Sir John Maxwell still ruled in military matters and was not to be changed in his view that martial law was the best deterrent to revolution. The reaction among moderate nationalists, continually conscious of being regarded as revolutionaries, was to become increasingly resentful of the regime, of the government and, in many cases, of their allies the Redmondite party.

In these circumstances, it was not surprising that early in August there was established in one of the proposed excluded north-eastern countries, Tyrone, the Irish Nation League for the purpose of repealing the Act of Union. For some twelve months, this organisation developed clubs in various parts of the country and seemed more likely than was Sinn Féin, which had become disorganised since before the rebellion, to challenge the monopoly of the United Irish League. Not surprisingly, its legislative arm, the Parliamentary Party became more critical of martial law and of the Castle administration; on such matters its older critics like T. M. Healy and William O'Brien also became involved, the former acting frequently as a prisoners' friend for internees, deportees and other victims of martial law.

It was thus that Dillon, the most openly sympathetic of the Party towards the defeated rebels, together with Healy, took up, on 26 July, such examples of military excesses in Easter Week, as the illegal execution of Skeffington and others at Portobello Barracks and the unauthorized shootings at North King Street, Dublin. They forced the government to institute full scale enquiries. It was thus that, on 12 August, Devlin spoke of a post-war rapprochement bringing north and south together. It was thus that T. P. O'Connor demanded publicly, on 22–3 August, that Maxwell be recalled. If there was not much success, at least the Castle administration did not have it all its own way. Upholders of the Union were driven to working up a new agitation for the extension of conscription to Ireland, about which a veritable campaign was waged by the British press, except for some pronouncedly liberal papers, from the end of August to the end of October.

Meanwhile the Nation League sought to organise meetings to challenge the partition agreement, secured by Redmond in June. Led by Father Philip O'Doherty of Carndonagh, who had some considerable following among the Derry clergy, they organised a meeting in the Phoenix Park on 10 September; beyond interesting T. M. Healy it was not very successful. But this protest though largely ignored by the press led to a change of attitude on the part of the northern bishops who had at first, under the influence of O'Donnell of Raphoe, accepted Redmond's direction. Thereafter they turned against partition.

In October Redmond himself took the lead in a sustained criticism of the government's Irish policy. At Waterford, on the sixth, he announced his irrevocable hostility to conscription. Eight days later the general attitude among Cork nationalists was privately summed up, for America, by Consul William Frost, as one of 'never trusting England'. On 18 October, in the House of Commons, Redmond attacked the whole system of government, putting forward a constructive plea under four heads: no conscription; abolition of repressive government; renewed attempt to implement Home Rule; and then, but only after the implementation of the first three, consideration of the resumption of recruiting. So effectively was he followed up that the French historian Y. M. Goblet, in recollection of Parnellite obstruction in parliament, has described the occasion as 'La nuit Irlandaise'.

Although Asquith said nothing, in startling contrast to his habitual re-action of 'wait and see', events would appear to credit Redmond with some success. On 4 November, Maxwell was recalled. Twelve days later, much to the surprise of the Party's own paper, *The Freeman's Journal*, a by-election was won in West Cork which Healy bemoaned as the death blow to

Catholic Ulster. The success was more apparent than real. The seat had for long been held by a supporter of William O'Brien. Local interests split on the vacancy and the winner was an unofficial candidate in the United Irish League interest. The Party, however, was basking in the sunshine of an Indian summer.

Redmond's new programme was an attempt to meet the changes in the political climate. The objection to conscription was based upon the view that Home Rule had been conceded in theory and that the terms of military service were, as in Canada, to be settled by the local legislature. The abolition of repressive government was essential if the Castle were not to destroy the organisation of the United Irish League and drive most of its members into the arms of the Nation League, of Sinn Féin or of whatever quasi-constitutional party might be set up in the wake of Easter Week. The resuscitation of the demand for instant Home Rule, Redmond had not favoured two years earlier as a distraction from the war. Now he took the risk that Carson would keep him to the terms of June 1916. Even to Redmond it must have been clear that recruiting would gain little from himself unless his credit first revived with the Irish people.

If the result was not very successful, the hopes of the Party rose when Asquith was displaced as Prime Minister and succeeded by Lloyd George in December 1916. On 2 December, T. P. O'Connor telegraphed the *North American* that, with the rise of the War Secretary, the Irish Parliamentary Party had regained its preponderant position at Westminster. Five days later Asquith was out and Redmond did not hesitate to state publicly that the new Prime Minister was expected to announce his Irish policy. But Lloyd George, in making his cabinet-selection speech on 19 December, was content with pious generalities about Ireland. Perhaps he preferred to be judged by words rather than by deeds. Two days later the Chief Secretary, Duke, was able to announce that the prisoners deported to Frongoch would all be home for

Christmas. The auguries might be read as in favour of a return to government by goodwill; but there was little goodwill towards England in nationalist Ireland. The police had already noted that the mass of the nationalists had changed their outlook on the Rising and the deportees returned to Dublin as conquering heroes, much to the surprise of many of them whose last recollections of the city had been of jeers and hoots. To fear of the United States and not to good will was attributed the releases of Christmas 1916—American supplies could be cut off from England.

The war continued to absorb the attention of the Prime Minister, Lloyd George, in the new year. In so far as anything was said of Home Rule it was on the relatively unimportant Dublin administration level, and implied that the affairs of Ireland could be settled by the Irish, meaning the Unionists as well as the nationalists. It was in this manner that Chief Secretary Duke spoke, on 14 January 1917, much as Lord Wimborne had spoken at the Dublin Lord Mayor's banquet on the preceding 29 November. Though not obvious at the time, this was the line adopted when next the Irish question had to be faced and the Irish Convention was appointed.

Early in the new year another by-election took place and provided some indication of the changing attitude of public opinion. In North Roscommon the death of the sitting member, James J. O'Kelly, an ex-Fenian supporter of Parnell who had long been a trusted member of the United Irish League, provided the vacancy. The Party nominee was defeated by George Noble Plunkett, papal count, a rather venerable figure chiefly renowned as the father of Joseph, one of the executed signatories of the 1916 proclamation of the Republic.

On 3 February, Count Plunkett's victory over his two nationalist rivals proved to be the first public vote of sympathy with the Rising. Was it also a withdrawal of confidence in the Redmondite Party? Various qualifications could be made such as the abnormally wintry weather, the division between an official and unofficial parliamentarian; but the one thing which was indisputable was that Plunkett's return with a majority over his combined opponents was a notice of public dissatisfaction with the United Irish League. As yet there was no rival party; the Count was well served by young clergy, released prisoners, the Irish Nation League and Sinn Féin, Fr. M. O'Flanagan, Laurence Ginnell, M.P., and Seamas O'Doherty of the I.R.B. The United Irish League had few outstanding members present and Redmond himself was seriously ill. All the League's opponents were united on three things (anti-partition, anti-conscription, and anti-party) and the greatest of these was anti-party. Redmond to many nationalists was no more than the Irish lackey of successive British Prime Ministers. The future might well be with physical force. As if to give point to the view that the government favoured Redmond some thirty young men, many of them recently released deportees, were rounded up and imprisoned for being involved in an alleged German plot (the minor plot, to be distinguished from the major plot in the following year). Very wisely the Redmondites determined to bring this up in parliament and a further round of protests over coercion and demands for Home Rule was inaugurated. It was all the more necessary as their own efforts to diminish the censorship as well as other incidents of martial law had recoiled upon themselves. Among the recently released deportees were several able journalists and these, early in 1917, commenced to ventilate their bitterness not merely against England but also against the parliamentarians. It was perhaps natural to test one's courage, in the first instance, by attacking the weaker adversary and so it was that Redmond's speech on the news of the Rising was now in its turn denounced with such an intensity that, as Professor Alison Phillips says, the military and public authorities advised Duke unsuccessfully to take strong measures. The Chief Secretary could be less tolerant on the news of German arms

consigned to Galway particularly in the light of Birrell's careless-
ness a year earlier. But the evidence of complicity of those
arrested over this German plot was not convincing, and after a
while they were released.

On 7 March, the House of Commons heard T. P. O'Connor
move that the system of government in force in Ireland was
incompatible with the policy of the allies in their fight for small
nations against the central European powers. So far as the United
Irish League was concerned it was a resolution of action for
breach of contract against the government and a formal notification terminating the Liberal alliance established in the time of
Gladstone. It was also a declaration to the Irish nationalists that
they were at one in their protest against coercion and tyranny in
Ireland and an implied abandonment of the condemnation of
unconstitutional action though not of the condemnation of any
alliance with the Germans. It was not a gesture to the revolutionaries nor to rival groups connected with them nor to Healy or
O'Brien. But it was an appeal to the Irish nationalists, in the light
of the North Roscommon defeat, to rely upon the old firm for
the maintenance of the old ideal and in the effective resistance
to the new aggression.

The occasion was memorable for the last speech in the
Commons of Major W. H. K. Redmond, brother of the Party's
leader, the much beloved member for East Clare, one of a group
of elderly nationalists in the front line trenches in Flanders and
on leave of absence, a few weeks before he was killed. In a
moving appeal to Carson and to the Ulster Unionists, he spoke
of that struggle in Europe and of their common affection for
Ireland and urged them to trust their fellow countrymen and
identify themselves with the demand for self-determination for
Ireland. On behalf of the Unionists, Ronald McNeill had given
notice of an amendment that as Ireland was over-represented in
parliament and Irishmen enjoyed all the liberties of British
subjects, there was no relevance in the Irish situation to the

11

problems of nationalities subjected to the autocratic tyranny of the central powers. Major Redmond had so completely won the goodwill of the House that the opponents of his motion contented themselves with stonily urging postponement of the issue until the end of the war. The Prime Minister, however, for the first time publicly identified himself with the position of Carson, declaring that the ministry was ready to accord self-government to any part of Ireland which desired it, that it would not support any attempt to coerce any part of Ireland against its will and that he personally was convinced that there were two races in Ireland, both of which had the right to be considered in any future political arrangement, which the Irish themselves could settle.

It was a clear exposition of the case for partition and was recognized as such by the Irish Party's leader who almost roughly refused to negotiate. The Party, on the following day, issued a manifesto deploring the change of view by Lloyd George and more than hinted that the days of constitutional activity were numbered. Partly because of the urgency of the need to bring America into the war and partly because of President Wilson's restatement of the Monroe doctrine of the need to secure the consent of the governed, English opinion generally favoured another immediate attempt to settle the Irish question. Such an attempt was endorsed privately on Wilson's behalf and Lloyd George was so informed on 17 April. It led directly to the Irish Convention on 16 May.

The withdrawal of the parliamentary members of the United Irish League from Westminster might have had some further significance. In the revolutionary tradition, the constitutional element as far back as the days of Butt had accepted a theory that alliance with parliamentary nationalists depended upon a mutual acceptance of alternative exploitation of different means to the end: the independence of Ireland.

Men, who knew Redmond and loved him because they knew

how much he loved Ireland and who out of loyalty to him followed his lead even to Flanders, could now very well feel that withdrawal from Westminster was symbolic (and were to feel it all the more so in the following year when a more permanent withdrawal took place over conscription). Would Redmond go further and associate himself with a national council? It was here that the link in 1916 with Germany was a major difficulty and the revelation of a German plot in February 1917 revived it. Failure to establish complicity, of any of those arrested, in this plot did not mean that revolutionaries in Ireland were without some German contacts. Ironically enough the government had reason to suspect Count Plunkett's family. The American-Irish connection continued to be suspect until the entry of the United States into the Great War in April made it virtually impossible for the Irish-American elements to continue to be pro-German. Nationalists could come together once more.

On 19 April 1917, at the instance of Count Plunkett, a National Council was convened to decide on future political action. The proposition did not turn out precisely as Plunkett envisaged. The Irish Parliamentary Party was still far too strong and only a small proportion of local government bodies attended. Plunkett, however, had circularised some 70 national bodies and at the meeting it was decided to set up a committee to determine the best means for future action. It was this national committee which was responsible for putting up a candidate against the Redmondite nominee at the Longford by-election. Although the contemporary press used the terminology 'Sinn Féin', this title in fact was not adopted until the autumn.

The general feeling in nationalist Ireland was that Lloyd George would make some move once more to settle the Irish question; and, in fact, he was under pressure from President Wilson to do so and the President's London representative reported on relatively unsatisfactory conversations both with Lloyd George and with Carson on 4 May. The position became more fluid. To those with their ears to the ground, like T. M. Healy reporting on 2 May, it appeared that the younger generation had turned violently against the Redmondite Party. In these circumstances, the Longford by-election, on 9 May, was watched with very great interest and the nomination of Joe McGuinness, on sentence in Lewes jail for his part in 1916, was salt in the wound for the Irish Party. On the day before polling, a statement condemning the partition of Ireland was issued over the signatures of Cardinal Logue and all his fellow Catholic bishops together with four Protestant bishops. The defeat of the Party's candidate by 37 votes was attributed by Redmond to the episcopal statement and in particular to an accompanying letter by the Archbishop of Dublin which appeared to be more positively aimed against the compromise agreed to by Redmond in the preceding summer.

With such a small majority, only the most irrational upholders of revolutionary nationalism could regard the result as a public endorsement of the Rising. There is no doubt that it was a blow to the United Irish League and to Redmond—the second blow, underlining the result in North Roscommon. The real significance was that the movement for the amnesty of the sentenced prisoners had now secured public endorsement, but as the questions of partition and conscription were vital issues, the victory was claimed by many forces. So far as the Party was concerned, a difficulty now arose about the new Franchise Bill then before Parliament. According to Healy, on 15 May, this measure would embarrass the Party which realized that the new voters would be overwhelming against them. In Healy's view, the Party wanted no fresh accession of young voters and were inclined to favour the exclusion of Ireland from the Bill. About the same time, and largely because of the Longford by-election, the government delay in announcing any proposals to deal with Ireland terminated with the Lloyd George announcement, on 16 May, of a convention of Irishmen to advise on the solution of Home Rule. As it turned out this body, which was carefully picked to make it as representative as possible of recognised interests north and south, was instrumental in securing the amnesty of the sentenced prisoners who were duly released in the middle of June. Immediately after, these met and decided to ignore the convention, an attitude largely imitated by the Ulster Unionists.

On 18 June, there was signed in Dublin and despatched to the United States a document representing the political views of some twenty officers of the Volunteers recently released, beginning with Eamon de Valera and Eoin MacNeill. This document is significant because it indicates the viewpoint of the released men in the context of American participation in the war. It was an implied abandonment of negotiations with Germany and it paved the way for an understanding acceptable to many former supporters of the Parliamentary Party who were prepared to accept a movement for a new constitutional party. It should be noted that the appeal to America also committed the signatories to a constitutional or at least a quasi-constitutional movement as only thus would there by any likelihood of their appeal being accepted by the new ally of England. The importance of this group became substantially enhanced by the victory of Eamon de Valera, on 10 July, in the East Clare by-election.

Of the East Clare election, it can be said that the overwhelming victory was a clear endorsement of the opponents of the Redmondite Party. Just as it can be said that T. P. O'Connor's motion on 7 March gave notice of a breach of contract, it can equally be said that such also was the verdict of Clare. Some two days later, Colonel O'Callaghan Westropp, writing to the London *Times*, declared that the election was a triumph against the principles of the old Party which had created a low level attitude in elections involving personalities. Westropp had contested the constituencies in 1892 against Willie Redmond whose recent death in action in Flanders had created the parliamentary vacancy. Westropp wrote as one who had abstained in the election and noted that some of his co-Unionists had supported the moderate nationalist, Patrick Lynch, though he himself, on reflection, considered the by-election likely to result in a situation in which a younger political party would permanently displace the United Irish League, largely because they were more likely to save the country from conscription.

Immediately after his election, Mr. de Valera declared that his Party would not be satisfied with Home Rule. They were determined to bring Ireland's case to the Peace Conference just as the 1916 men had been. In the month of August, in another by-election, William Cosgrave defeated the nationalist candidate in Kilkenny city. About the same date the government arrested one of the 1916 commandants, Thomas Ashe, on a charge of seditious behaviour at a meeting commemorating the landing in Kerry of Sir Roger Casement. Ashe's arrest was one of a number of such cases. Dublin Castle feared, however, at this stage to take similar measures against recently elected M.P.s like Eamon de Valera and William Cosgrave. As September dawned, the more romantically-minded supporters of the new regime believed they saw a peaceful solution of Anglo-Irish relations. Thus Eoin MacNeill contributed to the *English Review* an article arguing the likelihood of a settlement with the Irish Republic to the satisfaction of all concerned. He recalled Ulster's attachment to the republican idea and that in the good days to come a League of Nations would maintain peace and put practical limitations upon the sovereignty of all states, great and small.

It was in this atmosphere that Sinn Féin held a national convention in October 1917. The movement was expanded and re-organized and elected as its president, the recently elected member for Clare. Immediately before it, the Castle sustained a serious reversal in public opinion by the death through forcible feeding of Thomas Ashe who had been on hunger strike in Mountjoy Prison. It was considered at the time that the inquest and the verdict of the jury provided the most scandalous demonstration of British misgovernment since the Rising and emotionally it created a great upsurge of enthusiasm for the men in the Rising tradition. In these circumstances, a convention of the Volunteers also in October not suprisingly appointed as its president, de Valera, thereby linking personally Sinn Féin and the Volunteers. These bodies between them were now able to mobilize the ability, enthusiasm and resources to displace the old Party. Before the end of the year the Party's fate seemed sealed to discerning people like Healy, and William O'Brien. Early in 1918, the Irish Convention after some considerable delay supported by a majority a new plan for Home Rule devised by Lord Midleton. This plan had the advantage that it had the support of the southern Unionists who had been instrumental in torpedoing the Lloyd George proposals of the summer of 1916. Midleton, in particular, sponsored the idea of a substantial annual payment by Ireland to Britain as a set-off for the Customs revenue. When the proposal reached Lloyd George, he was so impressed that he wrote to Bonar Law urging that he should use all his endeavours to secure acceptance by the Ulster Unionists. To the Prime Minister the war situation was so bad, the Irish influence in Australia as well as in America so great, that an immediate solution of the Irish question was essential. Unfortunately, the northern leaders, Protestants and Catholics, were not prepared to give way. Then on 12 January 1918 the Prime Minister proposed postponement of the fiscal and other crucial aspects to the end of the war, whereupon the plan was defeated by a combination of the Unionists, Catholic bishops and William Martin Murphy, representing the independent capitalistic interest. At this point, on 6 March, John Redmond who had been deserted by the northern nationalists, collapsed and died. In the eyes of Lloyd George, his death was a serious loss, as his successor in the leadership of the United Irish League, John Dillon, was no admirer of the Prime Minister. To the Prime

Minister, however, the nationalists he was accustomed to in Parliament were preferable to those he regarded as extremists and by defeating Sinn Féin in three by-elections, they appeared to have gained a new lease of life since the beginning of 1918. The Convention having reported to the British government, it was decided to introduce conscription to Ireland immediately. There was an implication that the government also proposed to confer some sort of self-government on Ireland but this was extremely vague.

The reaction of all the nationalists at Westminster was to withdraw and join a conference summoned to the Mansion House, Dublin by the Lord Mayor, to consider the best means of defeating conscription. The conference drew up an appeal to the President of the United States and secured from the Catholic bishops of Ireland a condemnation of conscription. There then was signed throughout Ireland a solemn promise framed along the lines of the 1912 Ulster Covenant against Home Rule—in this case, to resist conscription. The resulting success in frustrating the government conscription plan was generally attributed to Sinn Féin and the bishops as well as to the labour movement which staged a one-day general strike. The Dillonite party got none of the credit. From this point one can clearly see the fall of the Irish nationalists at Westminster. The writing on the wall, however, was not evident to the Party's new leader or at least he would not admit it. As he determined to fight a by-election in East Cavan contested for Sinn Féin by Arthur Griffith, the government obligingly arrested Griffith, de Valera, and dozens of Sinn Féin supporters on the excuse of a new German plot, thereby assuring the return of Griffith if indeed this was not a foregone conclusion. The penultimate act was the denunciation by government proclamation under D.O.R.A. of Sinn Féin as a dangerous organisation. The final act was played in December, at the General Election when Sinn Féin won 73 seats and the nationalists 6. Once again, government had influenced public opinion in favour of the new movement by keeping in prison the Sinn Féin leaders until after the results had been declared. It marked the end of the Parliamentary Party and of Irish nationalist representation at Westminster.

The fall of the Irish Nationalists at Westminster had stemmed mainly from their failure to win Home Rule. Moreover because they gave way on partition they lost the confidence of the people when it came to resisting conscription; and after the war, just as Lloyd George won the General Election in Great Britain with a mandate to secure the best terms for England at the Peace Conference, so Sinn Féin in Ireland got a mandate to secure self-government which the Westminster parliamentarians had failed to attain.

R. DUDLEY EDWARDS.

BIBLIOGRAPHICAL NOTE

This essay is based upon sources available in print. Since it was first projected, the British Public Record Office has opened more recent files under a thirty-year rule restricting accessibility. This will enable future work on Ireland in the revolutionary era to be based on archival material.

The main works relied on here are indicated below in the chronological order of their publication. Thanks are due to His Excellency, President de Valera for making available printed documentation connected with the Mansion House Conference, 1918.

Gwynn, S. L. *John Redmond's Last Years*. (1919).
Goblet, Y. M. *L'Irlande dans la Crise Universella, 1914-20*. (Paris, 1921).
Phillips, W. A. *The Revolution in Ireland, 1906-23*. (1923).
Healy, T. M. *Letters and Leaders of My Day*. (1928).
Gwynn, D. R. *The Life of John Redmond*. (1932).
Carty, James. *Bibliography of Irish History, 1912-21*. (1936).
Lenin, V. I. *On Britain*. Edited by C. Leiteisen, T. Dexter and I. Lasker. (Moscow, n.d.? 1961).

Hayes, R. *Manuscript Sources of Irish Civilization.* (11 vols. Boston, Mass. 1966).

Savage, David. 'The Attempted Home Rule Settlement of 1916' in *Éire-Ireland.* (Autumn 1967).

MacGiolla Choille, B., *ed. Intelligence Notes, 1913–1916.* (1967).

Edwards, Owen Dudley and F. Pyle, editors. *1916: The Easter Rising.* (1968).

Laffan, M. A. *The Rise of Sinn Féin 1916–18.* (U.C.D. thesis, unpublished, 1968).

Lyons, F. S. L. *John Dillon, a biography.* (1968).

The Background to the Rising;
from 1914 until the issue of the
countermanding order on
Easter Saturday, 1916

by
MAUREEN WALL

(VII)

The Background to the Rising; from 1914 until the issue of the Countermanding Order on Easter Saturday, 1916

In dealing with an event like the Rising of 1916 the student of history is always tempted to try to trace the usually very complicated sequence of events leading up to it, and to try to understand the ideology and motives underlying the actions of the principal actors in the drama. The results of such a study can never be more than tentative, but an attempt will be made here, on the basis of published material, to examine some aspects of the following problems. How far was the thinking of the leaders influenced by the history of previous risings? Did a revolutionary situation exist in Ireland during the years before 1916? How did the plan for the Rising take shape, and what evidence is there that the original choice of date was autumn 1915? Were the leaders clear on their aims—were the activists seeking a military success or would they have been satisfied with a blood sacrifice and another glorious failure? Were the stated aims of those who opposed immediate action any more practical? What part did the I.R.B. as such play in bringing about the Rising, and to what extent was the I.R.B. taken over by a few determined men? What was Connolly's role during the period? What were the circumstances surrounding the issue of the countermanding order on Easter Saturday, 1916.

In popular histories of Ireland the reasons for the collapse of the various movements and planned uprisings against English rule are usually listed. The activities of informers, the intervention of the Catholic clergy, the non-arrival of foreign aid, the harshness of the weather and several other causes are advanced to explain the repeated failure to bring about nation-wide rebellion. Pearse and Connolly, the two chief propagandists among the leaders of the Rising, referred again and again to what they believed to be the real causes of these failures in the century or so before 1916, and they insisted that their generation must not repeat the errors of the past. For instance, in January 1914, Pearse wrote:

'The leaders in Ireland have nearly always left the people at the critical moment; have sometimes sold them. The former Volunteer movement was abandoned by its leaders; hence its ultimate failure. Grattan "led the van" of the Volunteers, but he also led the retreat of the leaders; O'Connell recoiled before the cannon at Clontarf; twice the hour of the Irish Revolution struck during Young Ireland days, and twice it struck in vain, for Meagher hesitated in Waterford, Duffy and Magee hesitated in Dublin. Stephens refused to "give the word" in '65; he never came in '66 or '67. I do not blame these men: you or I might have done the same. It is a terrible responsibility to be cast upon a man, that of bidding the cannon speak and the grapeshot pour . . . Now my reading of Irish history is that, however the leaders may have failed, *the instinct of the people has always been unerring.*'[1]

In November 1915, Connolly wrote:

'In 1848, as later, there were men who talked much of revolution, but when the spirit of the times called upon them to strike, they all began to make excuses, to murmur about the danger of premature insurrection, of incomplete preparations, of the awful responsibility of giving the word for insurrection, etc., etc.

In 1848, as later, the real revolutionary sentiment was in the hearts of the people, but for the most part they who undertook to give it articulate expression were wanting in the essential ability to translate sentiment into action. They would have been good historians of a revolutionary movement, but were unable to take that leap in the dark which all men must take who plunge into insurrection.'[2]

Pearse was writing six months before the outbreak of the first World War, when he thought of a rising as an event which must take place at some vague time in the future, while Connolly's views were expressed at a time when he was actively preaching revolution at the earliest possible date lest the Great War— England's difficulty and Ireland's opportunity—should come to an end before a blow had been struck. The writings and speeches of these two men also stressed their belief that in the past Ireland had always 'struck too late' and they used this argument from history to support their call for immediate action.[3]

Eoin MacNeill, on the other hand quoted Davis to prove that in the past Ireland had lost 'through inadequate preparation'. He warned also that the British government, in the past, had sown dissension among the Irish to break up their national movements, and argued that the Irish Volunteers in the eighteenth century had failed, not because 'they did not fight', but because 'they did not maintain their organization till their objects had been secured'.[4] It would be idle to seek to discover whether these men were influenced by their historical studies or whether they sought in history arguments to support the views they already held: on the one hand, that leadership had failed in the past and must not do so again, and that the important thing was to strike in time; on the other, that all could be lost through precipitate action, and that the 'watch and wait' policy was the only possible one for the Volunteers. MacNeill equally disagreed with Connolly and Pearse in their belief in the essentially revolutionary character of the Irish people. In February 1916 he wrote:

'I do not know at this moment whether the time and circumstances will yet justify distinct revolutionary action, but of
this I am certain, that the only possible basis for successful
revolutionary action is deep and widespread popular discontent. We have only to look around us in the streets to realize
that no such condition exists in Ireland. A few of us, a small
proportion, who think about the evils of English government
in Ireland, are always discontented. We should be downright
fools, if we were to measure many others by the standard of
our own thoughts.'[5]

At first glance it would seem that in many ways the climate for
rebellion had never been so favourable. The coercion weapon
which had been used, since the mid-eighteenth century, to
smother public opinion and to suppress agitation and rebellion,
had been set at naught by the activities of Carson and the Ulster
Unionists. In the nineteenth century coercion had been mainly
directed at the Catholic and anti-Unionist section of the population, and although it had been resisted down the years by secret
societies—agrarian, sectarian and political—and had been flouted
at times by constitutional movements like the Catholic Association, the Repeal Association and the Land League, successive
governments continued to pass coercion acts. When Unionists
and Protestants turned to treason, however, defying the government, instituting a rebellious provisional government and an
armed volunteer force, and threatened to call in the Kaiser, they
went unpunished, and so coercion as a means of ruling Ireland
ceased to be effective. The treason felony law and the arms
licensing laws had been defied with impunity. The R.I.C.—
upholders of law and order for three-quarters of a century—had
ignored the illegal importation of arms, the drilling, and the
treasonable words and actions of the Unionists.

Not only did they provide a headline for treasonable activities,
but the Ulster Unionists also influenced extreme nationalists in

another important way. By their general parading of emotion, their utter disregard for 'the done thing', their posturing and their inflamatory oratory, they helped to eradicate that fear of looking ridiculous which had entered deeply into the minds of the population during the late nineteenth and early twentieth centuries. Carsonism brought a great emotional release which was soon apparent in Dublin and throughout the country. Defiant gestures were no longer confined to a few political leaders and demagogues. Speeches and writings showed a rapid rise in temperature; uniforms were invented and worn without self-consciousness; public parades and manoeuvres took place without fear of either public ridicule or intervention by the police. James Larkin was the first to seize the opportunity provided by the breakdown of coercion in Ireland, when he set up the Citizen Army in the autumn of 1913, as the defensive military arm of the labour struggle then in progress; and before the end of the year the Irish Volunteers had been launched in the Rotunda. Soon more than 100,000 men were enrolled throughout the country, although the solid strength of the Volunteers lay from the beginning in Dublin.

In spite of all the martial fervour and treasonable activities, a revolutionary situation did not, however, exist in Ireland in the years immediately preceding 1916. Dublin had been a centre of intense social conflict during the terrible lock-out of 1913, but at no time was there any serious danger of a Paris-style revolution, with a rush to the barricades. Like the Citizen Army, the Volunteers were formed for defensive, not offensive action. Land reform and land purchase measures and other social and economic benefits, as well as the steady stream of emigration from the countryside, had gone far to eradicate the atmosphere of smothered war which had existed in rural Ireland since the mid-eighteenth century. The great bulk of the Irish population supported Redmond and his Home Rule policy, believing, despite or even because of the already very grave threat of

partition, that the party leaders were best equipped to assess the political situation, and that their policy of supporting the British war effort was the best in the circumstances; that the 'loyalist nationalist card' was the best reply to the 'Orange card' if Home Rule for all Ireland were ever to be achieved.

It was against what would seem to be a definitely non-revolutionary background that the architects of the Rising set out to formulate their plans. Emulation of the activities of the Ulster Unionists had been an important factor in moving them to decide that arms should once again be taken up in support of Ireland's right to nationhood, but the Ulster defiance, from the beginning, and more particularly after the Curragh 'mutiny' of April 1914, increased the difficulties facing anyone seeking to bring about an explosive revolutionary situation in Ireland. Since Carson's resistance to the government had not been crushed either by coercion or by military force, these could not be applied either, to any great extent, to the other irregular armies in the country—apart from which, the leaders of the Irish Parliamentary Party were insistent that no martyrs should be created. As a result, government tolerance was such that, despite sham battles and sieges, parades with arms, seditious and anti-recruiting speeches and countless other manifestations of what could be regarded as treason in the years between 1913 and 1916, scarcely more than a dozen of what might be termed prominent men in the militant movement were convicted, and their activities rated no more than sentences of three to six months, or deportation to England or to another part of Ireland.[6] Clearly it was going to be a difficult task to spark off a nation-wide rising against a government which tended towards permissiveness rather than tyranny,[7] but it would seem that the leaders drafting the plans continued to believe that once the signal was given from Dublin a general insurrection would take place. It is difficult to avoid the conclusion that they were basing their calculations more on their reading of past history than on a realistic assessment of the conditions prevailing in the Ireland of the second decade of the twentieth century.

When the split occurred in the Volunteers in September 1914, and the vast majority of the force, then estimated at 150,000, followed Redmond into the new National Volunteer organisation, unanimity on the desirability of revolution was far from prevailing among the members of the provisional committee now directing the policy of the minority which had remained faithful to the Irish Volunteers. A section of the committee, of which Eoin MacNeill and Bulmer Hobson were typical, believed then and continued to insist right up to the time of the Rising, that the rôle of the Volunteers was defensive and not offensive. These took the line that the Volunteers should bring their organisation into an ever greater state of preparedness, so that by the end of World War I when they would be joined, they expected, by thousands of Irish veterans, they could proceed to demand Home Rule with the assurance that their demand could not be resisted. Their strategy seems to have taken little account of the problem of partition, nor is it clear from the documents which survive, what these Volunteers proposed to do when confronted by the revived Ulster Volunteers, similarly augmented by World War veterans from Ulster and Great Britain. They were entirely unsympathetic to the view that an insurrection must be staged during the course of the European war, but they believed that resistance should be offered if the government created an explosive situation by attempting to enforce conscription, or to disarm the Volunteers. The landing of a German expeditionary force would have also been regarded by this group as an event which would automatically bring the Volunteers into the war against Britain.[8] If any one of these factors should precipitate military action by the Volunteers, they advocated defensive and guerilla tactics.[9]

Within the Volunteer Executive, however, was another group which believed in insurrection—win or lose—and they were

NB determined that their wishes should prevail. Indeed they believed that even if Germany lost the war, and even if the leaders were executed and many lives lost in a hopeless gesture of rebellion, it would be a victory for the soul of Ireland, and they did not count the cost for themselves or others.[10] Tom Clarke was, from the beginning, the centre of the plan to precipitate a rising, and he and his closest associate, Seán MacDiarmada, began at an early date to prepare a scheme by which they proposed to use the Irish Volunteer organisation, without the knowledge of MacNeill, its Chief-of-Staff, as an army which would challenge the British in open rebellion. Clarke and MacDiarmada had evidently drawn one definite conclusion from their reading of Irish history. They probably would have agreed with Pearse and Connolly that lack of leadership had been one of the main causes of failure in previous generations. Nevertheless, their actions make it clear enough that they believed that the activities of spies and informers in betraying plans had been perhaps of even greater significance, and they accordingly set out to plan a rebellion which would be entirely under their own control, the details being known only to them and to a few others.

Joseph Plunkett, who was taken into their confidence at an early date, had similar views on the importance of extreme secrecy in all that appertained to their plans. Not for them the ramifications of the United Irishmen with their secret, oath-bound society, and their periodic meetings of delegates, which ultimately led to the arrest of almost the whole Leinster Directory in Oliver Bond's house in March 1798, several weeks before the date fixed for the rising of that year. Nor did Clarke and MacDiarmada, although they were treasurer and secretary, respectively, of the I.R.B., adhere to the I.R.B. constitution, with its elaborate system of circles, centres and sub-centres, electoral divisions and conventions, a system which in the 1860s had failed completely in its declared object of defeating the British intelligence service in Ireland.

Studies in the History of the Rising

Several members of the I.R.B. had enjoyed very considerable influence in the Volunteers since their foundation and indeed regarded them largely as their own creation, which they could effectively control from behind the scenes. With the outbreak of war, however, it was clear that the lines of division were no longer going to be between I.R.B. and non-I.R.B. men, but between those who may be termed activists—those prepared to take advantage of the fact that England, for the first time since 1815, was embroiled in a major war in Western Europe, to strike a blow for Irish independence with some hope of success— and those who wished to continue a 'wait and see' defensive policy. The divisions which took place within the Volunteer Executive on the question of the expediency of a rising were by no means unique in Irish or in world history. It is a common characteristic of revolutionary groups, whether social or political, to divide along certain lines. One section—usually a small minority—favours action, often on the grounds that a struggle, however limited, will of itself produce revolution in the end. The other section tends to be vehement in its denunciations of the hot-heads and is content to build up the organisation, enrol new members, draft constitutions, theorise and evolve strict dogma, hold meetings, pass resolutions, and await the day of revolution without taking any overt action to bring it about. The absence of repressive or provocative measures by the government, on any serious scale, was bound to make the task of the activists exceedingly difficult in Ireland, but one factor which buoyed up their hopes from the beginning was their belief that John Devoy and Clan na Gael in America would not only be able and willing to give them practical assistance in arms and men, but would be in a position also to ensure that they would achieve belligerency status on the side of the central powers in the war.

Already in August 1914 a committee of Clan na Gael had presented Ireland's case to the German ambassador, telling him that their friends in Ireland aimed at setting up an independent government during the war, and asking for German assistance in arms and trained officers; and Tom Clarke, who throughout the following years was the central link between Clan na Gael and the activist group in Ireland, was immediately advised of the steps taken.[11] A meeting of 'physical force' men (not all of whom were members of the Volunteers or the I.R.B.) at which Clarke presided, took place on 9 September 1914, and it was decided to launch a drive for more recruits to the Irish Volunteers, the Citizen Army, Fianna Éireann and Cumann na mBan; to assist German forces in the event of a landing, provided they undertook to aid them in the fight for Irish freedom; and to resist any attempt to disarm the Volunteers or to enforce conscription. Most important of all in the light of after events, it was decided that if the war were coming to an end without any military outbreak in Ireland, a rebellion should be staged and Irish independence declared, so that Ireland's right to a seat at the peace conference would be assured.[12] Seven of those present at this meeting—Thomas MacDonagh, P. H. Pearse, Joseph Plunkett, Eamonn Ceannt, Seán MacDiarmada, Tom Clarke and James Connolly—would together form the group of determined men, who ultimately brought about the Rising.

When the decision for war had been taken on 9 September, the Volunteers had been estimated at 150,000 men and it was perhaps with the hope of precipitating rebellion before the movement could disintegrate that Connolly persuaded Clarke, MacDiarmada, and other members of the I.R.B. to stage a major manoeuvre on 24 September 1914 the day on which a section of the provisional committee of the Volunteers denounced Redmond's action in supporting Britain in the war. A recruiting meeting had been arranged to take place in the Mansion House under the auspices of Redmond and the British Prime Minister, Asquith, and the plan was to occupy and fortify the Mansion House on the day before the meeting, hold it and fight, if necessary, to the last man. Eighty Volunteers assembled in Rutland Square and about forty of the Irish Citizen Army at Liberty Hall, but when it was discovered that crown forces were already in position in the Mansion House, and that the forces at the disposal of the anti-recruiting party were so pitifully small, the manoeuvre was cancelled.[13]

This setback made it clear even to Connolly that some serious advance planning was necessary, and having taken up permanent residence in Dublin he took over the Citizen Army from Larkin in the autumn of 1914, and set out to perfect its organisation and build up its morale in preparation for the coming fight. The Citizen Army was revolutionary in a sense different from the other non-professional armies in the country. Disillusioned by the failure of international Socialism to prevent war, Connolly began to stress more and more in his teaching that the cause of labour was the cause of Ireland, and he plainly distrusted the ability of middle-class leadership—'physical force' as much as 'constitutional'—in what he called 'this crisis in our country's history'. In the first issue of the *Irish Worker* published after the outbreak of war he wrote:

'Let us not shrink from the consequences. This may mean more than a transport strike, it may mean armed battling in the streets to keep in this country the food for our people. But whatever it may mean it must not be shrunk from. It is the immediate feasible policy of the working-class democracy, the answer to all the weaklings who in this crisis in our country's history stand helpless and bewildered crying for guidance, when they are not hastening to betray her.

Starting thus, Ireland may yet set the torch to a European conflagration that will not burn out until the last throne and the last capitalist bond and debenture will be shrivelled on the funeral pyre of the last war lord.'[14]

It is difficult to estimate how much the rank and file of the

Citizen Army would have been fired by Connolly's concept of Ireland's role in the march of world democracy, but he succeeded in building up an army—small in numbers (not amounting to more than two hundred men) compact and efficient—whose members would be ready to leave their factories and workshops at a word from their commander, and man, not the barricades perhaps, but certainly Liberty Hall and defend it against all comers. Indeed this defensive strategy, this fortification of certain buildings, seems to have been Connolly's basic war strategy from the beginning. He probably realised that this was the only way in which the Citizen Army could ever hope to make a worthwhile revolutionary gesture. He had first expounded it during the Boer War;[15] it had been the basis of the plan to seize the Mansion House on 24 September 1914; he revived it in November 1914 when he urged the Volunteers to precipitate government action by defending Monteith from arrest and deportation;[16] it was the plan he outlined to MacNeill in January 1916[17] and it was the plan put into operation in Dublin in Easter Week. He would have been glad of the help of the Volunteers, but with or without them, he was prepared, if necessary, right up to the eve of the Rising,[18] to provoke the authorities into attacking Liberty Hall, and commit the Citizen Army to the defence of his little fortress to the last man, if this was the only way in which military action could be precipitated. From the outbreak of the World War, but particularly from the autumn of 1915 until the eve of rebellion Connolly continued to fear that the other 'physical force' men would back down in the end leaving him and the Citizen Army to 'go it alone'. Immediately before the planned attack on the Mansion House in 1914 he had written to William O'Brien:

'It is a desperate situation and I am afraid that our friends of the Conference have not got sufficient dash and desperation to deal with the matter. The meeting for Asquith will be a military affair, and the City will be in the hands of the military to carry it through. In a sense all our future is on the cast of that die. I am ready for the call.'[19]

But the events of Easter Week 1916 were to prove that 'dash and desperation' were not lacking in the majority of the men who had attended that Conference on 9 September 1914, six of whom together with Connolly, less than two years later, were to constitute themselves the provisional government of the Irish Republic.

If Connolly applied himself openly to perfecting the Citizen Army in the months which followed the outbreak of war, Clarke and MacDiarmada applied themselves with equal dedication to the preparation of their plans for an insurrection, using the Irish Republican Brotherhood as their instrument. By its constitution the I.R.B. was constrained to 'await the decision of the Irish nation as expressed by a majority of the Irish people, as to the fit hour for inaugurating a war against England' but Clarke and MacDiarmada cared little for the niceties of constitutions, and they brought the same singlemindedness, not to say ruthlessness, to bear on manipulating the I.R.B. as they did on manipulating other Irish-Ireland groups and organisations, in order to precipitate a rebellion while England was at war. They used such portions of the constitution as suited their purpose; in particular the section which decreed that the powers of the Supreme Council, when the Council was not in session, could be exercised by the I.R.B. Executive, though they disregarded the qualification which forbade the Executive to declare war or alter the constitution. The Executive consisted of the secretary, the treasurer and the president of the Supreme Council, and during the years before the Rising the posts of treasurer and secretary, respectively, were held by Tom Clarke and Seán MacDiarmada. The Supreme Council itself rarely met, and since a majority vote of the Executive was binding on all three members, Clarke and

MacDiarmada were in a position to exercise unlimited control, and to act as they saw fit in the name of the I.R.B. They recruited new members with little regard for outworn regulations concerning circles and elections and the limits of delegated authority.[20] Bulmer Hobson, who had been one of the best known and one of the most energetic workers in re-vitalising the I.R.B. in the early years of the century, lost the confidence of Clarke and MacDiarmada in 1914 and resigned from the Supreme Council. Thereafter, although he remained Chairman of the Dublin Board of I.R.B. Centres, he was kept in the dark about the plans for a rising.[21] Pearse, on the other hand, who had been distrusted by I.R.B. men of long standing, because of his support for the Irish Council Bill of 1907 and his willingness to accept Home Rule as an instalment of freedom was, nevertheless, brought into the very heart of the conspiracy because Clarke and MacDiarmada saw his immense value to the movement, and believed in his complete dedication to the cause of Irish nationhood, and trusted in his willingness to translate words into action when the time came.[22]

The original plans under discussion in 1914 and 1915 were evidently for a rising which would take place about September 1915, and it is not clear whether it was to have been confined to Dublin or to have included the rest of the country as well.[23] When Diarmuid Lynch returned from a mission to Clan-na-Gael in the end of 1914, he was told that an 'advisory committee' had been appointed to draft a provisional plan for a fight in the Dublin area.[24] This committee, which was evidently a large one, included a considerable number of Volunteer officers who were not in the I.R.B. Indeed Le Roux, in his life of Clarke, refers to it as the 'advisory committee of the Irish Volunteers'.[25] Lynch seems to imply that his own insistence on the need for a stronger emphasis on secrecy and his urging that the 'advisory committee' should be dissolved, played a part in a decision to allow the committee to lapse. Le Roux states that the committee 'was

allowed to lapse at the end of 1914' because it was too cumber-
some' and 'the I.R.B. wanted a body that would enforce I.R.B.
policy unknown to all non-I.R.B. members'. It would probably
be true to say, however, that by the end of 1914 the Volunteers
had completed the reorganisation necessary after the split with
the Redmondites, and when the General Council of the Volunteers met on 6 December 1914 and agreed to the appointment of
a headquarters staff,[26] there seemed to be no further need for the
'advisory committee'. Since it had not been exclusively under
I.R.B. control it seems unnecessary to attribute its disappearance
to I.R.B. influence, though Clarke and MacDiarmada were
probably glad to see it go. It does seem reasonable to suppose,
however, that Clarke who, according to Lynch, was very critical
of the draft plan for the Dublin rising, decided that he and Seán
MacDiarmada would endeavour to use all their powers as the
virtual government of the I.R.B. to get control as far as possible
of the now streamlined Volunteer organisation, while preserving
the strictest secrecy on crucial decisions even towards all but a
few of the I.R.B. members themselves. 'There must be no Red
Jim MacDermotts this time',[27] MacDiarmada is quoted as saying
in 1914, and in the event there were none.

By December 1914 Pearse was working closely with Clarke
and MacDiarmada and in his capacity as Director of Organisation he submitted detailed plans to the Volunteer Executive
which would be put into operation if the government should
decide to enforce conscription. These plans were adopted and
sent to the principal officers in different parts of the country and
were to be communicated to the rank and file of Volunteers if
the occasion arose.[28] In this manner plans, which were ostensibly
being perfected with a view to meeting either the threat of
conscription or a government move to disarm the Volunteers—
plans which could be discussed among all Volunteer officers
whatever their views on policy—could equally be held in readiness for an unprovoked insurrection when the 'war party' should

deem it necessary. Piaras Beaslaí has stated that the plans for the insurrection of Easter Week 'had taken definite shape before the end of 1914', and that he and Edward Daly 'as commandant and vice-commandant of the first battalion, had our positions allotted to us, and had started preparing plans for operations as early as December 1914'.[29] During the early months of 1915 a series of lectures was given at Volunteer headquarters in Kildare Street, by Connolly, MacDonagh and others, on practical aspects of warfare, including communications, mapping and street fighting.[30]

On 10 March 1915 officers were appointed to command the four Dublin city battalions. Edward Daly was to command the first, Thomas MacDonagh the second, Eamon de Valera the third and Eamonn Ceannt the fourth; while Pearse, Plunkett, Hobson and the O'Rahilly were appointed commandants on the headquarters staff.[31] With the exception of Hobson, these men, appointed more than a year before the Easter Rising, were at their posts when the Rising began. On 13 March 1915, two days after receiving their appointments, the four battalion commandants were called to a meeting at Volunteer headquarters to discuss plans for the Rising which was to take place in the following September. Pearse, who was in the chair, outlined the general plan, according to which each battalion was to be responsible for blocking one of the roads connecting the four military barracks with the city centre. Battalion headquarters were to be selected at points where food was available, and commandants were given details of passwords and of the type of notification they would receive when the Rising was about to begin. This account of the briefing of the Dublin commandants comes from President de Valera, the only member of the group to survive the Rising.[32]

At this time (March 1915) Seán T. O'Kelly was sent by MacDiarmada and Clarke on a mission to Clan-na-Gael in New York, to give them detailed information on plans for the Rising.

He was given no date, however, and one must assume that if a rising was intended for the following September the date was sent by another messenger.[33] In May 1915 MacDiarmada, on a visit to England, told P. S. O'Hegarty that it would take place in 'September or thereabouts' and is reported as saying 'We'll hold Dublin for a week and save Ireland'.[34] Connolly, Clarke, MacDiarmada, Pearse and Plunkett were evidently acting together, and although Connolly was not a member of the I.R.B. he was to be in command in Dublin. It is significant that in the lecture which Connolly delivered to the Volunteers at this time on street fighting, he stated his belief that the government would never permit the army to destroy capitalist-owned property in the main streets of the city.[35] All the Volunteer commandants appointed in March 1915, with the exception of the O'Rahilly and de Valera, were members of the I.R.B. and were in the confidence of the planning group to some extent. Although on the advice of MacDonagh, at some time after his appointment, de Valera reluctantly joined the I.R.B., he did not belong to and evidently had no wish to be admitted to the inner circle which was planning a rising, preferring to regard himself as a Volunteer officer, who would obey the orders of his superior officers when the time for action came.[36]

Various reasons may be suggested to explain why the plans for a rising in the autumn of 1915 had to be abandoned. One event, which must have caused confusion among the leaders, was the arrest of Seán MacDiarmada, for delivering an anti-recruiting speech in Tuam on 16 May 1915. He was sentenced to four months hard labour and was in Mountjoy prison until 18 September of that year. His biographer regards it as a grave mistake on the part of MacDiarmada to have made himself liable to imprisonment at this time.[37]

It seems probable that the main reason for the postponement, however, hinged on the question of arms from Germany. In March, Joseph Plunkett was sent to discover what progress had been made by Casement, who had gone to Germany towards the end of 1914, and to institute direct negotiations on behalf of the activists in Dublin for support in arms and men. Casement was pessimistic about the outcome of his own mission and warned Plunkett that to 'attempt a rising in the streets of Dublin in 1915' would be 'criminal stupidity'. No indication has emerged so far of the exact nature of the report made by Plunkett on his return from Germany, some time around the end of June 1915. Desmond Ryan states that he brought the news that the Germans 'only committed themselves to send captured arms to Ireland, and that no others were then available'.[38] No arrangements appear to have been made during the summer of 1915 for the landing of an arms cargo and one would be inclined to assume that those who favoured a rising had decided, on Plunkett's return, to alter their original plans for a September rising, were it not for the fact that Desmond Ryan has left it on record that, in early August, Pearse was still expecting a rising to take place before the end of September.[39] It is possible that they had decided, in the absence of a promise of strong German support, to confine the Rising to Dublin.

During the month of July the preparations for the funeral of O'Donovan Rossa occupied much of the time of the I.R.B. inner circle. Connolly, not surprisingly, suggested at first that they should stop blethering about *dead* Fenians' and 'get a few *live* ones for a change' but Clarke so far convinced him of the importance of the demonstration that he and the Citizen Army took a prominent part in the procession.[40] Irish nationalist public opinion had for a very long time been demonstrated through mass meetings and public funerals as well as through the ballot box. Their constitution laid down that the I.R.B. should 'await the decision of a majority of the Irish people, as to the fit hour of inaugurating a war against England'[41] but it laid down no special procedure for ascertaining the views of the Irish people. If Tom Clarke wished to fulfil the terms of the constitution and demonstrate that a majority of the Irish nation was in favour of a rising no better opportunity could have presented itself than the Rossa funeral. It is reasonable to suppose that he convinced Connolly that a funeral on the lines of Terence Bellew Manus's in 1861 could be looked upon as a demonstration that Irish public opinion was ready to endorse a policy of 'physical force'. Both men knew well that a procession which included representatives even of the Irish Parliamentary Party was much more likely to be a demonstration of the 'double think' which leads people to sympathise with dead heroes, while having no intention whatever of emulating them, but Connolly took care to point out in his article in the Rossa souvenir publication, that Rossa's title to honour was that he was in revolt against the British Government in Ireland, and he questioned whether those 'who accept what Rossa rejected' have any right to take part in honour paid to him. He made his own position clear when he stated:

'The Irish Citizen Army in its constitution pledges its members to fight for a Republican Freedom for Ireland. Its members are, therefore, of the number who believe that at the call of duty they may have to lay down their lives for Ireland, and have so trained themselves that at the worst the laying down of their lives shall constitute the starting point of another glorious tradition—a tradition that will keep alive the soul of the nation.

We are, therefore, present to honour O'Donovan Rossa by right of our faith in the separate destiny of our country and our faith in the ability of the Irish Workers to achieve that destiny.'[42]

It has been suggested[43] that by firing a volley over the grave of Rossa, the activists hoped to force the government to suppress the Volunteers, thus precipitating war with England on terms acceptable to all the members of the Provisional Committee including Hobson and MacNeill. Pearse in his graveside oration had, on the instruction of Clarke, 'thrown discretion to the winds'[44] and had hurled defiance at the government, concluding with the words:

> 'They think they have foreseen everything, think they have provided for everything; but the fools, the fools, the fools!— they have left us our Fenian dead, and while Ireland holds these graves, Ireland unfree shall never be at peace.'

Neither illegal use of arms nor verbal treason moved the government to take action against the Volunteers and so precipitate a rising. Within some weeks of the Rossa funeral it seems clear that those who had been planning a September rising had been forced, for whatever reason, to alter their plans. Connolly who had been satisfied since March that the Volunteers would go into action in the autumn, now seems to have come to the conclusion that the Fenian dead would continue to be the main preoccupation of the men on whom he had been relying to challenge the British government with more than words. During the last months of 1915 he kept advocating immediate insurrection; his pronouncements being a cause of grave concern, not only to MacNeill, but to the inner circle of I.R.B. and Volunteer leaders who favoured a planned rising, and who feared that Connolly would goad the government into proceeding against them before their new plan could be perfected.[45] In October he wrote:

> 'The Irish Citizen Army will only co-operate in a forward movement. The moment that forward movement ceases it reserves to itself the right to step out of alignment, and advance by itself if needs be, in an effort to plant the banner of freedom one reach further towards its goal . . .'

Again in November he wrote:

'Revolutionists who shrink from giving blow for blow until the great day has arrived, and they have every shoe-string in its place, and every man has got his gun, and the enemy has kindly consented to postpone action in order not to needlessly hurry the revolutionists nor disarrange their plans—such revolutionists exist only in two places—the comic opera stage, and the stage of Irish national politics.'

In the same article he speaks of 'that leap in the dark which all men must take who plunge into insurrection'.[46]

But Clarke, Pearse, Ceannt, Plunkett and those in their confidence had no intention of plunging into insurrection and they were not prepared to throw the Volunteers into any clash with the authorities that Connolly might choose to precipitate. They were still relying on help from Germany and, in the end of August 1915, Clarke sent Robert Monteith on a mission to Germany to assist Casement;[47] while in September Diarmuid Lynch was dispatched by Pearse to Kerry to consult with I.R.B. men there on the most suitable port in that county for the landing and distribution of a cargo of arms. He reported back to Pearse, Clarke and MacDiarmada (released from prison on 18 September) that the Kerrymen favoured Fenit.[48] In the same month Joseph Plunkett went to the United States presumably to complete arrangements for a German arms shipment.[49]

Planning was now in the hands of a small group of I.R.B. members who in the summer of 1915 had decided to set up a Military Council in an effort to tighten their control of the Volunteers. It would be inaccurate to regard the setting up of a Military Council, consisting of Pearse, Ceannt and Plunkett, in May or June 1915 as an act of the I.R.B. as such, although Diarmuid Lynch states that the Council was appointed by the I.R.B. Executive on a motion proposed by him.[50] It would be naive to assume on this evidence that Lynch was the originator of the scheme for a Military Council. Clarke was the only member of the Executive present, and there is little reason to doubt that Lynch proposed his motion on Clarke's instructions. Of the claimed members of the Executive who took this decision, one was Denis McCullough, who was not then president of the Supreme Council,[51] and hence not a member of the Executive, and the other was Lynch acting, he states, as 'a substitute for Seán MacDermott then in prison'. The constitution of the I.R.B. made no provision for the election of substitute officers in this arbitrary fashion, and it seems reasonable to assume that Clarke, Pearse, Plunkett and Ceannt decided that a Military Council was necessary, and convened what they called a meeting of the Executive of the I.R.B. in order to give some semblance of I.R.B. authority to their activities. The danger that the Supreme Council would subsequently question their action was virtually non-existent, since during the whole period it is clear that Clarke and his close associates were able to manipulate the I.R.B. machinery in any way they chose. (It seems not unlikely that Clarke's desire to get Diarmuid Lynch to court deportation to America in June 1915 stemmed from his belief that Lynch, who was a member of the Supreme Council, knew too much.)[5] The district, county, and provincial delegate system had little reality from the time Clarke and MacDiarmada were appointed treasurer and secretary to the Council, and it would be true to add that had delegates met at regular intervals, and deliberated and taken decisions according to constitutional procedure during the years before 1916, the likelihood of a rebellion's taking place would have been remote.

Lynch, whose account of the Rising is written with the emphasis on the importance of the I.R.B., implies that the original committee of three was widened later to include Clarke and MacDiarmada. Sometimes he speaks of them as co-operating with the committee; sometimes as '*ex-officio* members of the committee' and again he says: 'Some months later when Seán MacDiarmada was released from prison, he and Tom Clarke—

the two members of the Executive resident in Dublin, a majority of that body— acted as *ex-officio* members of the Military Committee, thus bringing the membership of the latter up to five'.[53] From Lynch's own account it seems quite clear that Clarke was probably the prime mover in establishing the committee and that MacDiarmada would have been in it from the start had he not been in prison. '*Ex-officio*' they could regard themselves as the I.R.B. during those years, and they acted in its name to take whatever steps they considered necessary to bring about a rising. All the members of the Military Council, with the exception of Clarke (who always remained completely behind the scenes), were on the Central Executive of the Volunteers, while three of them were on the General Council. With Pearse as Director of Organisation, Plunkett as Director of Military Operations, and Ceannt (from August 1915) as Director of Communications, it seemed as if the Military Council would be in a position at any time to stage a *coup* if necessary, and relying on the fact that a majority of Volunteer officers in Dublin and in the provinces were members of the I.R.B., they believed they would be able to commit the whole Volunteer force to rebellion when they chose to do so. They did not realise, however, it would seem, that the changes they had introduced into the I.R.B. organisation would necessarily weaken its force as an activist group within the Volunteers. The system of recruitment to the I.R.B. had altered and the basic organisation with its circles and its unswerving obedience to an immediate superior had been undermined. Now the Military Council—while maintaining a rigid secrecy about its existence and plans—expected to be able, at very short notice, to direct the Volunteers through the influence of roughly 2,000 I.R.B. men scattered throughout the country, but did not make it clear to them that an inner circle existed in Volunteer Headquarters, which would expect all I.R.B. men to act according to their instructions—and only their instructions—when the time came. In the event their expectations

were not justified. In 1916 the problem was not one of the
emergence of a Pierce Nagle or a Red Jim MacDermott who
would sell the secrets of the I.R.B. to the government, but rather
a struggle between men of integrity who held conflicting views
on the course to be followed by the Volunteers.

By the end of 1915 (largely through the efforts of Clarke, it
would seem, since MacDiarmada was in prison) the I.R.B. had
been reorganised. Seven provincial delegates had been elected
none of them resident in Dublin except Lynch, who represented Munster. MacDiarmada, Clarke and Pearse were co-opted
as well as Patrick McCartan, who then lived in Tyrone. According
to Le Roux, Clarke declined to accept nomination for president
of the Supreme Council, which carried with it the nominal
presidency of the Irish Republic,[54] and instead Denis McCullough
was unanimously chosen on the motion of Seán MacDiarmada.
McCullough represented Ulster and was normally resident in
Belfast. He had just been released from prison and was still liable
to deportation. In the circumstances, he seems a strange choice
for what should have been the chief post in the I.R.B. He himself
has recalled that he demurred at his nomination and suggested
Pearse instead, but MacDiarmada told him that they could never
control Pearse.[55] From this evidence it would seem that Clarke
and MacDiarmada were determined, as the only members of the
Executive resident in Dublin, to continue to act in the name of
the I.R.B. with as little consultation as possible with the other
members of the Supreme Council. Clearly Clarke was interested
in the reality of power rather than in prestige, and neither he
nor MacDiarmada, after working together for several years,
would have found it easy to share authority with Pearse, though
it was very important that he, who was to hold the supreme
command in the Rising, should be a member of the Supreme
Council of the I.R.B., thus underlining the Fenian tradition.

Clarke and MacDiarmada had some degree of personal connection with many of the members, and they used I.R.B. men

such as Seán T. Ó Ceallaigh, and members of the Supreme
Council such as Diarmuid Lynch and Patrick McCartan to carry
out important missions, while divulging nothing of their real
plans to them, or even to Denis McCullough, the third member
of the Executive and President of the Supreme Council itself.[56]
They worked tirelessly to prepare the public mind for insurrection by great demonstrations like the funeral of Rossa; by
engineering the take-over bid of the *Coiste Gnotha* of the Gaelic
League, and by getting into the hands of individual I.R.B. men
as much influence as possible in every Irish-Ireland organisation
in the country. Perhaps most important of all was the fact that
the members of the Military Council, particularly Clarke, were
in close touch with John Devoy in America, who was directing
the plans to secure German aid for the Rising. It should also be
mentioned, though this fact is often forgotten, that the members
of the Military Council (with the exception of Connolly), unlike
the organisers of the risings of 1798, 1848 and 1867, scrupulously
refrained from attacking what today would be called 'the
establishment'. They did not deliberately antagonise any section of Irish life, whether Irish Parliamentary Party, Catholic
bishops and clergy or any of the other customary targets of
revolutionaries.

MacCullough and Lynch agree in stating that the date of the
Rising was already fixed by the end of 1915.[57] The Supreme
Council met in January 1916 and passed a resolution proposed
by MacDiarmada, that they 'should fight at the earliest date
possible'. Lynch, who was there, states that Clarke and Mac-
Diarmada 'had the entire confidence of the Council' and he adds
that it was clear to him that they and Pearse were not prepared
to report their plans in any detail. He was of the opinion, at the
time and subsequently, that their decision to keep the plans
'within as narrow a circle as possible . . . was the part of common-
sense and wisdom'.[58]

However confident the members of the Military Council

might feel about their ability to control and direct the Volunteers, they realized that Connolly's Citizen Army was completely outside their sphere of influence, and that their planning might go for nothing if they were forestalled by some precipitate action of Connolly. The danger of premature revolution was to a great extent averted, however, when the Military Council co-opted Connolly in January 1916, having evidently convinced him of the definiteness and feasibility of their plans for a rising. The Military Council of six now controlled, they believed, roughly 3,000 Volunteers in Dublin and 13,000 in the Provinces. The Citizen Army of about 200 men could be counted on to act only in Dublin.

While the members of the Military Council seemed to have successfully gathered into their hands the control of the I.R.B. Volunteers, and the Citizen Army by January 1916, there remained the important question of German aid, which continued, for obvious reasons, to be largely outside their direct control. Casement's scheme for an Irish Brigade recruited from Irish prisoners of war, had not proved any more successful than similar schemes in earlier centuries,[59] and Plunkett's information in the summer of 1915 would seem to have given little grounds for hoping that the Germans would send artillery or officers. A cargo of arms and ammunition was promised, however, and a belief probably persisted that if a stand were made in Ireland, and if the Germans saw that the Irish were serious revolutionaries (a difficult enough proposition for Germans who were daily confronted by Irish regiments in the war), they would render assistance in force.[60] The belief persisted also among Irish revolutionaries, both at home and in the United States, that it was to their advantage to achieve belligerent status as an ally of Germany during the war, and so ensure that their case for independence should be considered at the peace conference.[61]

The decision to include the provinces in the insurrectionary plan seems to have been contingent from the beginning on the landing of a considerable quantity of German arms on the west coast of Ireland, and in the autumn of 1915 Diarmuid Lynch, in consultation with prominent Volunteers in Kerry had, as we have seen, decided on Fenit as the most suitable port for the landing and distribution of the arms. Lynch's testimony would indicate that plans for a country rising proceeded rapidly, since he was, he said, commissioned by Pearse early in January 1916 to issue instructions to 'the Cork, Kerry and Limerick Brigade Commandants respecting the positions to be occupied by their forces over Easter Sunday'.[62] John Devoy has stated that he was informed by the Military Council early in February that the Rising had been fixed for Easter Sunday, 23 April, and they asked that a shipment of arms should reach Ireland between 20 and 23 April. In consultation with the German authorities the arrangements were completed and confirmation was sent to Ireland that the arms would be landed at the port of Fenit between those two dates. On Friday, 14 April, however, Philomena Plunkett, sister of Joseph Plunkett arrived in John Devoy's office, asking that arms should not be landed until the night of Easter Sunday.[63] The ship had already sailed before these new instructions could be given to her commander, but the Military Council proceeded with its plans on the assumption that the German ship would not only successfully run the British blockade, but would reach port in Kerry punctually on Sunday night, on which night, and not before, the local Volunteer commandants, allowing no margin for possible early arrival or possible delay, would expect her, and stand by to make arrangements for unloading the arms.

As the date fixed for the Rising approached, however, it had become increasingly evident that there was a limit to the degree of secrecy which could be maintained in planning something so complicated as a nation-wide insurrection. As early as September 1915 MacNeill's suspicions had been aroused, and he continued to suspect that Connolly and some of the Volunteer Executive believed that it was absolutely essential that they should fight before the war ended, and were making preparations to take the initiative rather than wait upon events. In February 1916 he drew up a memorandum clearly stating his views on the role of the Volunteers, and repudiating any suggestion that a rising must of necessity take place during the war, or that a blood sacrifice was essential to the preservation of Irish nationality. In spite of the reassurances, particularly of MacDonagh, who was not yet a member of the Military Council, MacNeill continued to distrust the intentions of what he rightly suspected to be an activist group within the Volunteer Executive. He stated after the Rising that he had been 'supported without reserve by Hobson' who had 'constantly insisted' that MacNeill should 'demand a clear and binding statement of policy at executive and staff meetings'. Hobson had been far too long a member of the inner core of the I.R.B. to be easily put off the scent. MacNeill called a meeting of the Volunteer Headquarters Staff, on 5 April 1916, in an effort to clarify the position, and it was agreed that, apart from matters of routine, no order would be issued to the Volunteers without MacNeill's countersignature. Those present at this meeting were Pearse, O'Rahilly, Ceannt, MacDonagh, Hobson, O'Connell and MacNeill,[64] and it is clear that the 'wait and see' group on the Headquarters Staff equalled or outnumbered the activist group and that the contemplated *coup* which would give effective control to the activists was going to prove a good deal more difficult than had been expected.

It seems possible, though there is available no documentary evidence to support the thesis, that the meeting of 5 April convinced the activists that MacDonagh must be co-opted to the Military Council.[65] The plan for insurrection in Dublin at least, would seem to have been completed when MacDonagh joined the Military Council, for they now had direct command of the four city battalions. That plan was the same in essentials as the one outlined by Pearse and Connolly in March 1915, and was based on Connolly's oft-suggested scheme of fortifying certain buildings and holding them against all comers.[66] Ned Daly, Tom Clarke's brother-in-law who resided with the Clarkes was completely in the confidence of the leaders, and had been preparing for his part in the Rising since the end of 1914. He had already given up his post in March to devote his whole time to final preparations and could be absolutely relied on to lead the first Dublin Battalion to their positions at the appointed time.[67] Eamonn Ceannt, as a member of the Military Council since its inception would certainly not fail in his command of the fourth battalion. Now that MacDonagh had accepted nomination to the Council he would answer not only for his own second battalion, but also for the third battalion, commanded by Eamon de Valera. The Volunteers were not, however, a regular army, and leaders by themselves without the rank and file could not make a rising. The group in the Volunteer Headquarters Staff who opposed a rising was still a powerful one and attitudes had been hardening since February. Would their influence operate to reduce the muster roll or would they try to block the Rising at the last moment when the plans could no longer be kept secret?

The tide began to flow strongly in favour of the activist group when soon afterwards the famous 'Castle Document' appeared. Alleged to be based on information from the files of Dublin Castle, it revealed detailed plans for a British military occupation of Dublin; for the arrest of persons prominent in Irish political and public life and in Irish-Ireland movements; and for disarming the Volunteers and Citizen Army.[68] On Tuesday and Wednesday of Holy Week the document was discussed at a meeting of the Headquarters Staff, and orders were issued by MacNeill to the Volunteers throughout the country to prepare themselves to resist any attempt to disarm them—a step which might have led to the 'defensive war' for which MacNeill had always declared himself to be prepared. When he discovered for the first time on the night of Holy Thursday, however, that the activist group was engaged in making preparations for war, and under cover of the Easter manoeuvres announced in the *Irish Volunteer* (of which he himself was editor) had issued orders for insurrection, he immediately challenged their right to do so. Throughout the following days a series of discussions and arguments took place between him and the activists, represented by Pearse, Plunkett, MacDiarmada and MacDonagh, and when they told him of the expected arms landing at Fenit, they succeeded for a brief period in convincing him that a general clash between the Volunteers and the British forces was now inevitable. Then came the news of the arrest of Casement, and with it the certainty that the government must now be on the alert. MacNeill's own account of these affairs states that even after hearing 'some sort of news about the failure and arrests in Kerry' he was still prepared 'to take part in the Rising'.[69] He believed, he wrote, that the Volunteers were 'entitled to protect' themselves if the government attempted to disarm them. He believed also that he was now being kept fully informed of events, but when The O'Rahilly and Sean Fitzgibbon and he were in consultation on the Saturday morning he discovered that Fitzgibbon had been sent by the activist group a few days before on a mission to Limerick, a mission which he had been incorrectly assured had MacNeill's sanction.[70] During the same meeting MacNeill became convinced that the 'Castle Document' was bogus and had been manufactured to deceive him and make him the unwitting tool of those who were determined to precipitate insurrection. He and his advisers came to the conclusion that no immediate swoop by the Castle was intended and that it was still possible to avert insurrection, and they believed it was their moral duty to do so.[71] When they came to this decision they were not yet aware that the arms ship had been lost and it is difficult to follow MacNeill's reasoning here. He had been persuaded when he had heard that an arms ship was expected that a clash with the government forces was inevitable. When he took the decision that it was possible and proper to call off the Easter manoeuvres the prospect of that clash between the Volunteer forces and the authorities still remained. He could, of course, have quite simply been relieved of what he regarded as his moral responsibility, by the Military Council, had they arrested him as they did Hobson, but, whatever their reasons, they did not attempt to solve the problem in that way.[72] In conjunction with The O'Rahilly and Seán Fitzgibbon and in consultation with others, not all of whom were members of the Volunteers,[73] MacNeill drafted the order countermanding the mobilisation announced for Easter Sunday, and special messengers were sent late on Saturday to bring it to strategic points throughout the country. By then the news had broken that the German arms ship had been captured by the British, and Austin Stack—one of the key-figures in the insurrection plan—had been arrested. The plan for the south and west had been based on the assumption that an arms landing would take place, and this had been largely set at naught before MacNeill dispatched his messengers or delivered the countermanding order to the *Sunday Independent*.

The events of those days—the failure of the activists to commit MacNeill finally to a Rising, the failure of foreign aid, the cancellation of the original date, and the repetition of so many of the circumstances which had allegedly prevented any serious attempt at insurrection on previous occasions in Irish history— might have been expected to produce once again a damp squib, another fiasco. Whereas, however, on previous occasions many of the leaders of activist groups had been arrested before the time fixed for insurrection, the government moved too late and the leaders in Dublin were still in a position to make a decision for or against action. They decided not to be deflected by the misfortunes which had overtaken them, and they put into opera- tion the Dublin plan which had been in preparation for more than a year, and which could not be affected in its early stages by the loss of the arms ship. On Easter Monday in Dublin about a thousand men and some women answered the call, and an Irish Republic was declared and defended for nearly a week. On Tuesday, Pearse's manifesto to the citizens announced: 'The country is rising in answer to Dublin's call and the final achievement of Ireland's freedom is now, with God's help, only a matter of days';[74] but apart from a few isolated minor incidents no support came from the country to ease the pressure on Dublin.

Pearse seems to be the only member of the Military Council to have left a written statement of his views on the cause of the failure of the country rising. These are contained in the following lines from his final bulletin from the G.P.O.:

'I am satisfied that we should have accomplished more, that we should have accomplished the task of enthroning, as well as proclaiming the Irish Republic as a Sovereign State, had our arrangements for a simultaneous rising of the whole country, with a combined plan as sound as the Dublin plan has proved to be, been allowed to go through on Easter Sunday. Of the fatal countermanding order which prevented those plans from being carried out I shall not speak further.'[75]

Although Pearse added: 'Both Eoin MacNeill and we have acted in the best interests of Ireland', the previous statement tends to place the entire responsibility for the failure of the country rising on the shoulders of Eoin MacNeill. When one examines the history of the preparations for the Rising one must regard this as an over-simplified explanation. What were the other factors which led to the almost complete collapse of the insurrection plan in the provinces, and why, despite the countermand, did Dublin rise? Was the 'combined plan as sound as the Dublin plan'? Was the plan for the south-west capable of being put into effect when the initial phase of the plan—the landing and distribution of arms—could no longer be put into action? Was it reasonable to blame MacNeill when the Military Council's whole strategy was based on the assumption that MacNeill was a figurehead, and that they would be in a position to take complete command of the Volunteer force when the time for action arrived? Why did the infiltration by the I.R.B. of the Volunteers not operate, as intended, to undermine MacNeill's authority? Why were I.R.B. men among those who carried the countermand through the country? Why did the two members of the Supreme Council who were in charge of the Northern Volunteers decide not to carry out the directions of the Military Council, even before the countermand reached Tyrone?

An attempt will now be made to suggest answers to some of these questions and to assess the significance of the countermand issued on Easter Saturday 1916.

MAUREEN WALL.

1. P. H. Pearse, 'From a Hermitage' (January 1914) in *Collected Works of P. H. Pearse: Political Writings and Speeches*, p. 209.

2. *Workers Republic*, 13 November 1915, quoted in *Labour and Easter Week 1916*, ed. Desmond Ryan, p. 102.

3. F. X. Martin, 'Eoin MacNeill on the 1916 Rising' in *Irish Historical Studies* xii, pp. 235, 241 gives examples.

4. *Ibid.*, pp. 236, 237–8, 242.

5. *Ibid.*, p. 240.

6. See *The Royal Commission on the Rebellion in Ireland* and Breandan MacGiolla Choille, ed. *Intelligence Notes 1913–16* for accounts of legal proceedings against Pim, MacDiarmada, Blythe, McCullough, Mellows etc. See also F. X. Martin, 'Eoin MacNeill on the 1916 Rising' in *Irish Historical Studies* xii, p. 242.

7. Piaras Beaslaí, *Michael Collins*, i. pp. 58–9 states: 'As one who was working tooth and nail to bring about an insurrection, I can testify that the biggest obstacle that we had to contend against was the cleverness of

Birrell's policy. The one thing that would have rallied support to our side was drastic coercion on the part of the English government; but Birrell cleverly contrived to appear as not interfering with us, while taking care that we were effectually silenced'.

8. Bulmer Hobson, 'The Origin of Oglaigh na hEireann' in *An tOglach*, June 1931, p. 12.

9. *Ibid.*, and see also Desmond Ryan, *The Rising*, p. 22 n. 9 and F. X. Martin, 'Eoin MacNeill on the Rising' in *Irish Historical Studies* xii, pp. 234–40.

10. See F. X. Martin, 'Eoin MacNeill on the 1916 Rising', pp. 236, 241, n. 7 and Pádraig Ó Snodaigh, *Comhghuaillithe na Réabhlóide 1913–1916*, pp. 62–4 for examination of the 'blood sacrifice' idea.

11. John Devoy, *Recollections of an Irish Rebel*, pp. 403–4.

12. Proinsias Ó Conluain ed. *Seán T.*, pp. 138–9; Desmond Ryan, *James Connolly: Labour and Easter Week*, pp. 2–3.

13. *Ibid.*, pp. 5–6; Piaras Beaslaí, *Michael Collins*, i. pp. 46–7, 56; Ailbhe Ó Monachain, 'Seachtain na Cásga i nGaillimh' in *Ar Aghaidh*, Eanair 1967, p. 7.

14. Desmond Ryan ed. *James Connolly: Labour and Easter Week*, p. 2.

15. Geo. A. Lyons, *Some Recollections of Griffith and his Times*, p. 13 states that on the way home from a meeting of the Transvaal Committee Connolly suggested to Griffith that certain buildings in Dublin should be captured and fortified as well as possible and a republic proclaimed. This plan was allied, as was always the case with Connolly's plan, with a belief in a spontaneous rising in the country once Dublin had taken action. (My attention was drawn to this reference by Commandant W. J. Brennan-Whitmore).

16. Lynch, *The I.R.B. and the 1916 Insurrection*, p. 70.

17. F. X. Martin, 'Eoin MacNeill on the 1916 Rising' in *Irish Historical Studies* xii, p. 252.

18. See *Labour and Easter Week 1916*, ed. Desmond Ryan, pp. 12–13.

19. *Ibid.*, p. 5.

Studies in the History of the Rising

20. Lynch, *The I.R.B. and the 1916 Insurrection*, p. 22 refers to 'unattached members' and notes pp. 35 and 36 that he enrolled four men in Valentia and a man in Carrigaholt. P. MacCartan wrote: 'Connolly was brought into the organization as a member at large, that is he was not attached to any circle but took the oath as a member at large. So Tom Clarke told me. I think Thomas MacDonagh and Joe Plunkett were also brought into the I.R.B. in the same way, as members at large, and about the same time'. See F. X. Martin ed. 'Extracts from the Papers of the Late Dr. Patrick McCartan' in *Clogher Record* (1964), p. 193. Pearse was said to have been refused membership by a club in the ordinary way and was 'co-opted' into the I.R.B. See Le Roux, *Tom Clarke*, p. 127. De Valera reluctantly agreed to take the I.R.B. oath in 1915 but attended no meetings and took no part in ordinary I.R.B. activities. See Tomás Ó Néill and Pádraig Ó Fiannachta, *De Valera*, p. 44. This evidence would indicate that five of the men most active in the conduct of the Rising were nominees of Clarke and MacDiarmada rather than ordinary members of the I.R.B. It has also been stated that most of the Volunteer officers were taken into the I.R.B. shortly before the Rising. See Proinnsias Ó Conluain, ed. *Seán T.*, pp. 155–6.

21. For Hobson's account of his disagreement with Clarke and Mac-Diarmada see F. X. Martin, *The Irish Volunteers 1913–1915*, pp. 49–50. See also Bulmer Hobson, *Ireland, Yesterday and Tomorrow*.

22. Even before Pearse joined the I.R.B. in the end of 1913 Clarke had chosen him to give the Emmet and Tone commemoration lectures. See Louis Le Roux, *Tom Clarke*, pp. 119–22 and *Collected Works of P. H. Pearse: Political Speeches and Writings*, pp. 53–75. See also Lynch, *The I.R.B. and the 1916 Insurrection*, pp. 111–2.

23. Diarmuid Lynch, P. S. O'Hegarty and others speak of a Dublin rising only, while, according to President de Valera, the plan outlined to the Dublin commandants on 13 March 1915 laid down that Connolly was to be in command of the four city battalions, and Pearse was to be in charge of all the Volunteers throughout the country. See Tomás Ó Néill and Pádraig Ó Fiannachta, *De Valera*, p. 41. It is possible that Connolly was to be in control in practice while Pearse had nominally the highest command or it may be that Connolly was determined that he would be in a position to ensure that a rising in Dublin would take place, irrespective of what should happen in the remainder of the country. By December 1914 Pearse had drafted plans for the country districts in the event of conscription being enforced. See n. 28.

24. Lynch, *The I.R.B. and the 1916 Insurrection*, p. 25; M. Ó Dúbhghaill, *Insurrection Fires at Easter*, p. 135 quoting from Seán T. Ó Ceallaigh, *An*

191

The Making of 1916

Poblacht, 30 April 1926; P. S. O'Hegarty, *A History of Ireland Under the Union*, p. 700 quotes Seán MacDiarmada as saying to him in May 1915: 'We'll hold Dublin for a week and save Ireland'. O'Hegarty gives the proposed date as 'September 1915 or thereabouts'.

25. Le Roux, *Tom Clarke*, p. 153.

26. F X. Martin, *The Irish Volunteers 1913–1915*, p. 202. The head-quarters staff consisted of Chief of Staff Eoin MacNeill; Director of Organization P. H Pearse; Director of Military Operations Joseph Plunkett; Director of Training Thomas MacDonagh; Director of Arms The O'Rahilly; Quartermaster General Bulmer Hobson.

27. Rev. J. Travers, *Sean MacDiarmada*, pp. 21-2. Red Jim had been a notorious Fenian spy.

28. Pádraig Ó Snodaigh, *Comhghuaillithe na Réabhlóide 1913–1916*, p. 91, quoting from the Hobson MSS.

29. Piaras Beaslaí, *Michael Collins*, i. p. 56.

30. Tomás Ó Néill and Pádraig Ó Fiannachta, *De Valera*, p. 40 and Pádraig Ó Snodaigh, *Comhghuaillithe na Réabhlóide 1913–1916*, p. 95.

31. *De Valera*, p. 40 quoting from *Irish Volunteer*, 20 March 1915.

32. *Ibid.*, pp. 41-2.

33. Proinsias Ó Conluain ed. *Seán T.*, p. 143. Le Roux, *Life of P. H. Pearse*, p. 317 states that Patrick McCartan went to the U.S.A. at the same time as O'Kelly in March 1915, but MacCartain's memoirs refer to a trip in 1914 and not in 1915.

34. P. S. O'Hegarty, *A History of Ireland Under the Union*, p. 700.

35. *De Valera*, p. 40.

36. *Ibid.*, pp. 41, 43-4. No date is given for de Valera's admission to the I.R.B., but it was evidently after his appointment as commandant in March 1915. He states that he discovered that Volunteers in his battalion knew more about the plans than he did, and when he complained to MacDonagh, he was told that those in the I.R.B. were given more information than others. Of the other commandants appointed in 1915 O'Rahilly does not seem to have joined the I.R.B. (Marcus Bourke, *The*

Studies in the History of the Rising

O'Rahilly, p. 100), and was not in the confidence of the leaders, nor was Bulmer Hobson, who had been a key man in the I.R.B. for more than a decade.

37. Rev. J. Travers, *Seán MacDiarmada*, pp. 22–5.

38. The best account of Plunkett's German mission is in Pádraig Ó Snodaigh, *Comhghuaillithe na Réabhlóide 1913–1916*, pp. 98–100. See also Le Roux, *Life of P. H. Pearse*, p. 318; Lynch, *The I.R.B. and the 1916 Insurrection*, p. 113; Ryan, *The Rising*, pp. 15, 37–41.

39. Pádraig Ó Snodaigh, *Comhghuaillithe na Réabhlóide 1913–1916*, pp. 113–4.

40. Le Roux, *Tom Clarke*, pp. 163–8; Ryan, *The Rising*, p. 57; *Diarmuid Ó Donnabhain Rosa 1831–1915: Souvenir of Public Funeral to Glasnevin Cemetery Dublin, August 1st 1915*; Beaslaí, *Michael Collins* i, pp. 64–5.

41. For a discussion of the views of Hobson and others on this section of the I.R.B. constitution see F. X. Martin, 'Eoin MacNeill on the 1916 Rising' in *Irish Historical Studies* xii, p. 259.

42. *Diarmuid Ó Donnabhain Rosa 1831–1915: Souvenir of Public Funeral*, p. 19.

43. Le Roux, *Life of P. H. Pearse*, p. 321, quoting Darrel Figgis.

44. Le Roux, *Tom Clarke*, p. 168.

45. See F. X. Martin, 'Eoin MacNeill on the 1916 Rising' in *Irish Historical Studies* xii, pp. 245–6, 251–2; Le Roux, *Life of P. H. Pearse*, pp. 321–4; Pádraig Ó Snodaigh, *Comhghuaillithe na Réabhlóide*, p. 117; Ryan, ed. *Labour and Easter Week*, p. 9.

46. *Workers Republic*, 30 October 1915 and 13 November 1915, quoted in Ryan, *Labour and Easter Week*, pp. 93, 102, 103.

47. Lynch, *The I.R.B. and the 1916 Insurrection*, p. 28; Pádraig Ó Snodaigh, *Comhghuaillithe na Réabhlóide*, p. 131.

48. Lynch, *The I.R.B. and the 1916 Insurrection*, p. 29–30; 135.

49. Pádraig Ó Snodaigh, *Comhghuaillithe na Réabhlóide*, p. 116.

14

The Making of 1916

50. Lynch, *The I.R.B. and the 1916 Insurrection*, pp. 25, 47, 102, 113, 131, 132.

51. McCullough became president of the Supreme Council in December 1915. See his letter to *Irish Independent*, 12 March 1966. His predecessor, S. Deakin, had been inactive for some time. See Le Roux, *Tom Clarke*, p. 170.

52. Lynch, *The I.R.B. and the 1916 Insurrection*, p. 26, writes: 'Tom Clarke was of opinion that I should refuse to register [as a "friendly alien"]; that deportation to the U.S. was certain to follow, and that this would afford the Clan material for anti-British propaganda . . . I preferred to register as ordered and remain in Ireland'. This was in June 1915.

53. Lynch, *The I.R.B. and the 1916 Insurrection*, pp. 25, 47, 102, 113, 130, 131, 132, 151. Lynch seems to suggest that MacDiarmada could only have been appointed to the Military Council when he returned from prison, but it is not clear whether or not Joseph Plunkett had returned from Germany at the time of his appointment to it.

54. In *The Record of the Irish Rebellion of 1916*, p. 13 published by *Irish Life* very shortly after the Rising a picture of Clarke appears with the description 'President of the Republic'.

55. Lynch, *The I.R.B. and the 1916 Insurrection*, pp. 28–9; Le Roux, *Tom Clarke*, pp. 174–6. McCullough's recollections were given in a Radio Eireann broadcast, edited by Proinsias Ó Conluain, 17 March 1966. In *Irish Independent*, 12 March 1966, McCullough gave December 1915 as the date of his election as President of the Supreme Council.

56. See pp. 172, 216–7.

57. See Lynch, *The I.R.B. and the 1916 Insurrection*, p. 48 and Pádraig Ó Snodaigh, *Comhghuaillithe na Réabhlóide*, p. 134, quoting from a letter he received from McCullough. Cathal O'Shannon got the distinct impression from a conversation with Connolly in January 1916 that the date of the Rising had been fixed by the Military Council before they took Connolly into their confidence. See *Evening Press*, 9 August 1968.

58. Lynch, *The I.R.B. and the 1916 Insurrection*, pp. 30–31; 131–3.

59. Similar unsuccessful attempts had been made to recruit Irish prisoners in France during the Seven Years War, 1756–63; and Tone had tried to recruit a regiment from among the prisoners in preparation for the French expeditions to Ireland in the late 1790s.

Studies in the History of the Rising

60. Whether the members of the Military Council really believed that German help other than arms might be expected is of course open to doubt. They may have been using the suggestion as another part of their strategy for committing the Volunteers to a rising. The Volunteers who were opposed to taking the initiative did intimate their intention of fighting should the Germans land an expeditionary force. (See note 8). It may also have been suggested to members of the Supreme Council for the same reason. On Holy Thursday Tom Clarke told Patrick McCartan that at least 5,000 Germans would be coming, and he 'was enthusiastic about how thorough the Germans were'. (F. X. Martin, ed. 'Extracts from the papers of the late Dr. Patrick McCartan' in *Clogher Record 1964*, pp. 197–8). On the previous Monday MacDiarmada had told Denis McCullough that 'a ship was to come up the Liffey with help'. (Denis McCullough, 'The Events in Belfast' in *Capuchin Annual 1966*, p. 382). Did Clarke and MacDiarmada believe that the northern leaders did not want to embark on a rising without some reasonable chance of success? At the last meeting of the Supreme Council in January 1916 McCartan had made it clear that he didn't want 'any more glorious failures' (*Clogher Record 1964*, p. 194). Pierce McCann was told on Easter Saturday: 'the Germans are to launch a big air-raid on England to cover the landing of German officers, arms and ammunition in Ireland.' See *Cluain Meala 1916*, p. 11. See John de Courcy Ireland, *The Sea and the Easter Rising 1916*, pp. 36–7 for an account of a German naval demonstration on 25 April 1916.

61. See account of John Devoy's speech at the Irish Race Convention on 4 March 1916 on the need for 'Ireland to take action as a belligerent—establish a national government and hold military posts'. (See Dorothy Macardle, *The Irish Republic*, p. 148).

62. Lynch, *The I.R.B. and the 1916 Insurrection*, pp. 49, 134.

63. John Devoy, *Recollections of an Irish Rebel*, pp. 458–63.

64. F. X. Martin, 'Eoin MacNeill on the 1916 Rising' in *Irish Historical Studies* xii, pp. 235, 236, 245–7, 255–6.

65. Lynch, *The I.R.B. and the 1916 Insurrection*, pp. 130, 132 gives the date of MacDonagh's co-option as the 'first week in April 1916'. Mac-Donagh had evidently been committed to the plan for a rising in the autumn of 1915, though as late as May that year he had expressed the hope that it might never be necessary to use arms. (See Francis Sheehy Skeffington, 'An open letter to Thomas MacDonagh in *1916: The Easter Rising*, ed. O. Dudley Edwards and Fergus Pyle, p. 149). His article in the Rossa souvenir publication in August 1915, however, echoes Pearse's sentiments when he speaks of 'a holy cause that will be served and served

only in blood, and served still though it be betrayed by every man and woman of us but one'. Again he says: 'With this spirit moving them or troubling them, the Irishmen of this generation have grown up. Most of them have anxiously prayed that when their destined duty arrives their eyes may be made clear that they may know it, and their hands made cunning, that by some wild luck they may be skilled to serve it'. The other six probably relied completely on MacDonagh to stand with them when the final decision had to be made, but as Director of Training and commandant of the Dublin Brigade he would have to be taken into their complete confidence in advance. Because of his close connection with MacNeill in University College they may have been delaying his co-option until the Easter holidays. Eamonn de Valera had made it clear that he would obey the orders of his superior officer, a course he was to maintain right up to the surrender in Easter Week. (Tomás Ó Néill agus Pádraig Ó Fiannachta, *De Valera*, p. 41). See also Marcus Bourke, 'Thomas MacDonagh's Role in the Plans for the 1916 Rising' in *The Irish Sword* viii, 178–85. MacDonagh's position is further discussed on pp. 245–6, note 66.

66. See p. 168.

67. Piaras Beaslaí, *Michael Collins*, i. p. 56. Very Rev. C. J. Travers, *Seán MacDiarmada*, p. 28.

68. For MacNeill's account of the document see F. X. Martin, 'Eoin MacNeill on the 1916 Rising' in *Irish Historical Studies* xii, pp. 247–8, 250. Its authenticity is still a subject for discussion and argument though the weight of evidence seems to indicate that it was a forgery. See Ryan, *The Rising*, pp. 64–75; Dorothy Macardle, *The Irish Republic*, pp. 158–9; P. J. Little, 'A 1916 Document' in *The Capuchin Annual 1942*, pp. 454–62; M. Ó Dúbhghaill, *Insurrection Fires at Eastertide*, pp. 196–203; John Brennan, 'The Castle Document' in *Irish Times*, 28 March 1958; Lynch, *The I.R.B. and the 1916 Insurrection*, pp. 133–4, 137; P. S. O'Hegarty, *A History of Ireland under the Union*, pp. 699–70; F. X. Martin, 'Myth, Fact, and Mystery' in *Studia Hibernica 1967*, pp. 119–21. See also Leon Ó Broin, *Dublin Castle and the 1916 Rising* for the inside story of the activities and decisions of the Castle authorities at the time.

69. MacNeill states that he 'did not see the least prospect of success for it'. See F X. Martin, 'Eoin MacNeill on the 1916 Rising' in *Irish Historical Studies* xii, p. 249. The non-activist group in the Volunteers had always insisted that they were aiming at success.

70. For Fitzgibbon's mission see Mannix Joyce, 'The Story of Limerick and Kerry in 1916' in *The Capuchin Annual 1966*, pp. 342, 351.

71. See F. X. Martin, 'Eoin MacNeill and the 1916 Rising' in *Irish Historical Studies* xii, pp. 247–50, 257–68.

72. Until Saturday the Military Council believed that they had committed MacNeill to participation in the fight, and the O'Rahilly's threat to shoot it out with whoever tried to kidnap himself could possibly have deterred them from attempting any further kidnappings. See Ryan, *The Rising*, pp. 93, 116. Liam Ó Briain reports MacNeill as agreeing with him in a conversation on Easter Monday morning that had they arrested him he would have had no further responsibility. See 'An tEirí amach mar do chonnacsa é' in *The Easter Rising 1916 and University College, Dublin*, ed. F. X. Martin, p. 61.

73. *Ibid.*, pp. 59–60; Proinsias Ó Conluain, ed. *Seán T.*, p. 162; F. X. Martin, 'Eoin MacNeill on the 1916 Rising' in *Irish Historical Studies* xii, p. 266.

74. Le Roux, *Life of P. H. Pearse*, p. 388.

75. *Ibid.*, pp. 396–7.

The Plans and the Countermand:
the Country and Dublin

by
MAUREEN WALL

The Plans and the Countermand:
the Country and Dublin

PEARSE'S assertion that there were in existence 'arrangements for a simultaneous rising of the whole country, with a combined plan as sound as the Dublin plan', is supported by Liam Mellows, who had left St. Enda's on Holy Thursday to take command in Galway, and was presumably in Pearse's confidence. He described the plans as being 'carefully prepared months ahead, every detail that would ensure success and co-ordination being worked out'.[1] So far the evidence for such planning has not come to light and one is left with the impression that this belief in a perfectly co-ordinated plan must have rested on the assumption by members of the Military Council, that they had in the I.R.B. membership an instrument, which would respond without question or hesitation and at the shortest possible notice to any order they might issue; an instrument, moreover, capable of committing the whole Volunteer organization to a rising.[2] Although they were aware that MacNeill, Hobson and other prominent Volunteer leaders were vehemently opposed to an unprovoked rising[3] they seem to have had no doubt whatever that the members of the I.R.B., who had infiltrated the Volunteers, would carry out their instructions, even though they had apparently taken no steps to inform I.R.B. officers or rank and file that they should disregard all orders except those emanating from known I.R.B. men. The I.R.B. strategy is outlined by Diarmuid Lynch as follows:

The method by which the effective participation of the whole

Volunteer force could be arranged without exposing the secret purpose of the Military Council was a problem of prime importance. Mindful of the 1914 capitulation to Redmond—contrary to the judgment of the I.R.B. Executive—the question of such participation could not safely be left to a vote of the governing body of the Irish Volunteers. A simple and what at the time seemed an effective solution was decided on; Pearse, besides being a member of the secret revolutionary group, was also Director of Organization on the I. V. Headquarters Staff, and in this latter capacity it was one of his functions to order any general exercises or manoeuvres by the Volunteers throughout the country. The issuance by him of such an instruction for Easter-time, 1916, was calculated not to arouse the least suspicion and to ensure a general mobilization under arms at the opportune moment.

Lynch goes on to discuss the order for the Easter Sunday manoeuvres published by Pearse in the *Irish Volunteer* for 8 April 1916, and states:

This was published with the approval of the Volunteer Executive and of Eoin MacNeill, Chief of Staff, but Pearse did not tell them that he had already issued secret orders to the Brigade Commandants as to the areas in which their respective 'manoeuvres' were to be held. Nor did he inform them of the ultimate purposes which those manoeuvres were intended to serve.[4]

It would seem, however, that Pearse and those who were acting with him believed that they would be able to secure the co-operation of MacNeill before the Rising began, and so considered it unnecessary to apprise the brigade commandants of possible divisions at command level. They probably relied on the fact that the 'wait and see' section of the Volunteers had declared their intention to resist in the event of any attempt by the government to suppress them; and if the Military Council manufactured the 'Castle Document' (which threatened suppression and disarming of the Volunteers) with the hope of bringing about this situation, they were eminently successful for a brief period. At a meeting of the Volunteer Executive on Tuesday of Holy Week, MacNeill drafted an order, which was acceptable to Pearse, ordering the Volunteers to prepare themselves to resist suppression. This document, dated 19 April, included the following instructions:

> Your object will be to preserve the arms and the organization of the Irish Volunteers, and the measures taken by you will be directed to that purpose.
>
> In general you will arrange that your men defend themselves and each other in small groups so placed that they may best be able to hold out.
>
> Each group must be provided with sufficient supplies of food, or be certain of access to such supplies.[5]

These orders correspond very closely to the plan already worked out for Dublin and, as if to underline the similarity of the plans for Dublin and the country, the *Irish Volunteer* for Easter Saturday, 22 April 1916, carried the following announcement:

> Arrangements are now nearing completion in all the more important brigade areas for the holding of a very interesting series of manoeuvres at Easter . . . As for Easter, the Dublin programme may well stand as a model for other areas.[6]

If the Dublin plan was indeed to be a blue-print for use in other areas, there is little evidence that it had been explained to the officers in the provinces; and the lateness of its announcement would have left little time for working out details with regard to selecting, seizing, provisioning, fortifying and defending specific buildings in other cities and towns, on the lines of the Dublin plan, which was being perfected for more than a year.[7] Country units had had little experience in reconnoitring the areas where they might be expected to set up their headquarters during a rising,[8] or indeed in making public appearances at all in the towns and cities they were to take over, except on the few occasions when prominent Volunteers from headquarters came to a district to inspect and encourage them. The evidence for any supervision or initiation of plans by headquarters staff for most areas in the country is slight[9] apart from vague generalised instructions about 'holding the line of the Shannon' and 'relieving the pressure on Dublin'.

The Military Council did take steps, however, to organise Volunteer movements in the south-western and western area which was to be the main centre of action outside Dublin. They knew, from the end of 1915, that the German arms were to be landed in Kerry, and the commanding officers of the Cork, Kerry, Limerick and Galway Volunteers were ordered to occupy positions in the event of a rising, which would enable them to cover the landing, protection and distribution of the arms. The positions were as follows:

> The Cork brigade was to move into positions on the north and north-west of the county in a line extending from the Pass of Keimineagh to north of Newmarket, making contact with the Kerry brigade to the west. The Kerry brigade was to extend eastwards from Tralee to the Cork border, and in the north to link up with Limerick. The Limerick brigade, which included Clare, and the Galway brigade were to hold the line of the Shannon to Athlone.[10]

The line of defence for Connacht was to be complete when the

Belfast, Tyrone and Derry Volunteers arrived to co-operate with the forces of Liam Mellows in holding the line of the Shannon. Patrick McCartan, who was a member of the Supreme Council of the I.R.B., has stated that the plan originally was contingent on a German landing in the west, and if the Germans were not to come 'we would be given other plans'. 'But', he adds, 'we never got the other plans'.[11] Had this co-ordinated plan for using the line of the Shannon and for trying to prevent British forces from penetrating into Connacht been put into operation, it might have prolonged the Rising for a time and would certainly have given the Crown forces a more formidable task than the reduction of Dublin alone gave them. Like the Dublin plan it was a defensive one, but it is difficult to believe that the handful of Volunteers available, even with the addition of German armaments, would have successfully taken and held towns such as Limerick and Athlone. Michael Colivet who was in command in Limerick, and who was rather amused at the magnitude of the task allotted to them, is said to have told Pearse that his men would have to be spaced out, one man for every three hundred yards, along the Shannon.[12] Austin Stack was to be the key-man in organizing the arms landing, and was given his instructions by Pearse on 27 February 1916,[13] but the other commanding officers in the south-west do not seem to have been aware until very shortly before Easter that the 'manoeuvres' were in fact to be a rising.

Three weeks before Easter, Michael Colivet was completing his plans for holding the Shannon line from Limerick to Killaloe and for taking Limerick city, if possible, though since 800 British infantry and 100 R.I.C. men were stationed there, and he could call on only 200 poorly armed men at most, his chances of doing so would seem to have been remote. However he planned to hold the north shore of the Shannon around the city and retire into Clare if necessary. Other Limerick, Clare and West Tipperary battalions were to act on similar lines in their own immediate areas, all intending to carry out the original plan of holding the line of the Shannon. It was not until almost the eve of the Rising that these eight battalions, consisting of 1,600 men, were designated a brigade and placed under the command of Colivet. On Tuesday of Holy Week, however, a message was received from Pearse telling Colivet of the expected arms landing in Kerry, and instructing him to supervise the collection and distribution of arms for his own men and for the Galway Volunteers. Colivet, sensing that this meant an immediate rising, and realising that the new orders completely cut across the tentative plans he had been making, went to Dublin to consult with Pearse. Pearse told him the Rising would begin on Sunday at 7 p.m. and ordered him to cancel all previous plans; and so Colivet found himself, at four days' notice, faced with the task of organising the newly constituted brigade to take delivery of the arms at Abbeyfeale and forward part of them to Galway; to attack police and military barracks and cut telegraph, telephone and rail communications. When all this had been accomplished and the position in Limerick was under control, they were to march eastwards and relieve Dublin. Elaborate plans covering all these points were drawn up late on Wednesday, and conveyed to the local commanding officers during the next few days. It is difficult to understand why the Limerick Volunteers, so few in numbers, largely untrained, badly armed, never having experienced fire, and totally unaccustomed to acting together as a unit, should have been ordered by Pearse at four days' notice to go on the offensive and attack military and police barracks in this fashion. No such task had been allotted to the Dublin battalions who had been preparing for a rising in the city for more than a year. Even had the German arms arrived, the local Volunteers could hardly have been expert in handling them without some practice. But they were, in fact, scheduled to start their attack on Limerick barracks presumably with the rifles and revolvers and shotguns already in their possession, in order to create a diversion to cover the arrival of the German arms at Abbeyfeale. With the police and military in defensive positions, the losses among Limerick Volunteers and citizens might well have been considerable, had this scheme been put into operation.

On Saturday, however, news came of the sinking of the arms ship, the capture of Casement and the arrest of Austin Stack. Colivet sent two messengers to Dublin asking for instructions and suggesting that, in view of what had happened, the Rising should be postponed. When no news had come from Dublin by evening he cancelled all arrangements for the Easter Sunday mobilisation. At this time Colivet was still unaware of a split in the Volunteer headquarters staff, and although a member of the I.R.B. he was no more in the confidence of the Military Council than were the non-I.R.B. members of the Volunteer organisation. On Sunday morning The O'Rahilly arrived in Limerick with the MacNeill countermanding order, and for the first time Colivet heard of the clash between MacNeill and the 'war party'. Since he had already cancelled the Sunday manoeuvres, the arrival of the countermand did not influence the position in Limerick to any great extent. James J. Gubbins, one of the messengers Colivet had sent to Dublin, returned on Sunday with a message from Seán MacDiarmada that the Rising would still take place, that 'the lost German ship was only one of many such expeditions' and urging the Limerick Volunteers to resist any attempt to arrest them. Liam Forde, the second messenger, arrived at midnight with a direct message from Pearse saying that 'everything was off for the present', but telling Colivet to hold himself in readiness for further orders. Another messenger, Patrick Whelan, who had been dispatched to Tralee, returned on Monday morning with discouraging news. Monteith, who had arrived with Casement, had denounced the Germans bitterly, saying that no men were coming, and the arms cargo consisted only of 20,000 obsolete Russian rifles and ten modern machine guns. At 2 p.m. on the same day Agnes Daly arrived from Dublin with a dispatch from Pearse announcing that the Dublin brigade was going into action at noon that day, and the instructions to Colivet were: 'Carry out your orders'. Since these orders were no longer relevant, owing to the loss of the arms shipment, it is not surprising that the message did not result in a rising in the Limerick area. Having already been constrained to alter their plans five days before, were they now to revert to the sketchy plan which had originally been under consideration for defending the line of the Shannon? MacDiarmada's message had merely been to resist arrest, and no attempt in fact was made to arrest them. In the circumstances it is hard to see what importance if any should be ascribed to the MacNeill countermand, although those who have told the story of Limerick in Easter Week have made the following comment:

> Having regard to McNeill's dispatch, with its reference to the Volunteers being deceived and to the whisperings of friction in Dublin, it appeared as if some persons in Dublin might have kicked over the traces. If that was the case, it was clearly Colivet's duty to obey loyally the orders of McNeill, who was Chief of Staff. The unanimous decision of the Battalion staff was that Pearse's dispatch could not be acted upon'.[14]

Some observations may be made on this statement. Firstly the situation was chaotic. The hastily drawn up plans were useless. The expected arms were at the bottom of the sea; the police and military in the south-west were on the alert; already the military forces in the city had been augmented to 2,000; Monteith had counselled against a rising. It would have been madness in the circumstances to have gone out on an offensive war as distinct from the defensive one which was being carried out by the Dublin insurgents. Nevertheless, knowing that the Dublin Volunteers had risen it was hard for these men (who had been genuinely geared for a fight when there was some hope of success), to take the weight of the decision on their own shoulders when finally calling off the Rising in Limerick; and it was natural that they should seek consolation in the fact that they were obeying the orders of their Chief of Staff. The Chief of Staff's countermand, however, related only to 'parades, marches, or other movements of Irish Volunteers' on Easter Sunday, and contained no prohibition on Monday manoeuvres and it had been confirmed by Pearse. Moreover, if the I.R.B. infiltration scheme had really been effective, Colivet, as a member of that organisation, would have been expected to carry out the orders received from Pearse on Easter Monday.

Only a brief reference can be made to the situation in Kerry, Cork, Tipperary and the other counties which were to have been involved in the plan for holding the line from Cork to the Shannon, after the Volunteers in these areas had been furnished with arms from the *Aud*. The arrest on Good Friday of Austin Stack, the one man who seems to have been in the full confidence of the Military Council, and who alone knew the plans for Kerry, threw everything into disarray; and Monteith's denunciation of the Germans did nothing to improve morale.[15] In Cork the number of conflicting messages from Dublin seems to have exceeded that received at any other centre, but again the loss of the arms ship and the subsequent alerting of police and military in the area was crucial, and MacCurtain's I.R.B. membership had made no difference when the crisis developed.[16] In Tipperary, where the county commandant, Pierce McCann, was evidently not in the I.R.B., the situation was no better and no worse than it was in areas where the I.R.B. men were in command. McCann got the countermand from The O'Rahilly and was instructed to bring it to Limerick and thence to Killarney. Frank Drohan, who was in command in Clonmel and was also centre of the local I.R.B. circle, brought the countermand to Waterford and New Ross. On Tuesday night of Easter Week, McCann agreed with two local I.R.B. men, Seán Treacy and Eamonn O'Dwyer, that Tipperary should go into action if the Cork and Limerick men

15

would co-operate, but although Treacy and O'Dwyer made contact with the Volunteers in Cork and Limerick no action ensued.[17] In Ulster, Denis McCullough, President of the I.R.B. and Dr. Patrick McCartan another member of the Supreme Council, who had been ordered to march their men through largely hostile territory to join forces with Mellows, and help in holding the line of the Shannon, knew nothing of the countermand when they decided not to attempt to carry out this assignment. The Tyrone men were unwilling to participate in a scheme which seemed to them impracticable and it is doubtful if their decision was influenced at all by the loss of the arms ship. McCartan had never been interested in 'glorious defeats' and McCullough had been shaken when he heard Bulmer Hobson on Palm Sunday inveighing against a rising. He realized that there was a division on the question even among I.R.B. men.[18]

Liam Mellows, who seems to have been completely in the confidence of the leaders, and as determined a worker for a rising as any of the members of the Military Council, had returned from England whither he had been deported, to take charge in Galway. He was not deflected by either the countermanding order or the failure of the arms ship. He followed the Dublin pattern by taking over large buildings—first the agricultural station in Athenry and later Moyode Castle.[19] The Wexford Volunteers, on receipt of a direct message from James Connolly on the Wednesday of Easter Week, similarly garrisoned the Athenaeum in Enniscorthy.[20] Had the police or the military made an attempt to dislodge them, as was done in Dublin, Enniscorthy might have played a significant rôle in the Rising. Indeed, the same would have been true of Cork and Limerick, in all probability, had the authorities attempted to disarm the Volunteers in those cities forcibly, instead of prevailing on them to surrender their arms by agreement. One of the few places outside the south-west, to which the Military Council had given some attention, was Dundalk, where they had sent Dan Hannigan to take charge some weeks before the Rising. Here, however, the plan of fortifying a large local building was not followed and the Louth Volunteers acted rather aimlessly though a few of them managed to reach Dublin and take part in the fighting.[21]

The events of Easter Week in north County Dublin fall into a different category from those in other parts of Ireland. The Volunteers under the command of Thomas Ashe formed the fifth battalion of the Dublin brigade, and Ashe, like the other Dublin commandants, had been working on plans for the Rising since the early months of 1915. Moreover, he was in the confidence of the members of the Military Council to a considerable extent, and when the Rising began on Easter Monday he was in direct communication with Liberty Hall, and was able to send some of his men to reinforce the Dublin Volunteers. The North Dublin men took the type of offensive action which had been recommended to Volunteer commandants in other parts of the country, but there was a substantial difference between attacking a few isolated country barracks in that area and attacking large police and military establishments in places like Cork, Limerick and Tralee. By their successful ambush of the R.I.C. reinforcements on their way to Ashbourne they probably did to some extent relieve the pressure on Dublin, but by that time the Rising in Dublin was virtually over.[22]

Some attempt was evidently made by the Military Council to provide outside leadership or assistance to certain areas, though no over-all plan is discernible. Con Collins, a close friend of MacDiarmada, and William Partridge, described as one of Connolly's best-known organizers, were sent to Tralee to assist in the arms landing there, though their dispatch on Wednesday and Thursday of Holy Week[23] left them little time to study local conditions or to become acquainted with local Volunteers. The officers and men of the Dundalk Volunteers asked headquarters for a man to take charge of their unit and 'knock it into shape,' and Seán MacDiarmada sent them Dan Hannigan, a man close to the Military Council, who was in charge when the Rising began.[24] The question of holding the line of the Shannon at the Cavan end also seems to have received some attention from the leaders, though clearly the plan, if it existed, was subordinated to the Dublin plan, at the last moment, when Seán MacDiarmada withdrew Seán O'Sullivan from Ballinagh and brought him to Dublin to assist Ned Daly. Denis McCullough was asked to send Seán Cusack (a British army sergeant and I.R.B. man) to replace O'Sullivan and to 'take charge in Ballinagh'. Even had Cusack reached Ballinagh on Easter Saturday or Sunday he would have had considerable difficulty in carrying out his mission of taking over leadership at the eleventh hour.[25] It is possible, too, that when Dr. Patrick McCartan was told by Pearse 'a long time before the Rising' that the Volunteers from Ulster were to 'concentrate at Belcoo and hold the line of the Shannon', some tentative plan for this area may have been under consideration. Belcoo is close to MacDiarmada's home town of Kiltyclogher, and he had sent twelve Howth rifles and some ammunition there in 1914.[26] If a co-ordinated plan for the Shannon area existed, it is clear that its success was less important in the eyes of the leaders than ensuring that the Dublin Rising got off to a good start. Indeed the insistence in the instructions to all county commandants that no action should be taken before 7 p.m. on Easter Sunday, when the Dublin Rising would already be under way, shows that Dublin was placed in the forefront of the plans, and initiative taken out of the hands of local officers.[27] The presence of organisers from other parts of Ireland would have been of primary importance to the Volunteers in provincial centres, but the scheme of appointing organisers had begun to break down from 1915 on, with the arrest, or banishment from their areas of action, of Robert Monteith, Ailbhe Ó Monachain, Liam Mellows, Ernest Blythe, Desmond Fitzgerald and Alf Cotton. Few would deny that the activities in Galway in Easter

Week were directly connected with the return of Mellows and Ó Monachain to an area where they had been active as organisers.

Adequate communication between the Military Council and the provinces was lacking, and this must be reckoned as an important factor in the collapse of such plans as did exist for a provincial rising. Although code telegrams were sent in some instances,[28] and although Pearse used the *Irish Volunteer* to convey directives about the Easter manoeuvres, under cover of which the Rising was to take place,[29] no detailed or well-digested system of communication seems to have been perfected, and it was Eoin MacNeill who saw the possibilities for disseminating information provided by the national newspapers. The police and military, on the other hand, could rely on the vital telephone and tele-graphic system to alert their men at very short notice, and this had already been done in the south-west before Easter Sunday, and an alert went out to the police throughout the country on Easter Monday morning.[30]

Although the police were everywhere on the alert they seem to have received instructions to keep things under observation rather than to take any overt steps against the Volunteers. Accounts of events in Limerick on Easter Sunday, for instance, paint an extraordinary picture of men from Tournafulla, Templeglantine, Killoughteen, Newcastle West, Killeedy, Monagea, Dromcollogher and Broadford drilling in a field at Glenquin, while twelve R.I.C. men with carbines stood on the road and watched them.[31] Had the authorities not adopted the policy of generally refraining from provoking incidents in other areas until they had got the Dublin Rising under control the outcome might have been very different, not only in areas like Enniscorthy, Cork and Limerick, but in many country districts as well. Had the police pursued others as they did Michael O'Callaghan in Tipperary, who shot and killed a sergeant and a constable who had come to arrest him,[32] fighting of a guerilla type might have broken out in several areas.

One field in which, despite the failure of the arms landing and the last-minute confusion, one might have expected the country Volunteers to have rendered valuable assistance to the Dublin insurgents was that of cutting road, rail, telephone, and telegraphic communication between outlying areas and Dublin. Although directives were sent out by Pearse for the seizure of railways and the dynamiting of bridges, this aspect of warfare seems to have taken second place in the general preparations to activities connected with actual fighting. In the event, the plan for capturing the central telephone exchange in Dublin, which was expected to paralyse the system throughout the country, miscarried and there seems to have been little sabotage of the system in other areas. Although several not very successful attempts were made on the perimeter of Dublin and in counties Wexford and Galway to put the railways out of action, the value of gelignite, for other than the manufacture of home-made bombs, does not seem to have been fully recognised, though there must have been many quarrymen and others in the country, who had practical experience in the use of explosives. There is little evidence, however, that advance preparations had been made in any area, even in Dublin, for demolition work, or that special groups had been trained for such work, though the Volunteers and Citizen Army seem to have had considerable quantities of explosives in their possession.[33]

Perhaps the most significant factor in the failure of the plans for a country rising, however, was the evident non-existence of the control claimed to have been wielded by the I.R.B. over the Volunteers.[34] Apart from the very general secret instructions issued by Pearse to some of the I.R.B. Volunteer officers early in 1916 and which were not understood by even all the senior commanding officers to be definite plans for a rising, I.R.B. officers in the Volunteers, and indeed the members of the Supreme Council itself, knew practically none of the secrets of their organization.[35] The ordinary rank and file members of the

I.R.B. seem to have been kept completely in the dark.

The evidence indicates that as early as 1908, and increasingly from 1914, when the decision in favour of a rising had been taken by the Supreme Council of the I.R.B., Clarke and Mac-Diarmada had begun gradually to alter the character of the organisation until by the eve of the Rising it had virtually lost most of the attributes which normally characterise a secret society carrying on effective revolutionary activities.

For such a society to have any real value on a national scale it must constitute a network of command, based on delegates elected or appointed on a regional basis, and must act as a grapevine along which orders, issued at very short notice, can descend through the various levels of command to the rank and file members, who like all grades in the society are pledged to complete unquestioning obedience to their superior officers. Such a society, however, had been shown in many countries to have been a hunting-ground for spies and informers. This had been particularly true in Ireland, in the United Irishmen in the 1790s and in the Fenians in the 1860s. Clarke and MacDiarmada were determined that history should not repeat itself in their day, and so they endeavoured to control to a great extent admission to the society throughout the entire country. The system of circles was in a great measure abandoned, and chosen individuals were sworn into the I.R.B. if they passed the tests of acceptability demanded by Clarke and MacDiarmada. In the last weeks before the Rising, officers in the Volunteers were taken into the I.R.B.—a seeming reversal of the normal secret society infiltration idea—and men were even sworn as members immediately before undertaking particular missions.[36] One of the few instances on record where the forms of the secret society were preserved was the meeting of the Leinster Executive of the I.R.B., called on Good Friday 1916, to effect the arrest of Bulmer Hobson,[37] and it is not unreasonable to assume that the Leinster Directory was acting under express instructions from the Military

Council which was not a part of the I.R.B. system as such.

Because of the breakdown of the normal secret society network, its value as a means of communication between headquarters and the provincial areas was greatly diminished. There was no arrangement for the efficient each-way exchange of information between leaders and led, and the days before Easter saw a procession of prominent I.R.B. men from the country to Dublin, seeking information about the Rising in which they were expected to take part, or perhaps it would be more correct to say that they were seeking denial or confirmation of rumours of an impending rising. This traffic had begun well before there was any question of a countermand, and it continued until the Rising began on Easter Monday morning. The visitors to the city included Denis McCullough, President of the Supreme Council, who had to force an interview with Seán MacDiarmada on the Monday of Holy Week, and was then told of the proposed Rising and the general plans, as well as a story which must have had little foundation, about a ship which was to come up the Liffey with help.[38] Dr. Patrick McCartan, another member of the Supreme Council, was not in the confidence of the leaders either, but Joe McGarrity of the Clan-na-Gael in America, two weeks before Easter, sent a message to McCartan for delivery to Clarke. The message reached McCartan by word of mouth (having been confided to at least two other persons on its way) and he learnt from it, for the first time, that the Rising was about to take place. He went to Dublin, on Holy Thursday, for more detailed information and was told by Clarke, among other things that 5,000 Germans were expected to land.[39] Diarmuid Lynch, who represented Munster on the Supreme Council, was told on Spy Wednesday.[40] Alasdair MacCába, the Connacht representative on the Supreme Council read in the newspapers of the arrest of Casement, journeyed from Killybegs to Dublin and was let into the secret on the night of Easter Saturday. He has placed it on record that there was a 'complete lack of communication' outside the Dublin area before the Rising.[41] Michael Colivet, an I.R.B. member, who was to occupy the key command position in the Limerick, Clare, West Tipperary area, went to Dublin on Spy Wednesday to try to get clear and definite instructions from Pearse, and was given a distinct impression that a German expeditionary force was expected.[42]

Communication in the Dublin area itself was little better and members of the I.R.B., who were destined to play an important part in the Rising, were not confided in until very late in the day. Among these were Eamon de Valera and Garry Holohan who were told on Spy Wednesday and Holy Thursday respectively, and Seán Heuston who got his first official knowledge of the date of the Rising on the morning of Easter Monday.[43] Similarly Liam Ó Briain, Seán T. O'Kelly, James Ryan, and members of the I.R.B. who were in close touch with the leaders in Dublin had so little knowledge of the situation that they approved of MacNeill's action, and accepted missions to carry the countermand to Volunteer officers throughout the country.[44] Frank Drohan, head of the I.R.B. in Clonmel, brought the countermand to Waterford and New Ross,[45] while Tomás MacCurtain, an I.R.B. man who was on terms of close friendship with Seán MacDiarmada, visited the various Volunteer centres on the Cork-Kerry border to put the countermand into operation.[46] Eamon O'Dwyer, county centre for the Tipperary I.R.B., and Dan Breen and Seán Treacy, enthusiastic rank and file members, had no inside information which could have led them to ignore orders coming from any source other than the Military Council.[47] This was true of I.R.B. men in the other counties where, according to Military Council theory, the Volunteers were to have been committed to the Rising through the instrumentality of members of the I.R.B.

Summing up the work of Seán MacDiarmada, his biographer states: 'he had formed the I.R.B. into a real instrument of active revolution, and to an almost absolute degree he had preserved secrecy, the most difficult thing for any revolutionary organisation. He had won where the original Fenians lost'.[48] It is difficult to agree with this conclusion. Absolute secrecy maintained by a tiny group of men, who were relying on the unquestioning obedience of the members of a nationwide revolutionary organization, was bound to defeat their object of bringing about a revolution, except in Dublin, where these men were, in fact, in a position to control events. The 'original Fenians' had at least produced sporadic risings in several parts of the country in 1867, despite the activities of spies and informers, and would probably have produced a much more formidable one in 1865 had their leaders been willing to take the field. It was useless to place I.R.B. men in high positions in the Volunteers without letting them know of the existence of the Military Council and its plans, or of the deep division of opinion existing at the top level in the Volunteer organisation. When the time for action arrived the I.R.B. men in the Volunteers outside Dublin, whether officers or rank and file, were as much at the mercy of events as the ordinary non-I.R.B. members; equally disheartened by the failure to land the German arms; and equally thrown off balance by the conflicting orders from Dublin.

Commenting on the fact that 'neither the leadership of the I.R.B. in 1916 nor that of the other organizations which participated in the Rising of "Easter Week" was cursed by either spies or traitors', Diarmuid Lynch says:

Herein we have splendid testimony to the extreme care in recruiting exercised by the men responsible for the I.R.B. over a generation (coupled with propitious circumstances), and in particular to the methods followed by the members of the Military Council who guarded their secrets so jealously that the insurrectionary forces were enabled to march unopposed into their several strategic positions on Easter Monday 1916.[49]

It is nonetheless true that, however carefully and jealously the

Military Council 'guarded their secrets', the British Admiralty had got information from its own intelligence in mid-April, of a German connection and an intended rising, but Dublin Castle discounted the information.[50] Moreover, the American end of the conspiracy had always been outside the control of the Military Council. Several people in Ireland were evidently aware of the message relating to the forthcoming rising sent by Joe McGarrity to Tom Clarke shortly before Easter,[51] and MacNeill had had a letter from an American correspondent early in March telling him that 'the project of an immediate rising was known to certain circles in America and was being rather loosely talked about'. It is worth noting also that, despite MacNeill's indignation with the militant group, when Pearse admitted that orders for an insurrection had been given, he threatened to do everything in his power to stop it, except the one thing which would have made it impossible. He made it clear that he would not inform the government of the Council's intentions,[52] and neither he nor the group of Volunteer officers and others who agreed with the MacNeill point of view in the final crisis ever considered informing the government. The quarrel was a family one, and the countermanding order gave no hint to the government that one set of Volunteers was more to be feared than another.

The views of most of the members of the Military Council on the significance of the countermanding order have been frequently repeated since, though there is little first-hand documentary evidence on the subject, apart from Pearse's final bulletin issued from the G.P.O., and the letter written by Thomas MacDonagh on Easter Sunday night on the eve of the Rising. In this letter, MacDonagh writes of MacNeill and Fitzgibbon as 'two honest and sincere patriots, though I think, wrong in their handling of the present situation and in their attitude to military action'.[53] Plunkett has been reported as speaking to Pearse inside the G.P.O. 'of how much bigger an event it would have been had the original plans gone forward

unchecked'.[54] Countess Markievicz quoted Connolly as saying
that MacNeill had 'cut the ground from under our feet', while
Piaras Béaslaí, who escorted Tom Clarke to the Keating branch
of the Gaelic League after the historic meeting in Liberty Hall
on Easter Sunday morning, claimed to have heard him say:
'Our plans were so perfect, and now everything is spoiled. I feel
as if I'd like to go away in a corner and cry'.[55] Mrs. Clarke,
widow of Tom Clarke, stated that on the same day she heard
him denounce 'MacNeill's treachery'.[56] Liam Forde has described
Seán MacDiarmada's 'frantic' reaction when he was shown the
countermanding order in the *Sunday Independent*, and his bitter
bewailing of the fact that they had been 'betrayed again'.[57]
Eamon Ceannt, who at 3 a.m. on Sunday morning is reported
to have told his wife: 'MacNeill has ruined us, he has stopped
the Rising',[58] returned from the conference in Liberty Hall, after
the decision had been taken to strike at noon on Monday, and
was then confident that 'the cancelling of the manoeuvres would
lead the British to believe that everything was all right'.[59]
Diarmuid Lynch goes so far as to say that when the meeting of
the Military Council adjourned at 1 p.m. on Easter Sunday 'an
all important element in the situation was that Dublin Castle
should remain in blissful ignorance of the arrangements for
Monday and remain convinced that MacNeill's cancellation of
the Sunday "parades" had removed all chances of immediate
trouble. Otherwise, the plan of the Military Council to occupy
the G.P.O., Four Courts, Jacob's Factory, South Dublin Union,
Boland's Mills, etc., might have been made difficult, if not
impossible'.[60]

It is clear from the inside story of the situation in Dublin
Castle during Saturday and Sunday that Lynch's estimate of the
importance to the leaders of the MacNeill countermand was
correct. By Saturday afternoon Under-Secretary Nathan and
Wimborne, the Lord Lieutenant, had become convinced that the
danger of an immediate rebellion was over for the time being.

They assumed that, if such a step had been in contemplation, it had been contingent on the arrival of arms from Germany. They also believed that Casement was the key-man in the conspiracy, and they were further lulled into a sense of security by the fact that no attempt had been made that morning to rescue him on his way from Kerry, through Dublin, to London. The notice from MacNeill in the *Sunday Independent* next day counter-manding all parades and manoeuvres confirmed them in their belief that all immediate danger of a rising was over. On Sunday evening, at a conference in the Viceregal Lodge, however, the Lord Lieutenant pressed strongly for the arrest of from sixty to a hundred of the well-known leaders of disaffection, and offered to sign the warrants himself, and take full responsibility. But luck was on the side of the revolutionary leaders. This time Under-Secretary Nathan, unlike Cooke, his predecessor in office in 1798, counselled caution and delay. There was no immediate danger, he insisted, and it would be unwise to take any action without the authority of the law officers, the Home Office and Chief Secretary Birrell. The strongest argument of all, however, came from the military and police authorities, who stated that they needed a gun which would have to be brought up from Athlone, if they were to attack Liberty Hall and that 'the time was short for adequate preparations to be made to ensure complete success'. The conference finally came to the decision 'that Easter Monday would be a bad day to make a raid on Liberty Hall with the city full of Volunteers and holiday makers' and 'that action must be postponed until the whole scheme of arrests and seizures of arsenals could be carried out as a combined operation'.[61] Fate, for once, had decreed that the planners of an Irish revolution should be out of gaol when the time for action had arrived, and that government officials, police, and military, should be sufficiently off guard to ensure their non-intervention until the insurgents had taken up their position on Easter Monday.

On Easter Sunday morning when the six members of the

Military Council met in Liberty Hall to discuss the crisis which had developed they knew, if there was any basis at all for the 'Castle Document' or even if there was not, that the arrest of the leaders must follow swiftly on the Casement arrest and the discovery of their association with the Germans.[62] Their caution in not attempting to rescue Casement and the disarming of government suspicion by the MacNeill countermand had given them a short respite in which to review the position. The seizure of 250 lb. of gelignite from a quarry in Tallaght and its transfer to Liberty Hall on the morning of Easter Sunday very nearly lost them that respite, for the police followed the raiders there and were keeping the 'precincts under close observation'.[63] Opinion among them was at first somewhat divided. Tom Clarke's view that they should follow the original plan for a Sunday rising was overruled,[64] and it was decided to start the Rising at noon on Easter Monday. If, as has been stated, MacDonagh and Ceannt at first opposed a rising in the circumstances then prevailing,[65] their decision to abide by the majority vote deserves to be recognised as one of the more important decisions in the history of the Easter Rising. MacDonagh was Commandant of the Dublin Brigade and he, Ceannt and de Valera, who had declared his intention of acting on MacDonagh's instructions, together commanded three of the four city battalions. Although Connolly, without doubt, would have brought the Citizen Army into action, and Ned Daly, brother-in-law of Tom Clarke, would almost certainly have obeyed Clarke rather than the Brigade Commandant, nevertheless the withdrawal of MacDonagh[66] and Ceannt could have reduced the impact of the Rising enormously.

Although no one could possibly deny that the I.R.B. revival which had taken place in the years before 1913 had been the the prime factor in setting in motion the events which led up to the Rising, the fact that the seven men, who had constituted themselves a Military Council, had taken the I.R.B. oath was

largely irrelevant. What was important was the fact that these
men had gravitated towards each other in the years since 1913;
that they shared a common ideal and a common purpose and had
agreed to work together to bring about a rising. They had come
to trust each other, and none of them flinched when the time for
decision came. Since they were to form the provisional government, it was presumably considered necessary that they should all
remain in Dublin, and thus their undivided attention was given
to the Rising in the city while the country commandants were
left to 'play it by ear'.

From the foundation of the Volunteers in November 1913,
it was inevitable that Dublin would be the centre of anti-British
action. The great bulk of the Volunteers who remained in the
anti-Redmond group when the split came in 1914 were resident
in Dublin. Eoin MacNeill, addressing the Dublin Brigade in
February 1915, said:

Much has been due to the fidelity and staunchness of the men
of Dublin. Much will be expected of them. It is not only in
matters of national principle that they will be looked to for a
lead. On them also in a large measure will depend the working
out of the Volunteer programme in its many practical details.[67]

Exactly a year later, in February 1916, he again pointed out in a
memorandum addressed to his colleagues on the executive that
the headquarters staff had done almost all its work in Dublin.
'Outside of Dublin', he wrote, 'our training of officers is only as
yet begun'.[68] Apart from this comparatively highly-organised
body of nearly 3,000 Volunteers, a large percentage of whom
might be expected to follow the lead of their commandants,
the Military Council could rely on three small groups which
were directly under its own control. These were the Fianna,
I.R.B. members[69] and the 'Kimmage Garrison', a group of over
fifty Irish exiles, who had returned and had been encamped at

the Plunkett house in Kimmage for some months before the Rising.[70] Lastly, there was Connolly's Citizen Army, a compact miniature force, well accustomed to answering summonses at short notice from their commander.[71] All these had, by amateur standards at least, received a good deal of training. They had drilled and participated in manoeuvres and were accustomed to parading together. Many had bought their own guns—opportunities for buying guns presented themselves more frequently in Dublin than in country towns and villages—while many of the Howth guns seem to have been kept in the Dublin area. For a considerable time before the Rising Volunteers and Citizen Army had been mobilised at unusual hours, sometimes as a test, sometimes because of a rumoured arrest of leaders, or of raids for arms, and they had had a full-scale mobilisation in Dublin as late as 17 March 1916.

One might have thought that the proliferation of different groups would have made for disunion and divided councils in Dublin, but instead these groups gave each other moral support and created almost a spirit of competition and emulation which must have played a big part in ensuring that a respectable number answered the call of the Military Council on Easter Monday. Cumann na mBan were also numerous and highly organised in Dublin, unlike other parts of the country where the movement had not as yet made any considerable progress. In Dublin, too, the suffragette movement, which had the support of all the members of the Military Council, was not without its importance indirectly in influencing the attitude of wives, mothers and sisters, who encouraged their men-folk to answer the call when the time for action came, and more directly in placing women in prominent roles in nursing, catering, secretarial and communication services, and even in the fighting line itself, while the Rising was in progress.[72]

Dublin, also, by comparison with the country, provided a great number of 'centres of disaffection', as the government would term them, which proved of immense importance in the final days and hours before the Rising. Each battalion had its recognised headquarters, and the Gaelic League halls, the Foresters and other halls, and numerous cafes and hotels could be resorted to freely by those who were active in the preparations or awaiting instructions, at a time when a meeting of a few people in any country town would have caused comment among the inhabitants within an hour, and placed the R.I.C. immediately on the alert. St. Enda's school was another centre which kept a group of young activists together. Larkfield, Kimmage had a resident garrison and an arsenal, while Liberty Hall, for years the citadel of the Citizen Army, was the meeting place of the Military Council during their final deliberations on Sunday and Monday, and was the point from which messengers were dispatched continuously throughout the last twenty-four hours before the Rising. It was from Liberty Hall that the leaders set out on Easter Monday to put their plan for the Dublin rising into effect.

It would probably be true to say, however, that the willingness of the leaders to die, and in particular their decision to commit the lives of others to the hazard, was the chief factor which ensured that a rising did take place in Dublin. Although the unwillingness of leaders to shed blood, or to take responsibility for firing the first shot, are not often listed among the causes given in popular histories for the failure of previous revolutionaries to go into action, Pearse and Connolly were quite conscious of it.[73]

There is no indication that the leaders who took the fatal decision on Easter Sunday morning gave any thought, as a group, to the problem of whether or not their decision to rise conformed to the usually accepted teaching of the Catholic Church on what constitutes a just war. There is no doubt, however, that on the eve of the Rising there must have been serious heart-searchings among some, at least, of the members of the Military Council as

16

to the morality of their action.[74] By proclaiming the Republic, and by setting up their provisional government, and by adopting the attitude that they were defending that government rather than attacking the British government, they were able to place the onus on the British forces of 'bidding the cannon speak and the grapeshot pour'. By taking up defensive positions and garrisoning unfortified buildings they sought to ensure that the British military would be forced to take the initiative and fire the first shots.[75] Although the same cannot be said of the plans allegedly drawn up for country commandants, the plan for Dublin ensured that the minimum of initiative in shedding blood would be taken by the Republican forces. Thomas MacDonagh, Commandant of the Dublin Brigade, made it very clear in his orders for various operations that, above all, they must 'avoid all unnecessary bloodshed'. One of the senior members of Fianna Éireann has stated that when his group was directed to endeavour to take the Magazine Fort in Phoenix Park 'without loss of life', he was disconcerted. Having taken part in sham battles for so long he had been, he writes, 'conjuring up pictures of Volunteers and Citizen Army charging the British with gory results'.[76] But not one of these men had seen a shot fired in battle, and had his picture of raw amateurs 'charging the British' materialised, the results of the Rising might have been very different. Inside their respective strongholds the officers had a control over their men that they could never have had if they had attacked military positions. If they wished to make sorties, these were planned and directed by officers under conditions in which the details could be discussed and men picked and given advance instructions. The plan also avoided the very grave danger of groups of soldiers, unused to fire, breaking and running if one man should panic, as was likely enough in the case of untried soldiers fighting in the open against a concealed defending force.

Whether the leaders in Dublin consciously adopted defensive positions in order to avoid firing the first shots, it would be impossible to say. Military tacticians usually explain their plan by saying that the number needed to hold a position against attack is one-third of those needed to take the same position. This is how officers in a regular army think when deploying their forces, but it is not necessarily correct to assume that the leaders thought along those lines. It is clear, however, that the defensive strategy adopted in Dublin had for a long time been that favoured by Connolly. On several occasions since the time of the Boer War he had advocated taking up positions in certain previously selected buildings and holding them to the last man.[77] The Sidney Street siege of 1911, which needed a large force of military and police and the expenditure of a great quantity of ammunition to dislodge two anarchists who were resisting arrest, may also have influenced the planners of the Rising.[78]

The leaders also believed that government forces would never destroy capitalist property and they believed that the Rising would end with close-range fighting between British and Republican forces, almost certainly with a bayonet charge.[79] Apart from the fact that the Dublin plan had been under consideration for a very long time, the situation there differed vastly from that in the country in other ways. For instance on Spy Wednesday, Connolly and MacDonagh are said to have toured the positions to be taken up in the various parts of the city, while Commandant de Valera and his officers are said to have had detailed knowledge in advance of every step of their plan. Again those who were to occupy the Municipal Buildings in Castle Street had a key to the building, while sufficient supplies had been brought into the G.P.O. to last for five or six weeks.[80] Preparations of this nature simply did not exist in other centres outside Dublin, and it should be remembered, also, that the Dublin police, unlike the the R.I.C. were unarmed. Perhaps the most important factor of all which distinguished the Dublin situation from that of the country was the fact that the Dublin plan was free from the complications regarding foreign aid,[81] or co-operation with

The Making of 1916

units from other counties which had never acted together before. However harrowing the prospects for the end of the adventure in Dublin might be for those who participated in the Rising, at least in its initial stages the taking up of pre-arranged positions in unfortified buildings was considerably less daunting than were the tasks prescribed for country units.

The members of the Military Council and the commandants of the Dublin Brigade had been planning for a rising for a very long time. They formed a closely-knit group who could meet and discuss immediate action even at the last moment when their plans seemed to have gone completely awry. If many of the subordinate officers and of the rank and file did not report for duty on Monday morning, they did not necessarily stay away because of the MacNeill countermand. We shall never know how many of them would have mobilised on Sunday, had they had full knowledge of what the manoeuvres meant. Piaras Béaslaí, who was vice-commandant of the First Battalion under Ned Daly, and thus close enough to the centre of things, has stated that 'many of the rank and file who had been talking confidently of a coming rising, never dreamed that the Easter Week man-oeuvres, so audaciously announced, constituted the promised "day"'.[82] At the same time one might assume that any man who joined the Volunteers should have been preparing himself for fighting at some stage, whether as a man resisting disarmament or conscription or some other provocation, but it is certain that there were men in the Volunteers as in all such organisations who never seriously believed that they would some day shed blood or risk their lives. Diarmuid Lynch claims, however, that as a result of organisation and training, and particularly of the presence among officers and rank and file of many I.R.B. men, the Volunteers 'as a whole gradually, and perhaps unconsciously, became imbued with an "offensive" rather than a "defensive" concept'. He also attributes a 'powerful influence' in this respect to the writings and speeches of Pearse.[83] Lynch was of the opinion that the Military Council relied on Pearse to move the 'Volunteers *en masse*' steadily towards the idea of insurrection and that they gave their sanction to such statements as: 'If ever the Irish Volunteers went into action' being followed by: 'It would be wrong for me to say they might soon be called into action'. By such talk, Lynch believed, he 'succeeded in not alone conveying the desired idea to those who were ready to be impressed by it, but at the same time in minimising the full and immediate purport of his remarks from others'.[84] It would have been utopian to expect a full muster of Volunteers on the day of the Rising in such circumstances, other than by decoying a great part of the force into action without their knowledge. As it happened, the countermand gave an opportunity to most Volunteers to make a decision, whether or not they wished to fight, and it was probably greatly to the advantage of all concerned on Easter Monday morning that numbers of men who had volunteered for a certain type of soldiering, which they had never clearly defined to themselves, were not press-ganged into battle. There is also the fact that the Military Council persuaded MacNeill to issue an alert to the Volunteers on 19 April, after the publication of the 'Castle Document', an alert which must have given many Volunteers an opportunity of examining their attitude towards real soldiering, some days before the countermand was issued.

If words meant anything, however, Pearse, Connolly, and MacDonagh had given ample long-term warning to those who wished to receive it that they were not playing at soldiers, but that a day was coming when they would be expected to go into action.[85] There is, too, a great deal of evidence that despite the insistence on absolute secrecy advocated by MacDiarmada and Clarke, the commanding officers, in many cases, felt it their duty to give their men due warning before embarking on such an enterprise.

Brian O'Higgins has recorded that, a month before the Rising,

Pearse addressed the special reserve company to which he and others not equal to the rigours of ordinary Volunteer duty belonged, and told them to mobilise on Easter Sunday. If there was nothing more important than a route march they were to return home 'but if there was work to be done, we were to have our share of that work'.[86] On Spy Wednesday, MacDonagh made it clear to B Company, Second Battalion, that they would be going out on Sunday and that some of them might not come back. Peadar Kearney, who was present, is recorded as saying that if MacDonagh had been less blunt "many more might have turned out for the "manoeuvres"".[87] Liam Ó Briain, who took part in the discussions which preceded the sending out of the countermanding order, and who himself took that order to some country areas, has given the following testimony to the state of preparedness of Volunteers for the coming fight:

> For months before Easter the Volunteers were told (and agreed) that any time they went out they might never come back; that they might be attacked, or be ordered to attack. They accepted this absolutely, with utter faith in their chiefs and with a perfect sense of soldierly discipline . . . A fortnight before Easter our officers made their wills . . . At all company parades that last week the men were told to be ready for anything on Sunday. Confessionals were crowded on Saturday night . . .[88]

References to the large numbers of people, who went to confession before going out to risk their lives, occur again and again in memoirs of the period.[89]

It would be foolish to deny that the issue of the MacNeill countermand caused considerable confusion among the Volunteers in Dublin, although it did serve to throw the Dublin Castle authorities off guard, and was in a large measure responsible for the fact that no steps were taken to arrest the leaders on Sunday.

One is tempted, however, to contrast the strength of numbers, the comradeship, the opportunities for thrashing out the problems, and for taking instant decisions, enjoyed by the leaders in Dublin, with the loneliness, the lack of information, the indecision, the enforced waiting for orders from a distant headquarters, which were the lot of country commanders during those trying days. All through the day on Easter Sunday, the Military Council was in close touch with Ned Daly and Eamon de Valera, the two Dublin city commandants who were not themselves members of the Council. When Seán MacDiarmada told Piaras Béaslaí, second in command to Ned Daly, at the conclusion of the conference at Liberty Hall on Easter Sunday morning, that they had decided 'to call off the thing for the present', he told him at the same time to hold himself 'in readiness for further orders, and to keep our battalion staff together at headquarters'.[90] Thomas MacDonagh, Brigade Commandant, issued instructions to Eamon de Valera who commanded the Third Battalion, cancelling the Sunday manoeuvres, but adding that all Volunteers were to remain in Dublin until further orders. De Valera had also received a direct command from Eoin MacNeill, to the effect that no Volunteer manoeuvres should take place that day, and instructing him to see that this order was carried out by his own battalion, and was conveyed to the other commands.[91] A recent biography of President de Valera states that MacDonagh's order put de Valera completely at his ease because MacNeill's order was being carried out in full in relation to that very day. This underlines the fact, often forgotten, that the countermand referred to Easter Sunday only. MacDonagh's order to de Valera was countersigned by him and sent to all officers in the Third Battalion, but when word reached him about 5 p.m. that the Rising would take place at noon the following day, he was able to arrange that the officers of the Third Battalion should meet at a concert, already arranged to take place, at 41 Parnell Square that night. Most of the officers and many of the rank and

231

file were present and de Valera sought to inspire them with enthusiasm for the coming fight.[92] On the same night Piaras Béaslaí kept the men of the Second Battalion together at the Keating Branch of the Gaelic League until Ned Daly arrived at 10 p.m. and told him that they would be 'going out' at mid-day on Easter Monday.[93] A section of the Second Battalion, with Tom Hunter, Battalion Vice-Commandant under MacDonagh, and Lieutenant Leo Henderson, spent Sunday night on guard in Father Matthew Park in Fairview, while Seán Heuston, Paddy Stephenson and several others spent the night in the Colmcille Hall.[94]

Connolly's Citizen Army owed no allegiance to the Chief of Staff of the Volunteers. Its members made no claim to have been thrown off balance by the conflicting orders circulating in the city during the Easter week-end, and the number of absentees from its ranks was minimal on Easter Monday. Having been led by Connolly and Mallin on a route march from Liberty Hall through the principal streets of the south side of the city between 3 and 6 p.m. on Easter Sunday, Connolly addressed them and told them they would be 'confined to barracks' for the night, and any man wishing to leave would have to apply for special permission. The men are said to have cheered, when he told them that they were now under arms, and that they would not lay down their arms until they had struck a blow for Ireland.[95]

With the Volunteers and Citizen Army ordered to stand to in Dublin, and with the Military Council there to keep in close touch with battalion commandants and other officers, the task of rapidly circulating the order for a Monday mobilisation was got under way with commendable efficiency. The new summons to action was sent out to the various officers, and the task of mobilising the Volunteer units went on throughout the early hours of Monday morning. Even the invalid unit to which Brian O'Higgins belonged, got its summons on time.[96] Not all messengers, however, fulfilled their missions, and some Volunteers who had not received the order to remain in the city until further notice, were not there to receive the message when it did arrive.

Men from as far away as Maynooth and Fingall got into Dublin in time. Even those who had gone to Fairyhouse, or who had not been at home on Monday morning when the summons came, or even those who had got no summons at all were well aware by the evening of Monday that the Rising was on if they wished to take part in it.[97] Several of those who had believed that MacNeill was correct in his attitude, and some who had taken part in countermanding the Rising—people like The O'Rahilly, James Ryan, Liam Ó Briain and Michael Hayes— joined up when they found that the die was cast. Just as many British soldiers who had been away from their barracks when the fighting began were able to rejoin their regiments before nightfall, and just as the guard in Trinity College, which numbered only eight on Easter Monday morning, had increased to one hundred and fifty by Wednesday,[98] so those Volunteers, who unwittingly missed the start of the Rising, were able to join up during the early days of the week. About thirty of the Hibernian Rifles went to the G.P.O. at midnight on Monday, and played their part in the Rising until the surrender.[99]

It would be true to say that Eoin MacNeill's countermand stopped no Volunteer, who was anxious for war, from participating in the Rising.[100] It might be added that whoever was responsible for the chapter of accidents, which led to the sinking of the arms ship, it was not MacNeill. It was perhaps natural enough, however, that those who were convinced that the Volunteers could be controlled by the Military Council through the I.R.B., and who believed that MacNeill could ultimately be placed in a position of approving of the Rising, and who had planned a country rising which hinged on the successful landing of German arms, should seek someone to carry the major portion of the blame when these plans went awry. Had MacNeill and Bulmer Hobson joined in the Rising, when once it had begun, as The O'Rahilly did, they would probably have escaped all censure. Versions of Irish history too often tend to seek for scapegoats and simple explanations to explain circumstances which are often very complicated, or too painful to contemplate objectively. Priests and bishops, for instance, had come in for a good deal of the blame for the collapse of the risings in 1848 and 1867, yet, although priests here and there had inveighed against those taking part in the Easter Rising,[101] and priests and bishops had played a part in the agreements to surrender arms made by the Volunteers in Limerick and Cork,[102] no one has since suggested that they were responsible for the fact that the Rising was not as successful as it might have been. It is difficult to follow Dorothy Macardle's reasoning when she writes of the failure of the plans in the south-west as follows:

> The news of the captures on the Kerry coast, first, had warned them to be ready for the signal to rise; then MacNeill's countermand had forced them to resign themselves to the abandonment of all their hopes and plans.[103]

Many others have published similar comments.

And yet it is difficult to understand why MacNeill continued in his position as Commander-in-Chief of a military organisation which he very well knew included a number of determined men of high rank and of considerable influence, who differed fundamentally from him on the question of physical force. Perhaps being a historian he did not wish to see himself in the rôle of O'Connell driving out the Young Irelanders with a series of 'peace resolutions'. Again the word 'split' had sad connotations in Ireland since the days of Parnell, and the Volunteers had already had a split with Redmond in September 1914, and no one wanted to force another. The Military Council certainly knew that MacNeill and they were travelling different routes, but the Council members seem to have confidently believed that they would eventually swing MacNeill on to their path by one means or another.

It would be pompous and foolish to criticise the plans for the Rising or indeed for any rebellion or revolution. The leaders of a submerged nation or people are never in a position to control events or to make plans which cannot go awry. Indeed when one thinks of the miscalculations and the colossal blunders made by the high command in the armies of the first class powers in two world wars, it is abundantly evident that planning, even when done by experts commanding all the resources of great states, can have disastrous results. The leaders concentrated their efforts on making a success of the Dublin Rising; the country plans were very much secondary; and with the loss of the arms ship, the chances of a sizeable rising in the south-west were minimal. In the event, it was of primary importance that the forces of rebellion were concentrated in Dublin instead of being dissipated in isolated incidents such as those staged in the past in places like Ballingarry, Killenaule, Tallaght, Stepaside, or Kilmallock. The Dublin rising with its flags, its proclamation of the republic, its setting up of a provisional government, its open declaration of war and its adherence to the rules of war was a dignified protest which could never be written off as a popish massacre or as the activities of village assassins. The plan for the city rising could not have brought military success unless, perhaps, a German landing on a massive scale had taken place. Yet it was a success in a 'land where to fail is more than to triumph, and victory less than defeat'. The insurgents held the centre of Dublin for nearly a week and proclaimed to the world that there were people in Ireland who were not reconciled to letting the capital remain forever a provincial city in the United Kingdom. The originators of the plan for the Rising had been the people to pay the price. No one could charge them with self-seeking or worldly ambition. They died bravely, asking for leniency for those they had led into the rising.

Looking at the plans from a practical point of view one might be tempted to say that the leaders had erred in not confining the Rising to Dublin, as had evidently been their original intention. In retrospect, however, one is forced to the conclusion that the widespread ramifications of the plans for the country rising, impracticable as they turned out to be, did emotionally involve the Volunteers of the whole country in the events which took place in Dublin, especially as it was clear right up to the eve of the surrender that the leaders continued to hope for backing from the country.[104] Had the leaders been simply sentenced to long terms of imprisonment, the impact on those who had been expected to participate in a country rising would have been considerably less, especially as their hopeless gesture would certainly have been derided by conservatives and moderates and by the vast following of the Irish Parliamentary Party. As it was, the spectacle of the ruins of some of the finest buildings in the centre of Dublin, which might have been expected to call for general execration of the revolutionaries, served rather as a backcloth for the drama of the long drawn out series of executions.

When one considers the quite extraordinary effect on Irish public opinion produced by the execution of the 'Manchester Martyrs' in 1867—the last political executions (apart from the Invincibles) before 1916—there is no reason to be surprised at the effect produced by the executions in 1916.[105] There is something prophetic in Connolly's account of the Manchester incident, written in November 1915:

'We honour them because of their heroic souls. Let us remember that by every test by which parties in Ireland today measure political wisdom, or personal prudence, the act of these men ought to be condemned. They were in a hostile city, surrounded by a hostile population; they were playing into the hands of the government by bringing all the Fenians out in broad daylight to be spotted and remembered; they were discouraging the Irish people by giving them another failure to record; they had no hopes of foreign help even if their brothers in Ireland took the field spurred by their action; at the most their action would only be an Irish riot in an English city; and finally, they were imperilling the whole organization for the sake of two men. These were the sound sensible arguments of the prudent, practical politicians and theoretical revolutionists. But "how beggarly appear words before a defiant deed!"'[106]

MAUREEN WALL.

1. Mellows wrote an account of the Rising in an American newspaper in 1916, which is reproduced in part in *The Wolfe Tone Annual* (1946), p. 98. Mellows stated that it was then an inopportune time to disclose the nature of these plans.

2. When some time before the Rising William O'Brien questioned Connolly on MacNeill's attitude to a rising Connolly told him that MacNeill was not acting with them 'but that it would be believed that he was'. When O'Brien expressed alarm at this statement Connolly replied that 'it had been carefully considered and they [the Military Council] believed it would work out all right'. On Good Friday Connolly told O'Brien that members of the Military Council had told MacNeill 'that he was powerless to prevent the insurrection taking place, as all the officers would obey the orders issued by Pearse . . .' Ryan, ed. *Labour and Easter Week 1916*, pp. 15, 16–17. For several references to assertions by members of the Military Council, on Good Friday and Easter Saturday, that MacNeill was powerless to thwart their plans, see F. X. Martin, 'Eoin MacNeill on the 1916 Rising' in *Irish Historical Studies* xii, pp. 248, 249, 259, 263, 266, 267. Even on Easter Sunday, Pearse in a note to MacNeill stated: 'I confirmed your countermand as the leading men would not have obeyed it without my confirmation'. See Lynch, *The I.R.B. and the 1916 Insurrection*, p. 53. For alleged I.R.B. control over the Volunteers see also Le Roux, *Life of P. H. Pearse*, pp. 314, 326–7, 337, 343–4, and Proinsias Ó Conluain, *Seán T.*, p. 163. Writers on the Rising have since continued to repeat that the Military Council controlled the Volunteers through the I.R.B. For instance Dorothy Macardle, *The Irish Republic*, pp. 126–7 states: 'Other members of the I.R.B. were officers in units throughout the country and it was from Pearse or MacDermott that these would take their orders in a crisis, not from MacNeill'.

3. F. X. Martin, 'Eoin MacNeill on the 1916 Rising' in *Irish Historical Studies* xii, pp. 226–71.

The Making of 1916

4. Lynch, *The I.R.B. and the 1916 Rising*, p. 48.

5. F. X. Martin, 'Eoin MacNeill on the 1916 Rising' in *Irish Historical Studies* xii, pp. 248, 258; Le Roux, *Life of P. H. Pearse*, pp. 349–50.

6. Quoted in *Report of Royal Commission on Rebellion in Ireland*, p. 12.

7. See pp. 168, 172.

8. Clonmel may be taken as a fairly typical example of the extent of advance preparation in a provincial town. The accounts of survivors show that one full scale mobilization of the Volunteer unit there had taken place 'in the spring' which had revealed that 'there were scarcely fifty men who could be counted on to go out and fight'. The I.R.B. was in control of the unit and 'only these knew the exact situation' it is stated, though subsequent events show how limited their knowledge of the situation must have been. Not until 'early in Holy Week' did Frank Drohan, head of the local I.R.B. circle, and commanding officer in the Clonmel Volunteers, get the order to 'deliver the goods'. Each Volunteer already was in possession of some sort of gun, but only now did work begin on 'filling cartridges, preparing explosives and field kits'. The strategy for the Rising which was decided on Easter Saturday, was as follows: 'The British had large forces in Clonmel, Cahir and Fethard; to attack these barracks would have been lunacy, and so it was decided to march to Lisronagh, join up with the Fethard Volunteers and attack the R.I.C. barracks at Lisronagh; then, to take the Clerihan barracks and proceed to Cashel. It was hoped to join forces with Pierce McCann there, and capture the Cashel barracks. This would have disrupted British authority in the areas, and presumably would have forced the British to send small army units from the various garrisons. These could be ambushed where opportunity arose'. The startling comparison between what these men were expected to do and what the Dublin men were to do is underlined by the fact that McCann obviously did not know the plans of the Clonmel men, and that 'John Mackey was appointed to convey this strategy to Paddy Heneghan in Fethard, in the early hours of [Easter] Sunday morning'. See *Cluain Meala 1916*, pp. 10–11.

9. See pp. 211–2.

10. This account is transcribed from Florence O'Donoghue's foreword to Karl Spindler, *The Mystery of the Casement Ship* (1965), p. 17. See also Lynch, *The I.R.B. and the 1916 Insurrection*, p. 49, 152.

11. Denis McCullough says their destination was Galway and Patrick McCartan has stated that it was Belcoo. See P. Mac an Bheatha, 'Uachtaran an I.R.B.' in *Inniu, Uimhir 1916*, p. 28 and F. X. Martin,

Studies in the History of the Rising

'Extracts from the papers of the late Dr. Patrick McCartan' in *Clogher Record* 1964, p. 198.

12. Desmond Ryan, *The Rising*, p. 82.

13. See Florence O'Donoghue's foreword to Karl Spindler, *The Mystery of the Casement Ship*, pp. 19-22.

14. J. M. MacCarthy, ed. *Limerick's Fighting Story*, p. 37. For the Limerick account in general see *Ibid.*, pp. 31-40; Ryan, *The Rising*, pp. 82-3; 85-9; 233-6; 241-3; Mannix Joyce, 'The Story of Limerick and Kerry in 1916' in *The Capuchin Annual 1966*, pp. 339-44, 351-8.

15. Ryan, *The Rising*, pp. 78-83, 108-114, 237-241. Although Ryan refers to the 'split in the Dublin leadership' as one of the 'tragic events which crowded upon the Kerry Volunteers' there seems little justification for doing so, since Stack had been arrested on Good Friday, before any inkling of the split had reached the south-west. Ryan, on the same page, would seem to give a more accurate summing up of the position in Kerry when he states: 'The events that paralysed Kerry were: a tragedy at Ballykissane Pier, the sudden arrival of Casement, the arrest of Austin Stack'. See *The Rising*, p. 110. If a document alleged to have been found attached to a letter from James Connolly was taken seriously by Stack as a blue-print for a rising, one wonders how he could have brought himself to face the responsibility of leading a rising had he been at liberty on Easter Monday. An extract from this document published in *Sinn Féin Rebellion Handbook*, p. 106 runs as follows: 'The humanising of war—you might as well talk of humanising hell? When a silly ass at the Hague got up and talked about the amenities of civilized warfare, and putting your prisoners' feet in hot water, and giving them gruel, my reply, I regret to say, was considered totally unfit for publication. As if war could be civilized! If I am in command when war breaks out, I shall issue as my orders:—The essence of war is violence; moderation in war is imbecility; hit first, hit hard, and hit everywhere ... If you rub it in both at home and abroad that you are ready for instant war with every unit of your strength in the first line, and intend to be first in, hit your enemy in the belly, and kick him when he is down, and boil your prisoners in oil (if you take any), and torture his women and children; then people will keep clear of you'. Anything less like the reality of war as practised in Dublin in 1916 by the Volunteers and Citizen Army can scarcely be imagined. For events in Kerry see also Mannix Joyce, 'The Story of Limerick and Kerry in 1916' in *The Capuchin Annual 1966*, pp. 336-9, 344-51, Florence O'Donoghue's foreword to Karl Spindler, *The Mystery of the Casement Ship* (1965); and William O'Brien's foreword to *Labour and Easter Week 1916*, ed. Desmond Ryan, pp. 19-20.

16. Ryan, *The Rising*, pp. 79, 81–2, 230–233; Liam Ruiseal, 'The Position in Cork' in *The Capuchin Annual 1966*, pp. 275–80.

17. See Desmond Ryan, *Seán Treacy and the Third Tipperary Brigade*, pp. 17–22; J. M. MacCarthy, *Limerick's Fighting Story*, p. 33; *Cluain Meala 1916*, pp. 10–12; Colm Ó Labhra, *Trodairi na Treas Briogáide*, pp. 12–13.

18. Ryan, *The Rising*, pp. 267–8. Ryan's view that in the north the MacNeill countermand was 'even more effective than elsewhere' can hardly be sustained, in view of the statements of those who were present in Tyrone at the time. Cathal O'Shannon, who was there, states that he did not know of the countermand until the night of Easter Sunday, by which time he had returned to Belfast from Tyrone. See *Evening Press*, 16 August 1968. Denis McCullough in 'The Events in Belfast' in *The Capuchin Annual 1966*, pp. 381–4 and in *Inniu, Uimhir 1916*, p. 28 makes no reference to the countermand as a cause for the lack of action by the Volunteers of Ulster. See also F. X. Martin, 'Extracts from the Papers of the late Dr. Patrick McCartan' in *Clogher Record* 1964, pp. 196–203 and Proinseas Ó Conluain, 'Fir an Tuaiscirt' in *Inniu, Uimhir 1916*, p. 25.

19. Ryan, *The Rising*, 244–8, 265–7; Mattie Neilan, 'The Rising in Galway' in *The Capuchin Annual 1966*, pp. 324–6; 'An tEirí Amach san Iarthar faoi Ceannas Uí Mhaoilíosa' in *Inniu, Uimhir 1916*, p. 20; Ailbhe Ó Monachain, 'Seachtain na Cásga i nGaillimh' in *Ar Aghaidh*, Eanair 1967, p. 7.

20. Ryan, *The Rising*, 248–50; Séamus Ó'Dubhghaill, 'Activities in Enniscorthy' in *The Capuchin Annual 1966*, pp. 317–23.

21. Ryan, *The Rising*, p. 250; Seán MacEntee, *Episode at Easter*. pp. 63–5, 107–118.

22. See Lynch, *The I.R.B. and the 1916 Insurrection*, pp. viii, 24, 32, 137; F. X. Martin, 'Extracts from the Papers of the late Dr. Patrick McCartan' in *Clogher Record 1964*, p. 191; Pádraig Ó Snodaigh, *Comhghuaillithe na Réabhlóide 1913–1916*, pp. 94–5; [Seán Moran], ed. *Ashbourne Memorial Book* (1959); Joseph Lawless, 'Fight at Ashbourne' in *The Capuchin Annual 1966*, pp. 307–316.

23. Ryan, *The Rising*, pp. 78, 237; Florence O'Donoghue's foreword to Karl Spindler, *The Mystery of the Casement Ship*, p. 21; C. Desmond Greaves, *The Life and Times of James Connolly*, p. 325.

24. Seán MacEntee, *Episode at Easter*, pp. 63–5.

Studies in the History of the Rising

25. Denis McCullough, 'The Events in Belfast' in *The Capuchin Annual 1966*, p. 383. Cusack was on his way to Ballinagh when McCullough, whose men had already been ordered back to Belfast from Tyrone, thought it his duty to intercept Cusack on the Belfast train at Portadown and order him to return home.

26. F. X. Martin, 'Extracts from the papers of the late Dr. Patrick McCartan' in *Clogher Record 1964*, p. 198; Very Rev. Charles J. Travers, *Seán MacDiarmada*, pp. 19–20.

27. Ryan, *The Rising*, p. 87; J. M. MacCarthy, *Limerick's Fighting Story*, p. 33; Seán MacEntee, *Episode at Easter*, p. 69. The over-riding consideration with the Military Council was that nothing must jeopardise the Dublin rising. This was the main reason why Pearse confirmed the MacNeill countermand on Easter Sunday. Diarmuid Lynch states that the decision to confirm the countermand was taken in order to further lull the suspicions of government, and to 'obviate the possibility that units outside the metropolitan area might start operations before the Dublin battalions could occupy their allotted positions on Easter Monday'. See *The I.R.B. and the 1916 Insurrection*, p. 53. It was certainly to the advantage of the Dublin men that the Rising should not go off in the country at half-cock; but the confirmation of the MacNeill countermand by Pearse added to the confusion of country commandants.

28. A code telegram 'The books have arrived' meaning 'The Rising is on' was sent to Limerick on Easter Saturday. See Mannix Joyce, 'The Story of Limerick and Kerry in 1916' in *The Capuchin Annual 1966*, p. 352. Evidently a somewhat similar code, asking for the return of a particular book was to be used in the autumn of 1915 as a signal, if the Rising were about to start. See Pádraig Ó Snodaigh, *Comhghuaillithe na Réabhlóide*, p. 113, quoting from a letter from Desmond Ryan. Joyce cites another code telegram announcing the Rising, sent by Seán MacDiarmada to Eamon Dore, then a medical student, saying 'Grind commences on 24th'. The whole question of code messages was evidently not considered of great importance by the leaders. According to Tomás Ó Néill and Pádraig Ó Fiannachta, *De Valera*, pp. 41, 48, the password 'Howth' was fixed on as the signal for a rising already in March 1915. De Valera chose 'Bruree' as his reply also in March 1915, and these were, in fact, the passwords which were used in Holy Week 1916. At the Volunteer Convention in October 1915, Eamonn Ceannt, Director of Communications, reported that 'numerous lines of communication between Dublin and the provinces had been established'. See F. X. Martin, *The Irish Volunteers 1913–1915*, p. 200. At the time of the Rising communications seem to have depended to a very great extent on men and women who travelled long distances by train or bicycle.

17

The Making of 1916

29. *Irish Volunteer*, 8, 22 April 1916.

30. Breandán MacGiolla Choille, *Intelligence Notes 1913–16*, p. 278.

31. Mannix Joyce, 'The Story of Limerick and Kerry in 1916' in *The Capuchin Annual 1966*, p. 355.

32. Desmond Ryan, *Sean Treacy and the Third Tipperary Brigade*, pp. 18–19.

33. Orders had been issued by headquarters for dynamiting bridges, for seizure of railways and for cutting communications generally. See Ryan, *The Rising*, p. 90; F. X. Martin, 'Eoin MacNeill on the 1916 Rising' in *Irish Historical Studies* xii, p. 259; Piaras Béaslaí, *Michael Collins* i, p. 90.

Local units were also aware that this was to be part of their duty in the event of a rising. For example see J. M. MacCarthy, *Limerick's Fighting Story*, pp. 32–3; Desmond Ryan, *The Rising*, p. 243, and *Seán Treacy and the Third Tipperary Brigade*, 17, 20–21.

For seizure of explosives by the Volunteers and Citizen Army see Breandán MacGiolla Choille, *Intelligence Notes 1913–16*, pp. 159–62 and Leon Ó Broin, *Dublin Castle and the 1916 Rising*, p. 85. Damage was done during Easter Week to railways in the Dublin area—at Blanchardstown, Fairview and Donabate, but attempts on railway bridges at other points in and near the city failed. A railway bridge on the Barrow was damaged, and telegraph wires were cut and the railway torn up between Athenry and Galway (see *Sinn Finn Rebellion Handbook*, pp. 36, 216–7), but on the whole, this type of sabotage does not seem to have impeded the crown forces to any great extent. As late as Wednesday of Easter Week Connolly sent a message to the Wexford Volunteers to hold the railway line from Rosslare, to prevent reinforcements from reaching Dublin. See Séamus Ó Dubhghaill, 'Activities in Enniscorthy' in *The Capuchin Annual 1966*, p. 320.

34. See note 2.

35. For general instructions see pp. 6–7. Discussing these instructions, Le Roux, *Life of P. H. Pearse*, p. 343 speaks of 'Pearse's order of January, 1916, for a mobilization for "three days' manoeuvres," the full meaning of which is said to have been clear to most'.

36. See note 20, p. 191 Rev. Charles J. Travers, *Seán MacDiarmada*, pp. 10–11 writing of the meeting between Clarke and MacDiarmada in 1908 and the appointment of MacDiarmada as wholetime I.R.B. organiser

says: 'The recruiting policy of the organisation was such that mere members were not aimed at: what was sought was to bring to it the key men with influence in cultural, athletic and social circles; the great object being to get one such man in every small town and village'. For the swearing of officers into the I.R.B. immediately before the Rising see Pádraig Ó Snodaigh, *Comhghuaillthe na Réabhlóide*, pp. 148, 161; Proinsias Ó Conluain, *Seán T.*, p. 156. Samuel Windrim, who was selected to drive a car from Limerick to Killarney and thence to Tralee on Good Friday 1916, to take part in the expedition which was to set up a transmitter there, was sworn into the I.R.B. before being told his mission. See Mannix Joyce, 'The Story of Limerick and Kerry in 1916' in *The Capuchin Annual 1966*, p. 348. Diarmuid Lynch, *The I.R.B. and the 1916 Insurrection*, pp. 24, 35, gives 2,000 as the number of I.R.B. members in or about the time of the Rising, and this figure includes Great Britain. Patrick McCartan has stated that the 500 men who turned out in Tyrone at Easter were all I.R.B. men. See F. X. Martin, 'Extracts from the Papers of the late Dr. Patrick McCartan' in *Clogher Record 1964*, p. 200. It would seem that Lynch's computation underestimates the figures or else that Lynch was thinking of a more select type of I.R.B. member than was McCartan.

37. Seán Ó Lúing, 'Talking to Bulmer Hobson' in *Irish Times*, 6 May 1961.

38. Denis McCullough, 'The Events in Belfast' in *The Capuchin Annual 1966*, p. 382.

39. F. X. Martin, 'Extracts from the Papers of the late Dr. Patrick McCartan' in *Clogher Record 1964*, pp. 196–8.

40. Lynch, *The I.R.B. and the 1916 Insurrection*, p. 132.

41. Lynch, *The I.R.B. and the 1916 Insurrection*, p. 134. See also *The Irish Times*, 16 September 1968.

42. Ryan, *The Rising*, pp. 85–6.

43. Tomás Ó Néill agus Pádraig Ó Fiannachta, *De Valera*, p. 48; John M. Heuston, O.P., *Headquarters Battalion Easter Week 1916*, p. 51.

44. Liam Ó Briain, 'An tEirí Amach mar do chonnacsa é' and James Ryan, 'In the G.P.O.: The Medical Unit' in F. X. Martin, *The Easter Rising 1916 and University College, Dublin*, pp. 61, 83.

45. *Cluain Meala 1916*, p. 11.

The Making of 1916

46. Liam Ruiséal, 'The Position in Cork' in *The Capuchin Annual 1966*, p. 376.

47. Dan Breen, *My Fight for Irish Freedom*, p. 24; Desmond Ryan, *Seán Treacy and the Third Tipperary Brigade*, p. 17.

48. Very Rev. Charles J. Travers, *Seán MacDiarmada*, pp. 33–4.

49. Lynch, *The I.R.B. and the 1916 Insurrection*, p. 54.

50. Leon Ó Broin, *Dublin Castle and the 1916 Rising*, p. 80.

51. See p. 216.

52. F. X. Martin, 'Eoin MacNeill on the 1916 Rising' in *Irish Historical Studies* xii, pp. 247, 248, 256.

53. Facsimile in *Capuchin Annual 1942*, p. 368.

54. Desmond Fitzgerald, 'Inside the G.P.O.' in *Irish Times Supplement*, 7 April 1966, p. 1.

55. *Michael Collins*, i, p. 90.

56. For a discussion of statements alleged by the Countess and Mrs. Clarke to have been made by both Connolly and Clarke see F. X. Martin, ed. 'Eoin MacNeill on the 1916 Rising' in *Irish Historical Studies* xii, pp. 270–1.

57. Mannix Joyce, 'The Story of Limerick and Kerry in 1916' in *The Capuchin Annual 1966*, p. 353.

58. Ceannt, on Holy Saturday night, is alleged to have told Seán T. O'Kelly, who gave him the news of the sending of the countermanding order to the *Sunday Independent*, that certain people should be shot, and that perhaps they would be shot. *Seán T.* ed. Proinsias Ó Conluain, p. 165–6.

59. Desmond Ryan, *The Rising*, p. 96.

60. Lynch, *The I.R.B. and the 1916 Insurrection*, pp. 76–7.

61. Leon Ó Broin, *Dublin Castle and the 1916 Rising*, pp. 84–90. Clearly Nathan did not want to be later accused of provoking a rising. Heads had rolled after the police action taken at the time of the Howth gun-running, and no matter what action a government official took it was very likely to be condemned later by a higher authority. Arthur Hamilton Norway, secretary to the Post Office, who was called to the Castle from the G.P.O. shortly before the Rising began, subsequently speculated on what might have happened had he been present when the Volunteers took over the G.P.O. and tried to restrain them: 'The certain result would have been that I should have been shot at once, and the probable result would have been that the government in London would have declared the whole trouble to have arisen from my wicked folly in firing on a body of peaceful, if armed, citizens.' Birrell made the same point to Asquith when he said: 'The thing that has happened swallowed up the things that might have happened had I otherwise acted'. *Ibid.*, pp. 95, 118.

62. Joseph Plunkett was not present. See Dorothy Macardle, *The Irish Republic*, p. 165.

63. Leon Ó Broin, *Dublin Castle and the 1916 Rising*, p. 85.

64. Clarke probably still believed that the I.R.B. infiltration of the Volunteer command would commit the country Volunteers to a rising. The other members of the Council seem to have realised the truth—that country commanders, whether I.R.B. or not had been kept so much in the dark about the realities of the situation in Dublin—that some of them, at least, would fail to grasp the fact that as I.R.B. men they should ignore orders coming from non-I.R.B. members of the Volunteer Executive.

65. Dorothy Macardle, *The Irish Republic*, p. 165. Desmond Ryan, *The Rising*, p. 97–8, refers only to the fact that Clarke was overruled and to the fact that the 'decision to strike was unanimous'.

66. A report was received at the Castle on 16 March 1916 that MacDonagh had said it would be 'sheer madness' to attempt a rising if the help promised by Monteith was not forthcoming. (See *The Royal Commission on the Rebellion in Ireland*, p. 7). The statement composed by MacDonagh on Easter Sunday night seems to me to show clearly that when, at the last moment, in the first week in April 1916, he was asked to join the Military Council, he made a deliberate choice, and never wavered from his decision. The facsimile of this statement reveals that he first wrote the words 'my obligation to act with my own Council' and then changed the word 'obligation' to 'intention'. It was not his I.R.B. oath, I suggest, but his own

The Making of 1916

clear choice, based on what he thought best for Ireland, which moved MacDonagh to act with the Military Council and not with the MacNeill group, and to vote with the majority of that council on Easter Sunday. See facsimile in *The Capuchin Annual 1942*, p. 368.

67. F. X. Martin, *The Irish Volunteers 1913–1915*, p. 189.

68. F. X. Martin ed. 'Eoin MacNeill on the 1916 Rising' in *Irish Historical Studies* xii, p. 239.

69. The part played by the Fianna Éireann has not received the attention it deserves. The extreme youth of many of those who participated in the Rising may in part be traced to the existence in the city since 1909 of this highly-trained body, two of whom—Con Colbert and Seán Heuston—were executed, while six others, ranging in age from 15 to 20, were killed in the Rising. See *Wolfe Tone Annual 1935*, p. 57–8. No attempt has been made, so far as I know to list the names of those under 20 who participated in the Rising, but they include Tommie Keenan, a boy of 12, who did good service in the College of Surgeons (see Margaret Skinnider, 'In Stephen's Green in 1916' in *The Irish Press Supplement*, 9 April 1966), Eamon Martin, Eunan MacGinley, Andy MacDonald, Seán and Noel Lemass, Roddy Connolly and others. For an account of the Fianna see also Bulmer Hobson, *Ireland, yesterday and tomorrow.*

70. See Piaras Béaslaí, *Michael Collins*, i. p. 73; John M. Heuston, O.P., *Headquarters Battalion Easter Week 1916*, pp. 11, 15; Ryan, *The Rising*, pp. 172–3; Michael Hayes, 'Thomas MacDonagh and the Rising' in F. X. Martin, *The Easter Rising, 1916, and University College, Dublin*, pp. 44–5; Ernie Nunan, 'The Kimmage Garrison' in *An tÓglach* (winter 1967).

71. For example on Friday, 24 March 1916, more than 150 of the Citizen Army left their employment on receiving a summons from Connolly, and were garrisoning Liberty Hall against a possible attack, within an hour of being called. See *Labour and Easter Week*, ed. Desmond Ryan, pp. 168–172.

72. Connolly's last communique to the soldiers of the Republic on 28 April 1916 ends with a striking tribute to the 'splendid women who have everywhere stood by us and cheered us on. Never had man or woman a grander cause, never was a cause more grandly served'. See Ryan, *The Rising*, p. 149.

73. See for instance examples quoted on pp. 158–9.

74. The writings of Pearse and Connolly in the years before the Rising continually call for the shedding of blood in the cause of Irish nationhood,

nor is there evidence that Clarke and MacDiarmada were not equally committed to this theory. For Pearse, Plunkett and MacDonagh, however, men of a deeply thoughtful and religious turn of mind, there must at the last moment have been some doubts. Francis Sheehy Skeffington's letter to MacDonagh (see *1916: The Easter Rising*, ed. O. Dudley Edwards and Fergus Pyle, pp. 149–52) points to a conflict between militarism and pacifism in the mind of MacDonagh; and one survivor of the G.P.O. garrison testified that while the fighting was in progress, the burden of responsibility lay heavily on Pearse and Plunkett. 'Time and again', wrote Desmond Fitzgerald, 'we came back to one favourite topic which could not be avoided. And that was the moral rectitude of what we had undertaken . . . We each brought forward every theological argument and quotation that justified that rising'. (See 'Inside the G.P.O.' from an autobiographical account by Desmond Fitzgerald, *Irish Times Supplement*, 7 April 1966). In February 1916 Pearse wrote of Tone and Emmet: 'Both would have been ruthless in revolution, shedding exactly as much blood as would have been necessary to their purpose.' (See *Political Writings and Speeches*, p. 291). When it comes to the point of action, however, this word 'necessary' becomes the difficulty. Dr. James Ryan gives a sad picture of what bloodshed meant to the leaders in the G.P.O. when they saw three old men lying dead in Moore Street, who were shot down by British machine guns while fleeing from their homes, carrying white flags. He writes: 'Seán MacDermott came over to the window and pointed to the three dead men and said something like "When Pearse saw that and showed it to us we decided we must surrender in order to save the lives of the citizens". The order of surrender did, in fact, contain the phrase: 'In order to prevent the further slaughter of Dublin citizens . . .' See Dr. James Ryan, 'The G.P.O.: the Medical Unit' in F. X. Martin ed. *The Easter Rising and University College, Dublin*, p. 89.

75. It has been suggested that Connolly, when dispatching Seán Connolly to the City Hall area had stated that this was a post of honour, since their detachment was the only one which would attack, while all others would be taking up defensive positions. It is now generally accepted that the plans did not include an attack on the Castle. Seán Connolly's brother, who was present has stated: 'When we consider how Seán divided up his company into small groups, which were to occupy the various buildings, it is easy to see that an attack on the Castle was not intended, even though one group did overpower the guard and take possession of the guard room'. Matt Connolly also states that the group had been warned that no 'unarmed soldiers were to be fired on or interfered with'. It is true that the first shot on Easter Monday was probably fired by this group when they killed the policeman who tried to shut the gate. It may have been a panic gesture, or it may have been considered necessary in order to

prevent the gates being shut. They contravened their orders by firing on an unarmed man, but his action could have given the men in the guard room time to prepare for attack, and amateur soldiers would have neither the presence of mind nor the skill to shoot to incapacitate rather than kill. The shooting of the young boy from the Magazine Fort, who was running to give the alarm was done in self defence. Apart from these instances and perhaps one or two in the Stephen's Green area, it seems clear that the fighting done by the Republican forces in Easter Week was done in defence of the Republic which they had declared by their proclamation. According to Diarmuid Lynch 'the O/C of the guard on munitions left in Liberty Hall had strict orders from Commandant Connolly not to open an offensive on any enemy forces unless attacked by them'. (See Matt Connolly, 'Dublin City Hall Area', and Commandant Paddy Holohan, 'Four Courts Area' in *The Capuchin Annual 1966*, pp. 181, 195–6; Diarmuid Lynch, *The I.R.B. and the 1916 Insurrection*, pp. 77–8, 161; Ryan, *The Rising*, p. 117.

76. MacDonagh gave this order to Captain James MacCormack, on Easter Monday, when he was on his way with a section of the Citizen Army to take Harcourt Street Station. See Ryan, *The Rising*, pp. 120, 205; Commandant Paddy Holohan, 'The Four Courts Area' in *The Capuchin Annual 1942*, p. 231.

77. See p. 168.

78. See *A History of Ireland under the Union*, pp. 696–7. It is interesting to find Under-Secretary Nathan on two occasions comparing the Rising to a series of Sidney Street incidents. See Leon Ó Broin, *Dublin Castle and the 1916 Rising*, p. 111; *The Royal Commission on the Rebellion in Ireland*, p. 10.

79. A great deal of evidence can be cited to bear out this point. See for instance Tomás Ó Néill and Pádraig Ó Fiannachta, *De Valera*, p. 40; Michael Hayes, 'Thomas MacDonagh and the Rising', Liam Ó Briain, 'An tEirí Amach mar do Chonnacsa é', and James Ryan, 'In the G.P.O.: the Medical Unit' in F. X. Martin, *The Easter Rising, 1916 and University College, Dublin*, pp. 44–5, 74, 76, 78, 84, 85; Peadar Kearney, 'A Personal Narrative of Easter Week' in Seamus de Búrca, *The Soldier's Song*, pp. 122–4; P. S. O'Hegarty, *A History of Ireland under the Union*, p. 700.

80. See Desmond Greaves, *Life and Times of James Connolly*, p. 325; Tomás Ó Néill and Pádraig Ó Fiannachta, *De Valera*, pp. 49–50; William O'Brien's introduction to *Labour and Easter Week*, p. 18; James Ryan, 'In

the G.P.O.: the Medical Unit' in F. X. Martin, *The Easter Rising, 1916 and University College, Dublin*, p. 85.

81. For a discussion of this and of the German offensive which coincided with the Rising see John de Courcy Ireland, *The Sea and the Easter Rising*, pp. 7, 36–7; Dorothy Macardle, *The Irish Republic*, pp. 156–7.

82. *Michael Collins*, i. p. 84.

83. Lynch, *The I.R.B. and the 1916 Insurrection*, p. 46.

84. *Ibid.*, p. 222; Desmond Ryan substantiates this version of Pearse's broad hints to Volunteer officers about 'the day we rise in arms', but adds that Plunkett 'who preferred to keep his own counsel, was startled at Pearse's outspokenness, and remonstrated with him. Pearse made his stock defence that there had been so much talk of insurrection for years that neither Dublin Castle nor MacNeill would suspect anything amiss. Undoubtedly, Pearse lent himself on the eve of Easter Week to adroit moves to capture, control and compromise as many men as needed to ensure that the Rising would take place and that it should be general'. (*The Rising*, p. 84).

85. The list of quotations to prove this could run into many pages but the essays of Connolly and MacDonagh in the O'Donovan Rossa souvenir publication in August 1915, together with Pearse's graveside address would be good examples. Junior officers and rank and file might not all be expected to be familiar with the poems of Pearse, MacDonagh and Plunkett, which showed clearly their ideal of dying for their country. Neither, probably would all of them have been familiar with pamphlets such as Pearse's 'Sovereign People'. But Dublin Volunteers had easy access to the *Irish Volunteer*, the *Workers Republic* and similar periodicals, and they had heard many war-like speeches, and there must have been a good deal of discussion at firesides, in pubs and clubs and cafes on what the leaders meant.

86. Brian O'Higgins, 'The Soldier's Story of Easter Week' in *Wolfe Tone Annual 1935*, p. 62.

87. *The Royal Commission on the Rebellion in Ireland*, p. 8; *The Soldier's Song: the Story of Peadar Ó Cearnaigh*, ec. Seamus de Búrca, p. 108.

88. See 'The Historic Rising of Easter Week 1916' in *The Voice of Ireland* ed. William G. Fitzgerald, pp. 134–5.

89. For example see Brian O'Higgins in 'The Soldier's Story of Easter Week' in *The Wolfe Tone Annual 1935*, p. 63; Séamus Ó Dubhghaill, 'Activities in Enniscorthy' and Denis McCullough, 'The Events in Belfast' in *The Capuchin Annual 1966*, pp. 319, 382.

The Making of 1916

90. Béaslaí, *Michael Collins*, i. p. 89.

91. Dorothy Macardle, *The Irish Republic*, pp. 163, 165; Tomás Ó Néill and Pádraig Ó Fiannachta, *De Valera*, p. 51.

92. *Ibid.*, p. 52.

93. Béaslaí, *Michael Collins*, i. pp. 90–91.

94. John M. Heuston, O.P., *Headquarters Battalion Easter Week 1916*, pp. 19–20, 53.

95. Matt Connolly, 'Dublin City Hall Area' in *The Capuchin Annual 1966*, p. 194; Margaret Skinnider, 'In Stephen's Green' in *Irish Press Supplement*, 9 April 1966.

96. See 'The Soldier's Story of Easter Week' in *The Wolfe Tone Annual 1935*, p. 64.

97. Lynch, *The I.R.B. and the 1916 Insurrection*, p. 161, says that 'as the day [Easter Monday] advanced, men who were late for the forenoon mobilisation arrived at Liberty Hall'. Captain Harry Nicholls, who was furious that he had received no summons, was in Stephen's Green on Monday morning, and played his part in the Rising. Louise Gavan Duffy got no call but she made her way from Haddington Road to the G.P.O. without incident. See Liam Ó Briain, 'An tEirí Amach mar do chonnacsa é' and Lúise Gabhanach Ni Dhubhthaigh, 'Insan G.P.O.: Cumann na mBan' in F. X. Martin, *The Easter Rising, 1916, and University College, Dublin*, pp. 65, 93.

98. *Sinn Fein, Rebellion Handbook*, 9, 17.

99. See *Irish Press Supplement*, 9 April 1966. The writer suggests that Thomas MacDonagh was responsible for some friendly contact between them and the Volunteers towards the end. See also Pádraig Ó Snodaigh, *Comhghuaillithe na Rabhlóide*, pp. 74, 88, 170, 171; Ryan, *The Rising*, p. 135.

100. MacNeill's personal intervention did not prevent the members of Pearse's Rathfarnham company from marching into Dublin that Monday morning. See Joseph A. Sweeny, 'In the G.P.O.: the Fighting Men' in F. X. Martin, *The Easter Rising 1916, and University College, Dublin*, p. 99. See Michael Hayes, 'Thomas MacDonagh and the Rising' in F. X. Martin, *The Easter Rising 1916, and University College, Dublin*, p. 43 for an account

of one man, who denounced MacNeill's action with great vehemence on the morning of Wednesday of Easter Week to Hayes and John Mac-Donagh, but who, nevertheless, refused their invitation to return with them to Jacob's Factory when invited to do so.

101. See for instance Seamus de Búrca, *The Soldier's Song: the Story of Peadar Ó Cearnaigh*, p. 116.

102. J. M. MacCarthy, *Limerick's Fighting Story*, p. 38; Desmond Ryan, *The Rising*, p. 233.

103. *The Irish Republic*, p. 177.

104. Pearse's manifesto to the citizens of Dublin: 'The country is rising in answer to Dublin's call'. (See Le Roux, *Life of P. H. Pearse*, p. 388). On Tuesday night after midnight, a meeting of the headquarters staff in the G.P.O. decided to send Laura Daly to Limerick and her sister Nora to Cork, to persuade the Volunteers there to support the Rising even at that late stage. (See Mannix Joyce, 'The Story of Limerick and Kerry in 1916' in *The Capuchin Annual 1966*, pp. 361–2). The communique issued by Connolly on 28 April to the soldiers of the Republic speaks of the information they have received telling how the manhood of Ireland, inspired by our own splendid action, are gathering to offer up their lives if necessary in the same holy cause'. He writes in glowing terms of the great fight being put up in other areas by the men of North Dublin, Dundalk, Galway, Wicklow, Wexford, Cork and Kerry. (See Ryan, *The Rising*, pp. 148–9).

105. The extraordinary effect produced on Irish public opinion by the execution of Allen, Larkin and O'Brien has not yet received the attention it deserves from historians, though E. R. Norman, *The Catholic Church and Ireland in the Age of Rebellion*, pp. 120–9, has made an excellent contribution to the subject. The commemoration concerts, and the monuments erected in their memory, and the fact that 'God Save Ireland' almost achieved the position of Ireland's national anthem, bear tribute also to this fact. Seán MacDiarmada and Pearse were at one with Connolly in the importance they attached to this episode. See Pádraig Ó Snodaigh, *Comhghuaillithe na Réabhlóide*, p. 62 for MacDiarmada's view. Pearse in December 1913, wrote of it: 'I have often thought that that was the most memorable moment in recent Irish history; and that that ring of Irishmen spitting fire from revolver barrels, while an English mob cowered out of range, might well serve as a symbol of the Ireland that should be; of the Ireland that shall be'. (See *Political Writings and Speeches*, pp. 197–8).

106. *Workers Republic*, 20 November 1915, quoted in Ryan, ed. *Labour and Easter Week*, pp. 106–7.

A Military History of the

1916 Rising

by

G. A. HAYES-McCOY

(IX)

A Military History of the 1916 Rising

COUNTY Inspector Sharpe of Wexford, the highest ranking officer of the Royal Irish Constabulary in that county, conveyed a tantalizing piece of information to the Royal Commission appointed to investigate the circumstances of the 1916 Rising. He said that one of his men had found in the possession of a Volunteer who was arrested in Co. Wexford 'the whole programme of the rebellion in Dublin' written out in pencil in 'an old pass-book'. This document listed the places occupied by the insurgents in Dublin and was 'presumably a copy of a general order'.[1] Sharpe said that the pass-book had been produced at the court-martial of the Enniscorthy Volunteer leaders early in May 1916.[2] The only other reference to it that seems to remain on record occurs in the *Report* of the Royal Commission, where it is said: 'There is no doubt that the outbreak had been carefully planned beforehand. A pocket-book discovered upon one of the rebels who took part in the Rising in Wexford contained a list of the places actually seized in Dublin when the outbreak occurred.'[3] This book may still exist. It is a pity that we know nothing more of its contents. If we did, we might be able to answer some of the questions regarding the Rising which, fifty years after the event, still provoke us.[4]

The documentation of 1916 is quite unsatisfactory. We have— because of the circumstances of the Rising—very little contemporary material from the Irish side, and not much more from the British. In consequence, many of the events of the Rising are obscure; in particular, the dispositions which were made in Dublin by the Irish Volunteers and Irish Citizen Army—

dispositions which caused Sir Mackenzie Chalmers, a member of
the Royal Commission, to say that the Rising was 'exceedingly well
arranged'—can now be explained only by inference.[5] Pearse and
the other insurgent leaders do not remain on record as having
said why they acted as they did—why they arranged their forces
as they were arranged, or for what immediate purpose. We
can reconstruct only from the evidence available; and our
reconstruction must be incomplete because the evidence is
incomplete.[6]

First, we infer that the plan of the Rising as it occurred on
Easter Monday was not a totally new one, but was a modification
of the plan that had been worked out in advance for a greater
rising on the previous day, that is, the series of operations that
was forestalled by the countermanding order. This seems
obvious.[7] The forces that were available to the insurgents on
Monday were smaller than they had hoped to have; how much
smaller, they could not have known beforehand. The pattern of
positions occupied was, we infer, modified accordingly, although
we have no means of knowing the extent of the modification.
Whether the insurgents had to abandon proposals to occupy
buildings other than those which they did occupy we do not
know, although we suspect they had.[8] And the situation indicates
that changes had to be made in the plan at very short notice on
Monday morning.

There is therefore a possibility that the nature of the effort
made in Dublin by the insurgents was altered by the loss of
support that we believe was occasioned by the countermanding
order and by the confusion which followed its issue. The leaders
of the insurrection may originally have intended a more
aggressive action; we can never be quite certain what was in
their minds. Perhaps the biggest mystery of the Rising is not that
its seven promoters could have done what they did if they had
really regarded military defeat as inevitable, but that they could
have come to count—as they certainly appear to have counted—

on the ultimate support of men whom they had either kept in the dark as to their intentions or had deliberately misled.

Nor can we be quite certain who the real leaders were, that is what part each of the seven members of the Irish Republican Brotherhood military committee, or military council—the seven members of the provisional government of the Irish Republic— played in framing and modifying the military plan.[9] Sir Mackenzie Chalmers's question, addressed to Wimborne, the Lord Lieutenant, and Edgeworth Johnstone, Chief Commissioner of the Dublin Metropolitan Police, at the Royal Commission's enquiry, if the insurgents had 'any old soldiers among them'[10] is, as far as the leaders are concerned, easily answered. They had not.[11] It is not so easy to suggest where their military competence came from. Not from Clarke, who showed no pretensions to it. Scarcely from MacDiarmada, who, although he was one of the founders of the Irish Volunteers and was a prime mover—indeed a vital inspirational and organising force —in the insurrection, was not a military leader.[12] Hardly from Pearse, who displayed no deep interest in military affairs. Connolly? Most likely. Connolly's service in the British army, if in fact he was a soldier,[13] cannot have taught him much, but he had a practical, highly intelligent mind and his record of very active soldiering during the week of the Rising is quite outstanding.[14] MacDonagh did not join the military committee until a few weeks before the Rising, so the planning can not have been his. Ceannt and Plunkett formed, with Pearse, the original military committee and were both—as was MacDonagh— Commandants in the Irish Volunteers and members of the Volunteer headquarters staff.[15] Plunkett, whom Connolly called 'a brilliant military man',[16] was deeply interested in military theory. Ceannt fought well in the South Dublin Union, but there is nothing to indicate that, had his military career been a formal or a more extended one, he might have attained more than field rank. Of them all, Connolly and Plunkett are the ones

18

who have been credited with the formulation of the insurgent plan of operations, and they seem, on the very meagre evidence available, to have been responsible for it. P. S. O'Hegarty, a former member of the Supreme Council of the I.R.B., has said that Sean MacDiarmada told him in May 1915 that 'the plans were Plunkett's, and that he had already worked them out when they got in touch with him, and that they were adopted practically without alteration'.[17] According to Desmond Ryan, Connolly 'highly approved' of Plunkett's plan and he and Plunkett—presumably after January 1916—worked together to improve it.[18]

*   *   *   *   *

The Irish Volunteers were mobilised in Dublin on Easter Monday morning following orders issued by MacDonagh, who was Brigade Commandant of the five battalions forming the Dublin Brigade. The 1st Battalion, under Commandant Daly, was mobilised at Blackhall Place, less D Company, under Captain Heuston, which assembled in Temple Street and proceeded thence to Liberty Hall.[19] Daly set up his headquarters in North Brunswick Street (later in Church Street), occupied the Four Courts, on King's Inns Quay, and the North Dublin Union in Church Street and sent parties to throw up barricades in the streets to the westward and northward of these positions.[20] Daly had about 120 men. Of the 2nd Battalion we shall speak in a moment. The 3rd Battalion, under Commandant de Valera, was mobilised at Great Brunswick (now Pearse) Street, less C Company, which assembled at Earlsfort Terrace. De Valera, who had about 130 men, established his headquarters in Grand Canal Street and occupied Boland's bakery as his main post. He seized Westland Row Railway Station, occupied and in places destroyed the railway line as far out as Ballsbridge, and established outposts in some buildings in the vicinity of the bakery, including one which commanded the main entry to the nearby Beggar's Bush Barracks. Part of his C Company held positions at and near Mount Street Bridge, the next canal bridge upstream from his main post.[21] The 4th Battalion, under Commandant Ceannt, assembled about 130 strong in Emerald Square, Dolphin's Barn and occupied the South Dublin Union Work-house and, as outposts to the east and south-east of it, positions in James's Street, Marrowbone Lane and Ardee Street.[22] The 5th Battalion, which was drawn from North Co. Dublin, was mobilised in its own area and operated outside the city.

The Irish Citizen Army was mobilised under orders from Connolly at its headquarters at Liberty Hall.[23] The 200 or so men on parade were divided in three parties. One, the main body of about 100 under Commandant[24] Mallin, marched to St. Stephen's Green, which they occupied, sending forward an advanced detachment which set up outposts in Harcourt Street Railway Station and at Portobello Canal Bridge. Mallin threw up barricades[25] in streets adjoining the Green.[26] The second body of about 50 marched from Liberty Hall to Dublin Castle.[27] The third body, together with about 70 Volunteers, most of whom had in recent months returned from England and Scotland—they were known as the Kimmage garrison—remained in the forenoon at Liberty Hall. At noon about 100 of this mixed Citizen Army and Volunteer force, together with Pearse, Connolly and Plunkett,[28] marched to the General Post Office and occupied it as the headquarters of the insurrection.

Pearse, who read the proclamation of the Irish Republic outside the building, assumed the offices of President of the Provisional Government and Commander-in-Chief of what was named in the Fenian tradition the army of the Irish Republic.[29] Connolly became Commandant-General of the Dublin district[30] and exercised command of the insurrection in the city.[31] Out-posts were occupied at the end of O'Connell Street, facing O'Connell Bridge, at the corner of Lower Abbey Street and in some other buildings close to the G.P.O., and barricades were constructed in Lower Abbey and North Earl Streets.[32] Before leaving Liberty Hall, Connolly had sent D Company of the 1st Battalion, 16 strong, which, as we have said, had earlier been ordered to Beresford Place, to Usher's Island with instructions to take the Mendicity Institution.[33]

The 2nd Battalion of the Volunteers, which remains to be mentioned, presents something of a problem. Each of the other three city battalions was assigned positions in its own area, that is, the area in which its members lived and in which its peacetime headquarters were; but the 2nd Battalion, which was the Dublin north-eastern battalion, was, according to its orders for Monday, posted across the Liffey with its mobilisation centre at St. Stephen's Green and its position to be occupied at Jacob's factory in Bishop Street, off Redmond's Hill. As things turned out, MacDonagh, who was the battalion Commandant,[34] occupied the factory and a position in Fumbally Lane with something more than 100 of his men about noon.[35] Almost as many of the battalion who had assembled at their usual place of meeting, Fr. Matthew Park, Fairview, were subsequently ordered into the G.P.O. The battalion was thus divided. Its posting to the south side left the whole north-eastern quarter of the city bare of insurgent troops. Part of the battalion did not, as it happened, cross the Liffey, but neither did it remain in the north-east. Furthermore, if the 2nd Battalion men from Fr. Matthew Park had not been brought to the G.P.O. the force at insurgent headquarters must have been, even by the exiguous standards of the revolt, very small. One cannot dismiss the feeling that the posting of the 2nd Battalion to the south side was a modification of the original Easter Sunday plan made at a time when it had to be accepted as inevitable that the number of the insurgents must be reduced below the expected total.[36] The further modification brought about by sending part of the battalion to the G.P.O. appears to have been a still later compromise.[37]

One may explain the failure of the insurgents—having regard to their otherwise very extended deployment—to station part of their forces to the east of the G.P.O. by saying that, since there were no military barracks in that direction, no immediate attack was to be expected from there. This may indeed be so, but the pressure which eventually reduced the G.P.O. and crushed the Rising was largely exerted from that quarter.

The disposition of forces made by the insurgents on Monday morning placed them in a ring around the central part of the city with two positions north of the river—the G.P.O. and the Four Courts area—and four positions south of it—the South Dublin Union, Jacob's factory, St. Stephen's Green and Boland's bakery. Outposts were, as we have seen, organised by the forces holding these positions, and there were further small parties outside the Castle and the Mendicity Institution. The only position within this ring that was held by government troops was Dublin Castle; how weakly it was held we shall soon see. Outside the ring there were troops in Marlborough (now McKee) and Royal (now Collins) barracks on the north side and in Richmond (since demolished) and Portobello (now Cathal Brugha) barracks on the south side. Linenhall, Islandbridge, Wellington and Beggar's Bush barracks were held, the first by an unarmed party and the others by merely nominal forces. There were also small training camps at the Bull Island, Dolly-mount and in Elm Park.

The proposed function of each of the insurgent posts, save the G.P.O., might be defined in terms of the barracks.[38] Daly in the Four Courts area may be said to have been placed where he could interpose between the G.P.O. and the Royal and Marl-borough barracks. Ceannt at the South Dublin Union stood in the way of British forces working into the city from Richmond barracks. MacDonagh and Mallin at Jacob's and St. Stephen's Green could counter attempts to move troops from Portobello barracks towards the Castle and into the city generally. De

Valera at Boland's bakery obstructed egress from Beggar's Bush
barracks, which however—although this, almost certainly, was
not realised—were virtually unoccupied.

The insurgent disposition on the south side can be seen to
have held—at least in theory—even wider possibilities of obstruction. Each of the main roads into the city—those from Merrion,
Stillorgan, Dundrum, Rathfarnham, Naas and Lucan—and each
of the railways—the Dublin and South-Eastern lines to Westland
Row and Harcourt Street Stations and the Great Southern and
Western line to Kingsbridge Station—might, in ideal conditions,
be blocked.[39] There are, of course, infinite possibilities of entry
into a city as big as Dublin and the paucity of the insurgent
forces made it impossible effectively to block even the main,
roads and quite impossible to stop movements by rail, but the
positioning of Connolly's little army can, it seems, be explained
only by reference to its obstructive and defensive possibilities.
Nor should we forget the insurgents' initial fear that they would
be overrun at once; we must consider their dispositions primarily
in the light of that.

The insurgent position was weaker on the north side of the
Liffey, a matter which was to be of the greatest significance since
their headquarters were there. Why they attempted with so
small a force to hold so extended a perimeter, or why they did
not confine themselves to one side or other of the Liffey are,
apparently, matters that must remain conjectural.[40]

What, militarily, was the insurgent purpose? Speaking of the
situation on Monday morning, Diarmuid Lynch, who although
he was not within the inner revolutionary circle was a member
of the Supreme Council of the I.R.B., and who took part as a
Staff Captain in the Rising, has said: 'Clearly, none of the
prearranged positions could now be manned adequately to
ensure a prolonged defence. Even had Dublin mustered in full
strength, the hope of a military victory had already been dissipated over the week-end.' He suggests that Pearse and the

others had 'hope of a military victory' when they laid their original plans—and Pearse himself said as much[41]—but that the most they could expect on Monday was to hold out briefly.[42] Connolly was more outspoken, or more dramatic. He said on leaving Liberty Hall for the last time that they were 'going out to be slaughtered'.[43]

The accepted explanation of the Rising is that it was a gesture of protest, a sacrifice willingly suffered by the leaders, who knew that they had no hope of military success, but believed that their appeal to arms would further the cause of Irish independence. This is perhaps an oversimplification, but if these were among the ends envisaged by the insurgent leaders it is arguable that they could best be served by occupying positions in Dublin and by resisting for as long as possible the efforts that must be made to eject them.[44] The advantages of such purely defensive action were that it offered the only possibility of survival for the time required to give point to their enterprise, and that such resistance in their own capital city—particularly at a time of war—must have considerable propaganda value.[45] The disadvantages were that an insurrection of this kind meant an open disclosure of strength and that the insurgents courted a defeat which must almost certainly be followed by the death of their leaders, the loss of their arms and equipment and, possibly, the discrediting of the whole separatist movement.

The insurrection was, of course, an offensive action, indeed an act of aggression, but the insurgents' efforts were everywhere defensive save at the Magazine Fort in Phoenix Park and Dublin Castle. The Magazine Fort was captured by stratagem shortly after noon and some small arms were taken; the raiders found it impossible to get into the high-explosive store, which it was intended to blow up. What it was proposed to do at the Castle is far from clear. The first intimation of the Rising that was received at Headquarters, Irish Command was a telephone message from the Dublin Metropolitan Police at 12.10 p.m. to say that the Castle was being attacked.[46] The initial movement there certainly was an attack and was so described by the insurgents.[47] Part of Captain Seán Connolly's small detachment of the Irish Citizen Army, which was the attacking force, shot the policeman at the gate, rushed the sentry and entered the Upper Castle Yard. They then intimidated the guard by tossing a grenade among them, overpowered and bound them and occupied the guardroom. But Captain Connolly soon retired from the gate and seized the City Hall, which is just outside. His men had already entered the buildings at the south end of Parliament Street, so that he thus dominated the northern exits of the Castle. Those of his men who had entered the guardroom lay low there and eventually withdrew surreptitiously. The handful of police and officials who were in the Castle shut both northern gates and the building was not subsequently entered by the insurgents.

What had been the insurgents' intention? If they meant to seize the Castle, why had they not pushed on? Small though their force was, the government force was smaller. There were no troops within the Castle on Monday morning save the guard of six men—who were now trussed up—and there were only 2 officers and 20 or 25 men in the adjoining Ship Street barracks.[48] The capture of the Castle, the very heart and centre of alien government, would have created quite a stir; nor would it have been as seemly, or as easy, to have shot or burnt the intruders out of the Castle as it was to shoot and burn them out of the G.P.O. Never had Irish insurgency such a chance. James Connolly said of Robert Emmet that if he had pushed on and captured Dublin Castle he would have 'roused all Ireland by the blow'.[49] Had he himself really intended to stop short?

The British showed themselves at the time to have been uncertain of the insurgent purpose.[50] Most Irish writers have clearly been uncertain ever since. William O'Brien is, however, emphatic that 'it was never intended to seize Dublin

Castle'.[51] He says that Connolly told him this, saying that although it would be easy to take the Castle it would be hard to hold it, and that the Castle buildings could not be taken and burnt because there was a Red Cross hospital there.[52] On the other hand, Piaras Béaslaí says that 'an unsuccessful effort' was made to take the Castle.[53] P. Ó Cearnaigh agrees.[54] L. N. Le Roux[55] and Dorothy Macardle[56] hold that it was originally hoped to take the Castle, but that insufficient strength led to an alteration of the plan. Miss Macardle goes on to explain Monday's efforts as an attempt to prevent troops from leaving the Castle. She says that if the insurgents had known that the Castle garrison was so small they would, despite their own weakness, have reverted to their original plan and would have pushed on with their attack. D. Ryan holds the same view. He says[57] that Connolly thought the occupation of the Castle 'not feasible, and not desirable, even if feasible', and that his plan was therefore 'to seal [it] up'; but he adds that an attempt would still have been made to take the place if it was realised that the opposition would have been so small. Ryan explains the occupation of the guardroom as part of the 'sealing up', although he omits to say why, if this was so, the Citizen Army men who entered the guardroom lay low[58]; Fox makes the statement, which is certainly incorrect, that possession of the guardroom made it possible to occupy the City Hall and the buildings in Parliament Street.

Diarmuid Lynch was the most objective of those who tried to solve the problem of the Castle. Although, he argued, the small size of Seán Connolly's force certainly indicates that a seizure of the Castle was not intended, the fact that he 'did attack the guard at the Upper Castle Yard entrance and did "take" the guardroom complicates the matter'. Lynch comments on the failure to reconnoitre the Castle premises beforehand, a failure which left the small size of the guard undisclosed, and he points out that, even in the circumstances as they existed, the Castle could have been taken.[59] There is evidence that the Citizen Army force in St. Stephen's Green believed during Monday afternoon that the Castle was in insurgent hands,[60] and there is one important contemporary statement that seems to prove that Pearse thought the same. Desmond FitzGerald says that Pearse told him on Easter Monday afternoon that the Castle had been seized and that he gave a flag to FitzGerald's wife, asking her to bring it to the Castle so that it might be hoisted there. She brought it, and was amazed to find British troops on guard at the gates.[61]

In view of all this, while Nathan's report to Birrell, 'attack made on Castle but not pressed home', might fairly describe the morning's events in the historic centre of Irish government,[62] Professor Liam O Briain's 'It was bungled' is, militarily speaking, perhaps a truer statement.[63] Connolly's explanation, said to have been given to the nurses in the Castle hospital shortly before his death, rings true; he is quoted as having said 'that when they found no resistance, they thought it must be a trap to entice them in and ambush them, and that Ship Street barracks, at the back, would be too strong for them.'[64] If the struggle at the Castle raises many questions, it also, more than anything else that happened during the week, indicates that the insurgents were indeed amateur soldiers. Both there and at Beggar's Bush barracks—which was almost undefended, but which they believed to be otherwise—their system of intelligence was bad.[65]

★   ★   ★   ★

The insurgents who were in arms in Dublin shortly after noon on Easter Monday numbered much less than 1,000. About 800 more joined them during the next day or so.[66] They were distributed throughout the city and they showed from the start that they were prepared to go to extremes: policemen were shot in St. Stephen's Green, the Castle and elsewhere within minutes

of the outbreak of the revolt and a body of the British Volunteer
Training Corps was fired on in Haddington Road during the
afternoon with fatal results. This, of course, posed an immediate
problem for the military authorities, who for one thing were
ignorant of the insurgent strength.

According to the official statements, there were in Dublin on
24 April less than 2,500 troops available for action.[67] These
troops, most of whom were Irish—all the infantry were Irish—
and many of whom were recruits still undergoing training, were
in 4 main units. The composite 6th Reserve Cavalry Regiment,
made up of squadrons of the 5th and 12th Lancers and of an
available strength of 886 of all ranks, was in Marlborough
barracks.[68] The 3rd Battalion (Special Reserve) of the Royal
Irish Regiment, which had been embodied in August 1914 and
which was used to supply drafts to the other battalions of the
regiment, then on active service on the western front and in
Macedonia, was in Richmond barracks. It had a total available
strength of 403.[69] The 10th Battalion of the Royal Dublin
Fusiliers, 467 strong—a wartime service battalion that was soon
to be engaged in the battles of the Somme—was in the Royal
barracks.[70] The 3rd Battalion of the Royal Irish Rifles, an Ulster
militia battalion 671 strong, was in Portobello barracks.[71] An
inlying picket, or one which remained with barracks, of 100
officers and men of each of these units had been kept in readiness
for some days 'to aid the Civil Power in the enforcement of the
law.'[72] These 400 men of the 4 pickets were immediately available on Easter Monday.

Although the insurrection took the government and the
military authorities by surprise,[73] headquarters of the Irish
Command and of the Dublin garrison acted with great prompti-
tude in dealing with a totally unprecedented situation. Warned
by the police of an attack on the Castle and hearing further news
of the insurgents' activities as the minutes passed, Colonel
Cowan, Assistant Adjutant-General of the Command and

deputy in Dublin of the absent Commander-in-Chief, Major General Friend, took immediate steps to reinforce the Castle guard, to safeguard the Viceregal Lodge and to recover possession of the Magazine Fort.[74]

It was the Dublin garrison Adjutant, who was in garrison headquarters at the Castle and whose chief, Colonel Kennard, was also absent, who called out the troops from the four main Dublin barracks.[75] Richmond barracks was summoned to send 'all troops in barracks . . . at once fully armed to Dublin Castle'; immediately after the receipt of this order at Richmond barracks 'another telephone message was received from the General Post Office to the effect that "Sinn Feiners" had seized the Post Office and help was required'.[76]

The party from Marlborough barracks—a troop, or possibly more, of lancers—came to the north end of O'Connell Street and rode forward towards O'Connell Bridge. Fire was opened on it from the G.P.O. and several saddles were emptied. The lancers beat a hasty retreat to their barracks. Theirs was the only force of those which entered the city in the opening moments of the insurrection to proceed to a point other than the Castle. As it happened, a second party of lancers had ridden across the southern end of O'Connell Street just before this. This was a party of 50 men that had been sent that morning to escort a consignment of ammunition from North Wall to Marlborough barracks.[77] Unaware of what was happening around them, these men rode on towards the Four Courts; they were fired on at Ormond Quay by men of the 1st Battalion, who were erecting a barricade at the entrance to Church Street. The lancers turned into the side streets to their right. Some scattered and penetrated as far as North King Street; but the main body barricaded them-selves in buildings in Charles Street, where they held out—they were not greatly molested—until the following Thursday even-ing.[78] Cavalry, which at the opening of the twentieth century was still considered suitable for use in city streets against demonstrators and against those forces of insurrection which were employing what Lord Wimborne called 'the ordinary tactics of revolutionists'—as in St. Petersburg in 1905—clearly had no place in the kind of 'insurrectionary warfare' that Connolly had been preaching on the eve of the 1916 revolt.[79] G. F. R. Henderson said of the German cavalry in France in 1870–71 that 'a few francs-tireurs, armed with the chassepot, were enough to paralyse a whole brigade'.[80] The Dublin insurgents bore this out, and bore out much that had been said shortly before the insurrection by Lord Roberts, Erskine Childers and other opponents of the *arme blanche*. It was quite in keeping with contemporary—although obsolescent—practice that cavalry should have been used as they were in Dublin during the first moments of the revolt. If the insurgents had remained in the streets they would doubtless have tried to ride them down. After the first moments, however, the cavalry fought dismounted.[81]

The infantry pickets were ordered to the Castle. That from Richmond barracks—100 men of the Royal Irish Regiment under Major Holmes—moved eastward by Old Kilmainham. Holmes was aware that the G.P.O. had been seized and that he might expect trouble. He proceeded cautiously and, seeing some of Ceannt's men behind the wall of the South Dublin Union in front of him, halted where Brookfield Road opened to his right. He sent forward Lieutenant Malone and 20 men. These were fired on, but, with 3 casualties, broke into the buildings facing the wall of the Union and, having sheltered for a while, returned the fire from there. Lieut.-Colonel Owens, the battalion commander, who was following the picket, now brought up the main body of troops from the barracks—about 200 men—and soon launched an attack on the handful of Volunteers who were all that Ceannt could spare to defend that part of his position. Two companies were sent down to the right towards the Grand Canal. These assailed the gate at Rialto Bridge, leading into the

Union grounds, and spreading eastward along the canal—where they came under fire from Ceannt's outpost in Marrowbone Lane—outflanked the insurgents in the open space inside the Union wall. Owens had also sent a party with a machine gun to the Royal Hospital. This gun opened fire from the other flank and by about 3.30, after heavy firing in which the Irishmen on both sides—all of Ceannt's men and most of Owens's—had their first taste of war, and in which both sides suffered casualties, the troops had burst into the grounds and had captured that part of the Union which faced Brookfield Road and some of the main buildings. The unfortunate patients in the Union hospital and the other inmates were directly in the line of fire. Firing died down in the later afternoon and most of the troops remained where they were for the night.[82]

Ceannt's men had fought gallantly and they were by nightfall still holding up the greater part of the Richmond barracks force; but they were unable to deny a passage towards the Castle to all of Owens's troops. At 9.35 p.m. Colonel Kennard, the Dublin garrison commander, who had returned to duty about 1.0 p.m., when he arrived in Portobello barracks, and who had later joined the Richmond barracks force, succeeded in reaching the Castle. He entered by the Ship Street gate accompanied by 86 men of the Royal Irish Regiment.[83] This was probably the picket that had left Richmond barracks 9 hours earlier. And meanwhile the Castle had been relieved by the other pickets. That of the Royal Dublin Fusiliers left Royal barracks about 12.30, marching along Albert and Ellis Quays in a column of fours without an advance guard. When the column reached a point half-way between Ellis Street and Blackhall Place it came under fire from the Mendicity Institution and was halted. The troops sought shelter in doorways, behind the river wall and behind a tram which had been stopped by the firing and eventually, after a brief return of fire, withdrew into the side streets. Reinforced from the barracks, the Fusiliers next advanced probably by

Benburb Street—at any rate under cover of the houses—to Queen Street, from the end of which they opened fire on the Institution with a machine gun. Covered by this fire, they rushed across Queen Street bridge, passed cautiously westward below the front wall of the Institution, and entered Watling Street. Others may, while Heuston's men were forced to crouch down below their windows by the intensity of the fire, have crossed Watling Street bridge. The column, suffering no further interruption of its progress, went up Watling Street to Thomas Street and then on by High Street. The troops turned to the right to avoid the Citizen Army at Parliament Street and the City Hall and reached the Ship Street entrance to the Castle shortly before 2.0 o'clock. They were 130 strong. The insurgents in the Institution, amazed that no effort had been made to assault them, believed that the troops had returned to barracks.[84]

Fifty Royal Irish Riflemen of the picket from Portobello barracks reached Ship Street and entered the Castle at the same time.[85] When these men had left Portobello barracks more than an hour earlier they were fired on from the outpost which the Irish Citizen Army had just set up in a public house on the city side of the bridge. Reinforced from the barracks, the troops sheltered for a time behind the wall beside the canal; then, returning the fire,[86] they soon succeeded in dislodging their opponents, who fell back, in accordance with their orders, to St. Stephen's Green. The picket, which had been reinforced for a second time and was now more than 200 strong, continued down Camden Street, but its advance guard was fired on at the corner of Redmond's Hill and Bishop Street by MacDonagh's men, who were by then established in Jacob's factory and who had a picket of their own at the street corners in front of the troops.[87] The troops retired a little and then, working through the South Circular Road, succeeded in pushing 50 men forward to the Castle.

As a result of these movements, Kennard had by nightfall

about 300 men in Dublin Castle, the safety of which, as far as
the administration was concerned, was thus ensured. So far, the
main purpose of the military had been to relieve the Castle, not
to attack the insurgents. The engagement at the South Dublin
Union was primarily a struggle to break through forces that
were in the way of one column of the relief. Other military
movements undertaken on Monday to safeguard positions
included the sending of a detachment from the School of
Musketry at the Bull Island camp, Dollymount to North Wall
to secure the docks on the north side; the reinforcement of the
guard at Kingstown (Dun Laoghaire); and the occupation of
Amiens Street Railway Station,[88] the electricity generating
station at the Pigeon House, the telephone exchange in Crown
Alley,[89] and—during Monday night—the Custom House.[90]
While the Dollymount detachment was moving in, the part of
the Volunteer 2nd Battalion which had assembled in Fr. Matthew
Park, Philipsburgh Avenue and which had remained there to
protect stores was moving also, having been ordered—as has
been already mentioned—to come to the G.P.O. The Volunteers,
who were marching from Ballybough Road towards Summer-
hill, stopped when they became aware of the advancing troops.
It was then some time after 3.0 p.m. The troops, who were
moving along the Great Northern Railway line, soon opened
up on the Volunteers with a machine gun, and what had been
the advance guard of the latter moved to take intercepting
action at Annesley and Newcomen bridges over the river Tolka.
The main Volunteer body stayed by the canal, but the Dolly-
mount troops showed no sign of moving against them—in fact,
they were intent on their own purpose to move down towards
the docks and to Amiens Street Station—and the main body of
the Volunteers soon continued on to the G.P.O. The party of
insurgents at the Tolka remained there until Tuesday evening.[91]

Trinity College was also secured for the administration on
Monday. There was a guard of eight members of the Dublin

University Officers Training Corps in the College at noon.
When they became aware of the outbreak of the insurrection,
these men shut the front gate and sent to summon more of their
comrades. Many of these came in and some soldiers on leave
who were passing in College Green were also brought in and
were armed from the O.T.C. store. At 7.0 p.m. the garrison
stood at 44. The gates were guarded and a watch was maintained
on the roof. The greatest danger to the College was anticipated
from Westland Row Railway Station, and the defenders concentrated during Monday night in watching the eastern end of
the grounds.[92]

Colonel Cowan took steps during Monday afternoon to
advise London of the revolt and to summon what reinforcements
were available within Ireland. Because of the occupation of the
G.P.O., he was unable at first to use the telegraph to communi-
cate with Field Marshal Lord French, the Commander-in-Chief
of the Home Forces, but he had a message sent to the Admiralty
by wireless from a naval vessel in Kingstown.[93] This was transmitted to French in the early afternoon and conveyed by French
to Augustine Birrell, the Irish Chief Secretary.[94] Orders were at
once given to prepare to send reinforcements to Ireland and by
that night a scheme for the transport of troops from Liverpool
had been drawn up[95] and the troops who were to go had been
alerted.[96]

The first of the Irish reinforcements whom Cowan summoned
consisted of a mobile column 'which had been arranged for to
meet any emergency'[97] and which was standing by at the
Curragh training camp; its intended function was, in fact, 'to
repel a landing', that is, to resist a German invasion.[98] The
column was made up of the 3rd Reserve Cavalry Brigade of
1,600 of all ranks. It was called up at 12.30 p.m. by a telephone
message[99] and trains were sent from Kingsbridge Station to
transport it. The call was endorsed, this time in writing, by Sir
Neville Chamberlain, Inspector-General of the Royal Irish

19

Constabulary, whose message stated that 'a serious insurrectionary movement' had occurred in Dublin and that the Castle
was besieged; Sir Neville asked that 'the troops held in readiness'
should be sent 'as soon as possible'.[100] The first of the trains
conveying the mobile column, which was commanded by
Colonel Portal and which travelled dismounted, arrived at
Kingsbridge at 2.15 p.m. and the entire column had arrived by
5.20 p.m.[101] One train load was sent through by the loop line
to the North Wall; it brought its complement to reinforce the
Bull Island troops and some of the 6th Reserve Cavalry Regiment
from Marlborough barracks at the docks.[102] Some more of
Portal's men were sent to the Castle; the remainder were held
for the moment at Kingsbridge. A further message calling for
1,000 more men was sent to the Curragh by one of the returning
trains.

Colonel Cowan also called for artillery from Athlone, the
4th Battalion Royal Dublin Fusiliers from Templemore and
available troops from Belfast. The first of the Belfast troops—
150 men—reached Amiens Street Station on Monday evening.[103]
Cowan did not know the numbers of the insurgents, nor the
extent of the revolt which they had begun. As time went on, it
became the accepted British practice to regard the revolt as
having been inspired by Germany, and for all Irish Command
headquarters knew on 24 April the Germans might be about to
take an active part in the Irish fighting. It was therefore imper-
ative that every effort should be made to control the situation in
Dublin at once. Furthermore, an enemy barricaded in defensive
positions in a city was notoriously difficult to eject. It must have
seemed essential to build up the number of troops available as
rapidly as possible.

★   ★   ★   ★

By Tuesday the pattern which subsequent fighting was to take had been established. The military—after all, they were professionals—had reacted quickly to the situation, and the steps which they had already taken to safeguard themselves—that is, the relief of the Castle, the making certain of the security of the barracks and other positions on the perimeter of the revolt, and the summoning of reinforcements—provided a basis for the offensive action which could now follow.

It would be difficult to say how much the military knew by Tuesday morning. Although uniformed police had been withdrawn from the streets, men in plain clothes circulated freely and information was gathered in that way.[104] It might have been noted on the previous day that the insurgent headquarters were in the G.P.O., since it was there that the ceremony of the proclamation of the Republic took place; the fact was announced by the insurgents themselves about noon on Tuesday, when *Irish War News* appeared, bearing the statement 'The whole centre of the city is in the hands of the Republic, whose flag flies from the G.P.O.' Once the military could assume that no further insurgent movements were to be expected in Dublin—once the insurrection had established itself as an affair of defended positions— Irish Command could plan its countermoves. Obviously, they had to be directed towards the overthrow of resistance in the G.P.O.[105] Equally obviously, they had to be based on an urban topography the central feature of which was a river that bisected the built up area and on the circumstance that the only post held by the government within the circle of insurgent positions lay close to the river. Possession of the Castle, to the establishment of which the first day's military activity was so largely devoted, indicated the manner in which the revolt was to be suppressed— a fitting situation, in view of the place which the Castle has always occupied in Irish history.

The military began on Tuesday the establishment of control over the south bank of the river and the opening of a passage from west to east, from the Richmond barracks-Kingsbridge-

Parkgate area, where the expected reinforcements could be assembled, to the Castle and thence eastward to a position whence an attack might be mounted on the G.P.O. Such a position lay at hand in Trinity College. As this plan was developed, operations in other areas could be modified, or altogether suspended. In effect, once it was established that the G.P.O. was the centre of the revolt the remaining insurgent positions could largely be by-passed. The outcome of this was that the insurgent tactics were undermined, for their ring of posts did not do a great deal to fulfil their function, which, according to the evidence, was to delay the fall of Headquarters.

The architect of the military plan was apparently Brigadier-General W. H. M. Lowe, who was, in the Irish Command, next in seniority to Major-General Friend. Friend, who was a Royal Engineer and whose military career had lain in administrative posts, had gone on leave to London on Friday, 21 April. He had learnt of the Rising at the War Office on Monday and had returned to Dublin at once, arriving on Tuesday morning. Lowe reached Kingsbridge Station from the Curragh at 3.45 a.m. on Tuesday and took over command of the forces in the Dublin area from Kennard. With Lowe came the first of 840 men of the 25th Irish Reserve Infantry Brigade, made up of the 5th Battalion Royal Dublin Fusiliers and the 5th Battalion Leinster Regiment and representing the extra 1,000 men that had been asked for on the previous day. The remainder of the brigade followed later in the morning.[106] The plan of operations which was pursued from Tuesday was either Lowe's or Lowe's and Friend's.

Very naturally, the insurgents, once they had occupied their positions, expected immediate attack. A Citizen Army man told James Stephens in St. Stephen's Green on Monday afternoon 'We are expecting an attack from the military at any moment.'[107] They looked upon Monday's encounters with the troops as efforts to dislodge them. Tuesday's *Irish War News*, having related the occupation of some of the insurgent positions, said

that 'attacks were immediately commenced by the British forces
and were everywhere repulsed'[108]—a propagandist flourish
rather than a statement of fact. The planned attacks began early
on Tuesday morning. The military assumed the initiative then
and held it to the end.

First, it was necessary to dispose of those insurgents who still
threatened the Castle. The City Hall, from the roof of which
fire had been kept up on the Upper Castle Yard through
Monday evening and into the night, was attacked in the darkness
by troops of the mobile column and the lower part of the
building was cleared.[109] Soon after daylight the troops fought
their way onto the roof and cleared that too. Connolly had sent
a reinforcement of 9 men to the City Hall on Monday evening,[110]
and he tried to send another on Tuesday morning,[111] but without
success. After this building had been taken, there remained only
the two insurgent posts in the houses at the end of Parliament
Street. An attack was mounted on these by a party of 5th Royal
Dublin Fusiliers—who had, as we have seen, come from the
Curragh during the night—at 2.0 p.m. on Tuesday and, although
they were as fiercely defended by their few occupants as the
City Hall had been, the two buildings were taken within an
hour.[112]

A further aggressive movement was prepared by the military
in the early part of Tuesday morning. 100 men and a machine
gun unit, that had come from the Curragh with the mobile
column, left the Lower Castle Yard at 2.15 a.m. and proceeded
by Dame Street, Nassau Street and Kildare Street to the Shelbourne Hotel.[113] The hotel was occupied, as was the United
Service Club, which is also on the north side of St. Stephen's
Green. Commandant Mallin sent a picket on Monday evening to
man the rooftops in Leeson Street, from which direction he was
not attacked,[114] but did nothing to protect himself to the north.
One is again forced to the conclusion that the military intelligence
—although they were fighting in an Irish city—was better than

that of the insurgents. Mallin's men, the greater number of whom had spent the night in the Green, were surprised at dawn by machine gun fire from the hotel and club. By 7.0 a.m. they had been forced to retire into the College of Surgeons, where they were to remain for the rest of the week. Save that they held down the troops who continued watching them and occasionally firing on them, and that they, in due course, to some extent restricted the passage into the city of the reinforcements from England, they were unable to influence the further course of events.

Two other developments on Tuesday were the establishment of full military control from west to east as far as Trinity College and the commencement of the cordoning of the north city area from Parkgate to North Wall. Lowe ordered Portal to use the Curragh troops to set up a line of posts from Kingsbridge Station to the College. Portal had carried out his order by noon, although the completion of the line along Lord Edward Street and Dame Street had to await the clearing of the insurgent positions in front of the Castle at 3.0 p.m. Machine guns had been brought into the College early on Tuesday morning, probably at the same time as they were sent to St. Stephen's Green.[115] Regular troops—a detachment of the Leinster Regiment—relieved the College O.T.C. in the afternoon,[116] and when the artillery, which consisted of two sections or four 18-pounder quickfiring guns, arrived from Athlone two of the guns were sent through to Trinity in the evening.[117] Large numbers of troops were brought into the College on Wednesday and headquarters for military operations in Dublin were set up there.[118] These movements, as Friend's successor, General Maxwell, was later to claim, 'divided the rebel forces into two, gave a safe line of advance for troops extending operations to the north or south, and permitted communication by despatch rider with some of the commands'.[119] In fact, operations were not extended to the south; after the machine gunning of the park at St. Stephen's Green no further movement of any significance was made in that direction.[120]

The formation of the north side cordon was begun before 2.0 p.m. The troops available for the cordon included two units which had just arrived, the 4th Battalion Royal Dublin Fusiliers from Templemore and the remainder of a composite battalion made up of Royal Inniskilling Fusiliers, Royal Irish Fusiliers and other troops from Belfast. These battalions had come by rail, the Templemore troops to Kingsbridge Station and the Belfast troops, following their advance party of the night before, to a point beyond Amiens Street Station. They had come in without difficulty. Lusk Company of the 5th Battalion of the Volunteers had attempted to blow up Rogerstown Bridge, three-quarters of a mile south of Rush and Lusk Station, on Monday afternoon, but the explosion damaged only one of the two lines; the attempt to break the tracks at the Sloblands in Fairview also left one line usable,[121] but the small body of the Volunteer 2nd Battalion was still in action at the river Tolka outside Amiens Street Station when the trains conveying the composite battalion were coming in, so that the troops alighted somewhere beyond the river.

The troops establishing the cordon were assisted by artillery. The train conveying the guns from Athlone could come no further than Blanchardstown, the line having been blown up there.[122] The guns were brought from that point by road. Two were, as we have seen, sent on to Trinity College. The other two[123] were used to clear a way for the troops establishing the cordon. At 3.30 p.m. an insurgent barricade at the North Circular Road bridge, outside Broadstone Railway Station, was shattered by the first artillery fire of the week. A party of Royal Dublin Fusiliers occupied the station. A second barricade on the Cabra Road bridge was shelled and carried a little later. These were unsubstantial barricades; one 'consisted [on Monday evening] of house furniture and a few poles'; but at least Commandant Daly, by building them, showed that he had anticipated the military movement that had removed them. Some of their 1st Battalion defenders retired to the G.P.O.[124]

The troops pushed forward along the North Circular Road, establishing posts as they went. They met no further opposition, although the cordon could not be completed until the 2nd Battalion men had left their positions at the Tolka. These men had fought successfully during the day and had inflicted casualties and taken prisoners when the troops tried to overrun them from Amiens Street Station. Their service was some of the best of the street fighting that had so far taken place, but they were now completely outnumbered—there were only 65 of them. The troops advancing from the west pressed down towards them from Drumcondra, the Belfast battalion came in by the Howth and Malahide Roads and the troops from the docks continued their attacks. The 2nd Battalion men were ordered back to the G.P.O.[125] From now on, the fact that there was no strong insurgent post in the north-eastern part of the city would have momentous consequences. The military cordon was completed by evening and local military headquarters were set up in Amiens Street Station,[126] less than half a mile from the G.P.O., and about the same distance—save that the river intervened— from Trinity College. Martial law was proclaimed in Dublin that evening and was extended to the remainder of Ireland on the following day.[127]

*   *   *   *

The movements and encounters of Tuesday left Lowe strongly placed to begin his attack on the G.P.O. They left the insurgents correspondingly reduced. All the major positions initially taken up by the insurgents were still intact, but apart from the G.P.O. and the posts in the Four Courts area, they had lost much of their significance. Daly's positions in the Four Courts area still served, as far as the G.P.O. was concerned, a vital purpose, and they were to be the scene of much fighting. De Valera's posts covering the lower part of the Grand Canal and what Ceannt held of the South Dublin Union were also to see bitter struggles, but this was because of faulty British dispositions. With one exception, none of the bigger buildings that were held by the insurgents on the south side of the Liffey was attacked with the intention of reducing it after Tuesday. The exception was the Mendicity Institution. The others fell in the end without fighting, as the British planners clearly hoped they would. We have evidence of this in the withdrawal of Colonel Owens's force of the Royal Irish Regiment from the South Dublin Union on Tuesday morning. Owens, as we have seen, had taken a great part of the Union by nightfall on the evening before, and he hoped to take the remainder on Tuesday. Instead, he was ordered—as the regimental history puts it—'for some extraordinary reason' to withdraw to Kingsbridge Station. He did so under protest, and his men were held there until Wednesday evening.[128] The 'extraordinary reason' was that the Castle, which had been Owens's original objective, had been relieved by Tuesday morning. The Union had been by-passed and could for the moment be left alone.[129]

The Mendicity Institution was the only post still held by the insurgents on or near the south bank of the Liffey—save of course de Valera's posts below O'Connell Bridge—and it was necessary that Lowe should seek to eliminate it. Although it had lost much, if not all, of its significance for the insurgents now that Dublin Castle had been secured and Trinity College occupied, the Institution was a threat to Lowe's security. Connolly seems to have had the building occupied to obstruct military movements eastward along the quays.[130] It is close to the Royal barracks, but on the opposite side of the Liffey, and the fire of its defenders did in fact hold up the Royal barracks picket for some time at Watling Street bridge and Blackhall Place on Monday. Heuston received a reinforcement of twelve men from the G.P.O. on Tuesday and he held his post until Wednesday, much, as it appears, to Connolly's surprise.[131] It is not clear what Connolly hoped ultimately to accomplish at the Institution. He would have been naive indeed if he had thought that Heuston's retention of it could have had any effect beyond the first hour or so on the British ability to relieve the Castle. Nor is it likely that he believed Heuston to be prolonging Ceannt's line to the Liffey, that is, that Ceannt and Heuston between them were obstructing the main south city entry from the west. Connolly said on Friday that Ceannt held 'the South Dublin Union and Guinness's Buildings to Marrowbone Lane', and that he controlled 'James's Street and district'. He added that 'on two occasions the enemy effected a lodgment and were driven out with great loss'.[132] This last, as a reference to the fighting at the Union on Monday and Thursday, was a statement of fact. It shows that headquarters was sufficiently in touch with Ceannt throughout the week to know how his main force had fared. But Ceannt had never occupied Guinness's brewery. That much was untrue. Was Connolly under a misapprehension as to the effect of the resistance which Ceannt and Heuston were putting up?[133] We know very little of what was known at insurgent headquarters of the British movements; nor indeed are we aware how much Connolly and his colleagues knew of the movements of their own widely scattered forces.[134] Whatever further service the insurgents may have hoped for from the Mendicity Institution, the British attacked the building on Wednesday morning and forced its surrender.[135]

Lowe was either vindictive or else entirely mistaken regarding another building. Liberty Hall, for long, as the government believed, the headquarters of Irish intransigence, was unoccupied by the insurgents since Monday afternoon, and it seems unlikely that Lowe, whose men were close by in the Custom House from Tuesday evening, was unaware of this.[136] Whatever their information, the British, who might have marched across Butt

Bridge unopposed save by the snipers in Kelly's at the corner of Bachelor's Walk and Hopkins's at the corner of Eden Quay, deployed a formidable armament on Wednesday morning against Liberty Hall. It was as though, having decided to attack, they must follow Western Front practice by first putting down an artillery barrage.[137] The two 18-pounders were brought out from Trinity College at an early hour, unlimbered at the intersection of Tara and Townsend Streets and manhandled into position at the mouth of Tara Street. At this short range fire was opened about 8.0 a.m. across Butt Bridge on Liberty Hall.[138] The barrage was augmented by fire from H.M. Yacht *Helga*, which had already—on Tuesday—fired at de Valera's position in Boland's bakery. The *Helga* came up the river and, stopping near the Custom House, opened fire. She fired 24 rounds.[139]

Fire was also opened by machine guns from the Custom House, the tower of Tara Street fire station, and the roof of the Tivoli music hall on Burgh Quay and by troops on the south side of the river. Surprisingly, the outer walls of Liberty Hall withstood this barrage very well, although the interior was wrecked.[140] Troops from the south side soon passed over Butt Bridge and joined their comrades north of the Liffey.[141]

The remainder of Wednesday's fighting in the O'Connell Street area was less dramatic. Lowe proceeded to surround insurgent headquarters. He was no doubt warned by the fighting of the two previous days that he must expect a fierce and a costly struggle if he attempted without adequate preparation to close with the defenders of O'Connell Street. It behoved him to be cautious. He was engaged in severe street fighting that was without recent precedent in the history of the British army. There had been nothing quite like this in the warfare of the late nineteenth century in the Sudan, South Africa or elsewhere; nothing, perhaps, since the struggles in Delhi and Lucknow during the Mutiny. The British troops in the force that relieved the legations during the Boxer rebellion in 1900 did not have to fight their way into Peking. What the troops had to face in Dublin was, of course, as nothing to what they had been facing for the better part of two years in France, but it was of a different nature. Indeed there was no real precedent for the Dublin fighting of a later date than 1871, the year of the Communard barricades in Paris. Again, the Paris fighting at that time was infinitely more severe, but the method was the same; in France as in Ireland, the victor, determined 'to snatch Paris burnt and bloody'[142] from the Communards, forced his way by gunfire into the heart of an inhabited city.[143] The result of the Dublin fighting may have been a foregone conclusion, but there was much about it—very much—that was unpredictable. In the centre of the city Lowe took no chances.

By the afternoon the troops, using Trinity College as a place of assembly, had occupied the whole area behind Aston and Burgh Quays. They crept westward from Amiens Street and the Custom House. They moved down by Parnell Square. All of this they did surreptitiously, keeping well under cover. Pearse and Connolly waited in vain for a bayonet charge in the open.[144] Machine guns fired from Trinity College,[145] from the tower of Tara Street fire station, from Amiens Street, from the Rotunda (where the Irish Volunteers were born). Snipers plied their rifles from the rooftops. O'Connell Street, Marlborough Street, Talbot Street, Lower Abbey Street were swept by fire.[146] At 2.30 p.m. the artillerymen took part once more. One of the 18-pounders was brought into position between the junction of College and D'Olier Streets and Fleet Street and fire was opened on the insurgent post in Kelly's at the corner of Bachelor's Walk.[147]

The insurgents stood up well to this barrage, but they were soon forced to contract. The men whom they had withdrawn from Westmoreland Street on Tuesday had been placed in the Imperial Hotel on the east side of O'Connell Street.[148] Now some of the Lower O'Connell Street posts were also withdrawn. The artillery fire made Kelly's untenable and its defenders were brought back to the Metropole Hotel. Connolly had been particularly anxious to provide against an attack from Lower Abbey Street. His principal outposts were in the lower part of O'Connell Street and his best barricade was in Lower Abbey Street. He seems to have expected an attack there or over O'Connell Bridge, and when the outposts behind Eden Quay were evacuated in the afternoon he sent fifteen Volunteers by Earl Street and Marlborough street to restore them. But the troop movements of Wednesday soon showed him that he had to face threats from other quarters. The 3rd Battalion of the Royal Irish Regiment was activated again on Wednesday afternoon. It was moved from Kingsbridge to Trinity College and sent thence—in an incomplete movement to threaten Mallin— to seize Grafton and Kildare Streets and Merrion Square;[149] but it was soon moved again and sent by Butt Bridge, Gardiner Street and Great Britain (now Parnell) Street to Moore Street.[150] Connolly had no posts northward of Henry Street, and the troops, aided by the first of the improvised armoured lorries,[151] reconnoitred Upper O'Connell Street. This was ominous. So was the fact that Henry Street was, by 5.0 o'clock, raked by fire from the Capel Street direction[152] and that at about the same time a machine gun was in operation on the roof of Jervis Street Hospital. The penetration of the troops along Parnell Street and down Capel Street completed Lowe's cordon about the G.P.O. and soon cut Daly's 1st Battalion off from headquarters.[153]

The roof of the G.P.O. was soon swept by machine gun and rifle fire. It became increasingly difficult for the insurgents to move their men in Lower O'Connell Street. They intensified their efforts to secure covered ways by boring through from house to house and, still expecting a frontal attack, they developed a new outpost at the corner of O'Connell and Middle Abbey Streets.[154] The position of the G.P.O. made it difficult for Lowe to reach it by gunfire either from the north or the south, and it was completely covered to east and west; it also narrowed the defenders' field of fire. Pearse admitted in his bulletin or manifesto issued on Thursday that the British had succeeded in the course of Wednesday afternoon and evening in cutting communications between the G.P.O. and 'our other positions in the city', and that headquarters were isolated.[155]

It is curious that Lowe, who was so cautious in the centre of the city, and one of whose first actions on assuming the Dublin command had been to suspend operations at the South Dublin Union, should have ordered an unnecessary and apparently suicidal advance at Mount Street bridge on Wednesday afternoon.

The War Office decided on Monday to send at once two infantry brigades, the 176th and 178th of the 59th North Midland Division, to Dublin. The movement began on Tuesday and the 178th Brigade, consisting of four battalions of the Sherwood Foresters (Nottinghamshire and Derbyshire Regiment), arrived in Liverpool from Watford and other stations in Hertfordshire and Bedfordshire and, crossing in two Isle of Man Steam Packet Co.'s ships, reached Kingstown (Dun Laoghaire) that night.[156] The brigade set out to march to Dublin on Wednesday morning. The left column of two battalions was ordered to move to the Royal Hospital, Kilmainham by the Stillorgan-Donnybrook Road and the right column, made up of the 2/7th Battalion in advance and the 2/8th following, was ordered to Trinity College by Merrion Road, Ballsbridge and Merrion Square.[157] The left column got through without difficulty. The right did not.

The brigadier, Colonel Maconchy, marched with the right column. The men had no weapons other than their rifles and bayonets; their Lewis machine guns had been left behind in Liverpool.[158] They advanced slowly, knowing that they might be fired on—'it was known to a house where the column would first come under fire'[159]—although not expecting opposition before they reached Ballsbridge. The day was very hot. Lieut.-

Colonel Fane, the officer commanding the 2/7th, reached the junction of Pembroke and Northumberland Roads about 12.30 p.m. Here, almost half a mile from Mount Street Canal Bridge, he came under fire. Halting his main body, he led forward his advance guard, which consisted of C Company.

The outposts of the 3rd Battalion of the Volunteers at and near Mount Street Bridge were in Clanwilliam House—that is, at the corner of Lower Mount Street, overlooking the bridge— the Parochial Hall in Northumberland Road, and a house at the corner of Haddington Road. There were in these positions seven, four and two men respectively. Four more Volunteers were in a yard on the city side of the canal; there were thus 17 men defending the position, mostly of C Company of the battalion, the same letter as that of the company which was about to attack them.

Fane, following information which he had received, was particularly watchful on his right, where de Valera's main force was; but he was enfiladed from the left as he attempted to move along Northumberland Road. The two men in the house at the corner of Haddington Road opened fire. Those in the other insurgent positions joined in and Fane, losing men freely, was pinned down.[160] What followed was an extraordinary demonstration of street fighting; all the advantages were on the side of the insurgents, because they were in cover and were well placed and—although heavily outnumbered—were cool and resolute in action, and because too the troops were poorly equipped for what they had to face. Many of the Foresters were raw recruits. 'Poor boys', said a contemporary observer, 'many of them had only had six weeks' training, and some of them had never shot anything but blank cartridge before'.[161] None had been trained for street fighting; their exercises had been in marching, entrenching, musketry, bombing, bayonet practice, night movements and field engineering.[162] They had at first no grenades and at no stage had they a field gun. Their direction was

287

courageous but unimaginative, and, as perhaps fitted the prerog-
ative power that the army had always claimed in Ireland, it was
arrogant. This last was particularly noticeable in Lowe's handling
of the developing situation. The attackers of Mount Street
Bridge were, one may say, the contemporary British army in
miniature, the British army of attrition and 'all ranks go forward
to kill or be killed'; and there were too undertones of Breed's
or Bunker Hill, and of Colenso.

Unable either to take the house at the corner or to continue
along Northumberland Road, Fane sent C Company up
Haddington Road to Baggot Street Bridge; but this attempt to
outflank the insurgents by way of Percy Place came under fire
from Clanwilliam House and from the railway line spanning
the canal further down and was defeated with heavy loss. All the
company officers were either killed or wounded. Fane reported
his position to brigade headquarters—which had been set up by
Maconchy in the Royal Dublin Society's buildings—at 2.45 p.m.
and a request was sent to the bombing school at Elm Park for
guncotton and grenades. When these were received the door of
the corner house was blown in and the building was later
captured. Of the two Volunteers who had so ably defended it,
one was killed; the other escaped. Fane was wounded.

As the afternoon wore on, B Company was sent to reinforce
C at Baggot Street Bridge and A Company went to the right,
past Beggar's Bush barracks and up Grand Canal Street. B was
held in Percy Place; A was stopped by fire from the railway
line and from Boland's bakery. Part of D Company got on to
the roofs of Northumberland Road, but their fire made little
difference; nor did that of snipers in the tower of Haddington
Road church do much to disturb the Volunteers. Fane believed
until late afternoon that he was being fired on from the school
opposite the end of Percy Place, but the insurgent post there
had been abandoned before the action began. He lost many men
outside the school and in the approaches to the bridge.[163]

Maconchy conferred with Lowe on the telephone about 5.30 p.m. He reported his difficulties, but Lowe ordered 'that the advance to Trinity College was to be pushed forward at all costs'.[164] Lowe was not in immediate need of reinforcement. In the eyes of half a century later the storming of Mount Street Bridge does not seem to have been essential; indeed, Lowe's orders *prevented* the brigade from getting through that night— and he might have had what was left of them within an hour if he had permitted them merely to turn aside and come by Baggot Street.

Fane was unable to carry the bridge. The 17 men who opposed him—aided by fire from other units of de Valera's force—had, to that extent at least, incapacitated a whole battalion. If other outposts had behaved as well, and other attackers as wrong-headedly, the suppression of the Rising would have been costly indeed.

The 2/8th Battalion was ordered up about 6.0 p.m. By 7.0 the Parochial Hall had been cleared and several further attempts had been made to rush the bridge. Soon, a small party succeeded in crossing and bombing Clanwilliam House. By 8.0 the building was on fire and three of its defenders were dead; the four others escaped. The Sherwood Forresters lost about 230 of all ranks killed and wounded in the day's fighting. It has often been suggested that Commandant de Valera, the greater part of whose nearby force was not engaged, might have more forcefully assisted the 17 men at the bridge.[165] If he had tried to do so, he must have brought on a major struggle in which all the troops that had arrived from England might have been involved. None of the insurgent leaders acted in this way. The struggle for all of them was essentially defensive, and each defended his own position. Nor, if the 3rd Battalion had behaved differently, could its efforts have affected the ultimate result; de Valera could not, it seems, have delayed Pearse's surrender.

The troops remained for the night in billets about Mount

Street Bridge. The place of the Sherwood Foresters at the canal was taken on Thursday morning by the 2/5th Battalion South Staffordshire Regiment (part of the 176th Brigade, which had followed the 178th to Kingstown),[166] and they marched in the afternoon, not to Trinity College, but by the South Circular Road to the Royal Hospital. On the way, but this time—apparently—without direct orders to do so from Lowe, they repeated the unnecessary attack of Wednesday. They marched with the 2/8th Battalion in front. As they approached Rialto Bridge, they were fired on by Commandant Ceannt's men in Marrowbone Lane distillery and the South Dublin Union. Maconchy halted the column and assistance was called for from Portobello barracks. Major Sir Francis Vane brought up 50 men from the barracks. Vane found the column, which he says was part of 'an important convoy carrying ammunition',[167] in difficulties. The Foresters were 'very raw recruits', and Lieut.-Colonel Oates, who commanded the 2/8th, was 'very much distracted'.[168] Vane went forward with two companies of the 2/8th and his own men, and some of the troops entered the grounds of the Union and broke into the main buildings. A struggle followed in the lower part of the Nurses' Home, a struggle of grenades and point blank rifle and revolver fire that lasted until dusk. Not more than half a company of troops was involved, and they were opposed by no more than 27 insurgents, but the fighting was severe and the 2/8th suffered many casualties before they withdrew. On the insurgent side the wounded Cathal Brugha particularly distinguished himself.[169] During the late afternoon Maconchy brought the column to the Royal Hospital, whence these Englishmen, the survivors of so rough a baptism of fire, looked down on the blazing city.

This was the last of the fighting in the 4th Battalion area. Ceannt held his ground, and was not further molested, until his surrender late on Sunday afternoon.[170]

It seems clear from what happened in the various insurgent

posts that the plan of insurrection made no provision for action subsequent to the opening moves. It was the reverse—perhaps its very nature required it—of what Eoin MacNeill, writing in February, believed to be necessary: 'If we are to have a plan of action, let us have it complete—not breaking off at the end of the formula. Let us see what we expect to do first, and next, and next, and what alternatives there are, and what is our provision for them'.[171] As the days went by and the insurgent Commandants realised that they were not going to be overwhelmed immediately, as Emmet and the Young Irelanders and the Fenians had been overwhelmed, they showed signs—particularly those of them who had not been hard hit—of wanting to pass to the next phase of resistance. They sought by offensive movements to prevent the closer approach of their opponents, and they tried to work out methods of co-operation. But their efforts came to nothing. An attempt of Mallin's to burn buildings in Harcourt Street in order to threaten troops who had placed a machine gun on the roof of University Church was defeated by fire from other buildings in the same street.[172] Daly considered trying to break through the cordon in Capel Street so as to link up with headquarters, but abandoned the project.[173] De Valera, who was shelled ineffectually on Thursday morning by a 1-pounder naval gun firing from a truck at the corner of Percy Lane[174] and by the *Helga,* which fired from the Liffey,[175] similarly abandoned a scheme to work up towards the Shelbourne Hotel from Westland Row. MacDonagh sent 15 or more cyclists from Jacob's factory towards Merrion Square on Thursday morning. They fired on troops at the corner of Lower Mount Street. Their purpose was to assist de Valera and they probably delayed still further the advance into the city of the slowly moving troops from England, but their movement proved to be no more than a reconnaissance; it had little effect on the general course of events.[176]

The main British concern on Thursday was to develop the

attack on the G.P.O. Sheltering in the houses, the troops moved forward slowly in Lower Abbey Street and Talbot Street and with still greater caution in Upper O'Connell Street. They searched every house. Machine guns at the Parnell Monument, on the roof of the Gresham Hotel, in the building at the junction of Westmoreland and D'Olier Streets and elsewhere sprayed the streets and spattered the house fronts. One of the 18-pounders opened fire at noon, apparently from a position at the Parnell Monument; the first of several shells fell near the Metropole, close to the G.P.O.[177]

Connolly was very active during the morning. He placed men in the outposts in Henry Street, where one of the armoured lorries had appeared,[178] and superintended the erection of a barracade in Prince's Street. He was wounded slightly in the arm. Later, when he was busy placing another outpost in Middle Abbey Street he was wounded in the leg, this time seriously.[179] Connolly continued to direct operations, but he did so with less effect. A change becomes noticeable in the military capacity of the insurgents after Thursday afternoon; the western outposts, which had just been placed then and which extended as far as Liffey Street, were withdrawn hastily early on Friday morning.[180]

The 2/5th and 2/6th Sherwood Foresters had been moved from the Royal Hospital to the Castle early on Thursday morning. They were now placed with the 5th Leinster Regiment, the 3rd Royal Irish Regiment and the Belfast composite battalion under Colonel Portal and given the task of tightening Lowe's cordon.[181] The Foresters approached Grattan Bridge by Parliament Street and came under fire from Daly's men on the drum underneath the dome of the Four Courts. Most of them crossed the Liffey and occupied the quays from Liffey Street to O'Connell Bridge. They penetrated Upper Abbey Street and threw up barricades.[182] The armoured lorries gave much assistance here, as they did in Moore Street and on the south quays.

They were used to move and place men under heavy fire, to transport sandbags for the barricades, and to tow the field guns into position.[183]

During the afternoon a fire which began in Lower Abbey Street while 'the military were shelling that district'[184] spread rapidly. By nightfall all the buildings southward to Eden Quay and northward as far as the Imperial Hotel were blazing. The insurgents who still held posts on that side of O'Connell Street were forced out.[185] By Friday morning Connolly's garrison was confined to the Post Office, some buildings behind it and the Metropole block. All the posts that the insurgents had tried to set up behind them towards Capel Street were gone;[186] opposite them, across O'Connell Street, were the British and the fires.

*　　*　　*　　*

Lieut.-General Sir John Maxwell arrived at North Wall at 2.0 a.m. on Friday and took over the Irish Command from Friend. There were then about 12,000 troops in Dublin.[187] Maxwell had commanded in Egypt—where he was at the head of one of the three distinct British forces in that country, the one called irreverently 'the second incompetent'[188]—but he had been ordered home as part of the rearrangement which had followed Sir William Robertson's appointment as Chief of the Imperial General Staff. French had picked him when the government decided to send somebody who carried more weight than Friend to handle affairs in Ireland.[189] Maxwell conferred with Friend and Lowe at the Royal Hospital shortly after his arrival and 'instructed the latter to close in on Sackville Street from east and west;[190] he retained Lowe in the Dublin command and made no change in the plan of operations.[191]

The destruction of the O'Connell Street area was continued on Friday. Two 18-pounders, one in Upper O'Connell Street and the other in Westmoreland Street, shelled the Metropole and the G.P.O. 'The intense cannonading', as Diarmuid Lynch says,

'became deafening'.[192] The indomitable Connolly said in the last order of the day which he addressed to his men: 'We are here hemmed in because the enemy feels that in this building is to be found the heart and inspiration of our great movement'.[193] He was, of course, quite right. Knowing what they wanted to do, the British had closed in for the kill; the only other city area in which anything more than sniping was being carried on on Friday was the adjoining one held by Commandant Daly. Like many of his contemporaries, Connolly had a bayonet fixation. He still thought in terms of 'the final charge'. He said that the troops were 'totally unnerved' by the slaughter which they had suffered and that they would not dare to 'attempt again an infantry attack' on the insurgents; yet he (or perhaps those who exercised command during his incapacitation) ordered the construction of a barricade inside the main doorway of the Post Office 'from behind which the defence could be continued in case the men were beaten back from the windows'.[194] The centripetal tendency that had brought in the Henry and Abbey Street outposts earlier in the morning led to the withdrawal of the insurgents from the Metropole block before noon, but their position, which seemed vital for the defence of headquarters, was reoccupied following Pearse's intervention.[195]

The investment of the Post Office was intensified during the afternoon. Snipers appeared on the unburnt part of the east side of O'Connell Street. Machine gun fire and the bursting of shrapnel shells led to the withdrawal of the defenders from the roof. The troops edged closer from Capel Street and Parnell Street, where one of the 18-pounders was brought up, although there was a difficulty in finding a target for it. But the attackers remained under cover. There was no charge. It was fire that brought about the downfall of the headquarters of the Republic. Incendiary shells (probably smoke shells rather than the generally used high explosive shells) set fire to the roof during the afternoon and, despite the efforts of the Volunteers, the upper part of the building was soon ablaze.[196] The wounded and most of the women were evacuated, the explosives were placed in safety in the basement and, shortly after 8 o'clock, the garrison began to move out.

As with many of the events of the week, the details of the evacuation are obscure. We know that Pearse, Connolly and over 400 of their men, including those who had held the Metropole block, were driven out by the flames, and that their exit was hasty. What they hoped to achieve is uncertain, and they may indeed, in their dreadful predicament, have been extemporising. They did not behave like men who had been driven desperate; not by any means. Their sally, if confused, was clearly not purposeless. Nor was it a wild rush to come to grips with an enemy that had avoided coming to grips with them; they were carrying Connolly with them, and they had Clarke and MacDiarmada and other non-combatants. It seems that, having been driven from the Post Office, their intention was to get in elsewhere; but what they may have hoped to do after that is not so clear.

The evidence that the insurgents were making for Williams and Woods' factory in Parnell Street and that they hoped to establish themselves there seems conclusive.[197] Two further objectives are indicated: a junction with Daly's command in the Four Courts area[198] and an attempt to break out of the city to the northward.[199] Unfortunately, we do not know, nor does there appear to be any way of finding out, how much Pearse, Connolly and the others knew about the British penetration of their immediate surroundings. If we knew that we might speak with more confidence about their hopes and intentions.[200]

The O'Rahilly went first —about 7.0 p.m.—with an advance guard of some 40 men.[201] He, Captain Sean Connolly and Captain Tom Weafer were the only insurgents of rank to be killed during the week. The O'Rahilly's party made their way through their own barricade in Henry Street and then charged up Moore Street. It is perhaps ironical that, with the exception of Sherwood Foresters at Mount Street Bridge and the South Staffords at a time of exasperation in North King Street, the insurgents—who had been on the defensive, and who themselves expected to be overrun—were the only ones to make a charge during the insurrection. They came under heavy fire from the British barricade at the top of the street and were stopped, with many casualties. The O'Rahilly was mortally wounded at the entrance to Sackville Lane. The main body followed the advance guard about quarter of an hour later. They ran singly and were under fire from the direction on the one side of Amiens Street and on the other of Capel Street and, over the rooftops, from a machine gun at the Rotunda Hospital. Pearse went last with the rearguard. Most of the main body and rearguard got as far as Moore Street by way of Henry Place and Moore Lane. They burst into the houses and barricaded themselves there. They remained in these positions, in the no-man's-land between their blazing headquarters and the cordon in Parnell Street, until Saturday afternoon. No report came back to them from their advance guard, which had disintegrated.

Meanwhile, half a mile to the west, another struggle had taken place. Whether the encirclement of the Four Courts area as distinct from the area of the G.P.O. was part of the scheme upon which the troops had been operating during the week does not appear. It probably was not. Maxwell says that the arrival of the 2/5th and 2/6th South Staffordshire Regiment at Trinity College from the Mount Street Bridge area on Friday afternoon enabled him to begin forming an additional cordon around the Volunteer 1st Battalion.[202] He probably used these extra troops to complete the close investment of all the insurgent positions on the north side, deeming this expedient in view of the fact that the Post Office was unlikely to hold out much longer. He allocated the 2/4th Lincolnshire Regiment (177th Brigade) to assist in cordoning the Grand Canal, but no attempt was made to come closer to the insurgent south side posts. Two companies of the 2/7th Sherwood Foresters went from the Royal Hospital in the evening to reinforce the northern cordon on the North Circular Road. They were ordered to provide against the possibility of an attack from the north-west; Ashe's 5th Battalion had just then been successful in their engagement with an R.I.C. column at Ashbourne, Co. Meath.[203]

The 2/6th South Staffords followed what was by then the usual route for troops coming from Trinity College—Butt Bridge-Gardiner Street-Parnell Street—and were ordered to advance westward along North King Street from the top of Capel Street. The other Staffords battalion was later ordered to move in the other direction, that is, eastward from Arbour Hill. Daly, who had been but little pressed up to this, was still strongly posted in King Street. His men hotly contested the advance of the troops and made them fight through the night for every inch of the way. The sufferings of the residents, many of whom remained in their houses, were intense. Several men who had no connection with the insurrection were killed—public opinion was later to say murdered—by the troops.[204] The 2/6th South Staffords had more men killed during the week than any British battalion save those of the Sherwood Foresters, and most of their 40 or 45 casualties were suffered in King Street. Although they were assisted by an armoured lorry, it took them fourteen hours to advance 700 yards. They did not link up with the 2/5th until 9.0 a.m. on Saturday.

Fire, including that of a field gun,[205] was kept up during Saturday morning on the houses which the insurgents had entered in Moore Street. The Provisional Government decided to seek terms some time after noon. Miss Elizabeth O'Farrell was sent out under a white flag about 12.45 p.m. and was taken to Colonel Portal. Pearse surrendered unconditionally to Lowe about 3.0 p.m. on the north side of the Moore Street barricade.[206] The surrender of the whole insurgent force on the north side of the Liffey took place on Saturday evening. MacDonagh, de Valera, Ceannt and Mallin did not surrender until Sunday, but, save for sniping in some isolated positions, there was no further action after Pearse had agreed to submit. The insurgents, who had acted throughout as a disciplined force, obeyed orders to the end, and of course Maxwell's and Lowe's immediate object was achieved when Pearse signed the surrender order; it remained for the troops merely to see that Pearse's order was enforced, to take their prisoners into custody and transfer them to England, to organize the courts martial and implement their directions, and to indulge in the ostentation that, for the military machine, is the invariable consequence of victory.

*   *   *   *

Insurgent activities in other parts of Ireland—in 'the out stations', as Maxwell called them[207]—were slight, but they were the cause of much anxiety to the administration and they occasioned considerable movements of troops, naval forces and police. Fighting, or the appearance of the Volunteers in arms and with warlike intent, was confined to Cos. Galway, Wexford and north Co. Dublin, but uncertainty prevailed everywhere and much tension was experienced in Cork and Limerick.

It has been claimed that the insurrection was first planned as a Dublin one and that the decision to extend it throughout Ireland was taken later and was dependent on the expectation of the receipt of arms from Germany.[208] As far as is known, no documentary record exists of a plan for such a widespread insurrection. As in the case of Dublin, one can only seek hints regarding it, and since the Volunteers made few moves in other parts of Ireland there is even less to guide one here than there is regarding the plan of operations in the capital. The acting Vice-Commandant of the Tralee Battalion was told by Pearse as early as the autumn of 1915 that the Kerry, Cork, Limerick, Clare and Galway Volunteers would 'link up with' or be 'in communication with' one another and that 'a line would be held' from the Shannon to Macroom.[209] It was proposed to distribute the expected German arms, that is, the cargo of the *Libau* (alias *Aud*) by rail from Fenit. The train or trains were to proceed from Fenit to Limerick, and thence probably to Athenry.[210] Commandant Colivet of the Limerick Brigade had instructions to unload some of the weapons and ammunition for his own men and to pass the remainder through his area. He was at first told that he must 'hold the line of the Shannon' and later that he must prepare to attack the military and police in Limerick to ensure the safe passage of the arms.[211] Connolly told Denis McCullough, who was President of the Supreme Council of the I.R.B. but was not aware of the details of the plans for the Rising, that no fighting was contemplated in Ulster and that he would be instructed before the date of the Rising to bring the Belfast Volunteers to Tyrone to join the Tyrone Volunteers under their leader, Dr. Patrick McCartan. This Ulster force would then go to Galway to join the Galway Volunteers under the Volunteer organiser Liam Mellows. The mission of this combined force was 'to hold the line of the Shannon'.[212] Robert Brennan of the Wexford Volunteers has recorded, but without further details, that Kilkenny was to have 'worked in' with Wexford.[213] The small body of Volunteers in Clonmel, whose orders 'were known only to the sworn I.R.B. members', intended to 'link up' with other South Tipperary forces and to attack police barracks. They hoped—according to the recollections of fifty years later—to ambush military columns which might be sent against them.[214] The Dundalk Volunteers, together with other Louth and Meath companies, were to have destroyed Slane bridge; after that, apparently, they intended mustering on the Hill of Tara.[215] And so on.

These reports of intentions to distribute the German arms, to 'work in' with neighbouring Volunteer forces, to assemble and to hold 'lines' are clearly only vague statements of general arrangements. Only fragmentary evidence seems to exist of more detailed plans. Practically all that we know relates to the landing and distribution of the arms. The only proposed later general movements that are mentioned are a concentration of the local Volunteer forces and those of Tipperary—or all the west Munster forces—at Limerick, followed by an advance to the relief of the insurgents in Dublin.[216] There is also a still more vague statement that action was to be taken against the troops in their own areas (the Curragh?) by Volunteers in the counties adjoining Dublin.[217] Pearse is said to have directed country commanders to work out details for their own areas,[218] but one can scarcely suppose that the general plan was as vague as the evidence makes it sound; if it was, the Volunteers were merely told to 'rise', or to bring about an 'armed revolt'. It seems clear, both from the little we know of the planning and from the activities of the week, that the distribution of forces in the country, as in the city, contemplated a warfare of position and of concentrated bodies rather than a guerrilla warfare of small forces.[219] The possibility of breaking through the troops and taking to the hills and continuing the fight there was canvassed in more than one of the Dublin positions before Easter Week was out. When de Valera's Vice-Commandant made this suggestion on Thursday, de Valera told him that no such plan had been discussed beforehand.[220] Major MacBride advised his comrades in Jacob's factory never to allow themselves 'to be cooped up inside the walls of a building again'.[221]

Of all the Volunteer activities of 1916 the movements in Cos. Dublin and Meath, culminating in the fight at Ashbourne, approximate most closely to the hostilities of 1919–21. Ashe's 5th Battalion followed Connolly's orders to act in their own area with a view to aiding 'in the dispersal of enemy forces'; although they succeeded in their object,[222] their activities had no direct effect on the situation in the city. Ashe's men camped at first near Finglas. They failed in their attempts to interrupt communications on the Great Northern and Midland Great Western Railway lines. They seized Donabate, Swords and Garristown police barracks later on and, on Thursday, on their way to destroy the Navan branch railway line at Batterstown, near Fairyhouse, they attacked Ashbourne barracks. The Ashbourne police had been reinforced to a strength of a District Inspector and 15 men, but they were hard pressed by the Volunteers. A column of 2 Inspectors and 55 policemen which approached Ashbourne from Slane was surprised by the Volunteer rearguard at Rath crossroads. Ashe, who had in all 37 (later 44) men, immediately attacked the police column and forced its surrender after five and a half hours' fighting. 2 Volunteers were killed and 5 wounded and 8 policemen were killed and 15 wounded. Ashe surrendered, on 30 April, on orders from Pearse; he had by then captured almost 100 police carbines.[223]

The insurgents were led in Co. Galway by the Volunteer organiser Liam Mellows. Action commenced on Tuesday, 25 April when Gort, Clarenbridge and Oranmore police barracks were unsuccessfully attacked. Some policemen were made prisoners and the main Dublin railway line was cut at Oranmore. A column of police and military reached Oranmore from Galway, partly by road and partly by rail, at 7.30 p.m. on Tuesday and Mellows and the Volunteers withdrew to the agricultural station at Athenry. Galway, where there was a small military force in the depot of the Connaught Rangers, was much alarmed by these movements and a request for 200 troops was sent by wireless to the naval station at Queenstown (Cobh). A reconnoitring party of 24 police and 10 soldiers in 9 cars was engaged by Volunteers at Carnmore on the Tuam road outside the town early on Wednesday morning, and at 2.30 that afternoon the sloop H.M.S. *Laburnum*, which had just arrived in the roads from Cork harbour, fired 9 rounds on an imaginary force 'of rebels advancing on Galway town' by the Tuam road.[224]

The cruiser H.M.S. *Gloucester* reached Galway from Cork harbour on Thursday and landed 100 troops. Mellows had then —he was in the agricultural station until Thursday afternoon— between 500 and 600 men, who were armed with 25 rifles, 60 revolvers, about 300 shotguns and 60 pikes. The Volunteers skirmished with the police outside Athenry, but withdrew in the afternoon to Moyode Castle, 6 miles to the south. Mellows tore up the Limerick railway line near Craughwell, and, suffering by then from a shortage of food and other supplies, decided on Friday to move further south in the hope of spreading the Rising to Clare and Limerick. He marched with between 350 and 400 men to Limepark on the Clare border about 5.0 o'clock that evening. On the same day a small column of troops from Galway entered Athenry and the 2/8th Battalion of the Sherwood Foresters reached Athlone from Dublin. The local police, reinforced by 200 constables from Ulster, had meanwhile been concentrating at Loughrea. Mellows was aware of these movements of his foes—the government strength had indeed been greatly exaggerated by some of his informants—and it was decided in the early hours of Saturday morning to disband the insurgent force. The Galway insurgents had held together throughout and, after the initial moves, had acted on the defensive. Mellows seems to have extemporised rather than followed a prearranged plan; he appears to have made no attempt to move towards the Shannon.[225]

The Rising in Co. Wexford was characterised by a similar defensive concentration. The Enniscorthy Volunteers took possession of their town at 4.0 a.m. on Thursday, 27 April. Paul Galligan, the Wexford Brigade Commandant, had reached Enniscorthy from Dublin on the previous evening, bringing orders from Connolly that British reinforcements were to be prevented from passing from Rosslare to Dublin. The Enniscorthy police shut themselves up in their barracks, where, save for a few shots, they were not molested. The Volunteers, who were astride the main line, disrupted rail traffic. They were 300 strong. Galligan occupied Ferns, whence the police withdrew to concentrate at Arklow, and the military collected their strength at Wexford town. Enniscorthy surrendered on Monday, 1 May, following a visit by two of the Volunteer officers, under military escort, to Pearse to confirm the validity of his surrender order. Since no attempt was made to move troops through the county towards Dublin, the only discernible effect of the Wexford operations on the Dublin military situation was that they caused the despatch of a small force by sea on Thursday to reinforce the guard at the explosives factory at Arklow.[226]

*   *   *   *

The casualties of the Rising amounted to about 500 killed and 2,500 wounded. The insurgents had about 60 killed (exclusive of the 16 executions) and—it appears—more than twice that number wounded.[227] Civilian casualties were more than 300 killed and perhaps as many as 2,000 wounded.[228] The troops and police, according to the official return, had 132 killed and 397 wounded.[229]

Pearse said in his final manifesto: 'I am satisfied that we should have accomplished more, that we should have accomplished the task of enthroning, as well as proclaiming, the Irish Republic as a Sovereign State, had our arrangements for a simultaneous rising of the whole country, with a combined plan as sound as the Dublin plan has been proved to be, been allowed to go through on Easter Sunday.'[230] Pearse's statements during the week reveal him as a good propagandist, and we must accept this one, complete with its ambiguous reference to the plan for a country-wide Rising, as propaganda rather than a report of what Pearse believed to be fact.[231] Desmond Fitzgerald tells us that both Pearse and Plunkett, when in conversation with him in the G.P.O., 'spoke of how much bigger an event [the Rising] would have been had the original plans gone forward unchecked.

303

But,' he adds, 'they did not suggest that even in that case we might have expected a military victory.'[232]

The Rising was, like all revolutionary attempts, a gamble. It was launched by men who believed that any effort was better than none, but whose plan of operations had not been, and could not have been, fully worked out. All revolutionaries extemporise; it is only their determination to be revolutionaries that is fixed. Pearse and his comrades left many military details to be settled by extemporaneous arrangement. They displayed a boundless, almost an arrogant, self-confidence—a basic requirement, too, of revolution, and of leadership; a quality that Desmond Ryan has epitomised as an 'extraordinary one-ideaed outlook on insurrection'.[233] They were opportunists; and they pushed MacNeill aside because he was an opportunist of a less effective kind, one who was prepared to take advantage of tomorrow's situation, not—as they were—of today's. Although the I.R.B. men were not militarists, they were—of all those, British and Irish, whose eyes were fixed on the Volunteers—the only ones who were aware that an armed force can fulfil its purpose only in arms.

Pearse and Connolly were followed by the rank and file of the Volunteers and Irish Citizen Army with outstanding courage and devotion. On the whole, the insurgents showed, in a week of severe fighting, remarkable military competence. It was these things, almost as much as the execution of the leaders, that made a political success out of the military failure of Easter Week. The Irish public opinion that, as Parnell saw so clearly, measures everything for itself, soon saw that the Rising was something to be proud of.

G. A. HAYES-McCOY.

1. *Royal Commission on the Rebellion in Ireland. Minutes of Evidence, etc.* (1916) (Hereafter quoted as *Royal Commission. Evidence*), p. 83.

2. Result of the Enniscorthy Trials announced 15 May 1916—*Sinn Fein Rebellion Handbook* (*Weekly Irish Times*, 1916) (Hereafter quoted as *Rebellion Handbook*), p. 58. R. Brennan, *Allegiance* (1950), who describes the court-martial proceedings, pp. 84 ff, does not mention the pass-book.

3. *Royal Commission on the Rebellion in Ireland. Report* (1916), p. 12.

4. The book is presumably filed away in British custody with the remainder of the records of the courts-martial. One should, however, note the distinct possibility, apparently unseen by the Royal Commission, that the book contains a record, made after the event, of what had happened in Dublin on Easter Monday, rather than a plan drawn up beforehand. D. Lynch, *The I.R.B. and the 1916 Insurrection* (ed. F. O'Donoghue, 1957) (Hereafter quoted as D. Lynch, *I.R.B.*), p. 163 records that a messenger was sent from the G.P.O., Dublin to Co. Wexford at 4.0 a.m. on Tuesday, 25 April 1916. This was Vice-Commandant P. Galligan of the Wexford Brigade, Irish Volunteers, who arrived in Enniscorthy on Wednesday evening with a message from James Connolly—R. Brennan, *op. cit.*, p. 64; statement of the Enniscorthy Irish Volunteer Captain S. Ó Dubhghaill, *Irish Independent Golden Jubilee Supplement, 1966*, p. 20. County Inspector Sharpe said that the pass-book was found on one of a party which had fired on a police patrol. Since no such incident appears to have occurred in Enniscorthy, the arrest must have been made elsewhere in Co. Wexford. P. Galligan went from Enniscorthy to Ferns after Thursday.

There are at least two other references to documentary plans of proposed insurgent operations in 1916. J. Doolan (4th Battalion, Dublin Brigade, Irish Volunteers, 1916) says that Cathal Brugha (Vice-Commandant of that Battalion) claimed that he was given before Easter Week 'a copy of the plans for the Rising'—*Sunday Independent Easter Rising Commemorative Supplement*, 1966, p. 7; see also report of lecture by F. O'Donoghue, *Irish Times*, 26 April 1966, and *cf.* D. Ryan, *The Rising* (3rd edn., 1957), p. 229. William O'Brien, General Secretary, Irish Transport and General Workers' Union to 1946, claims that James Connolly told him of the insurgents' arrangements some time before the Rising, saying that only two other persons and himself were aware of the complete military plans, 'of which three copies only were made'—Introduction to D. Ryan, *Labour and Easter Week* (1949), pp. 11 f. What became of the copies mentioned by Connolly is unknown. Brugha's copy was, on his instructions, burnt by his wife. R. M. Fox, *History of the Irish Citizen Army* (1943), p. 131, outlines a vague and unrealistic plan said to have been related by Michael Mallin, Connolly's colleague in the Irish Citizen Army. Countess Markievicz claimed that she and Mallin had been entrusted by Connolly with 'enough of the plans of the Rising' to be able to carry on if anything happened to Connolly—memoir printed in R. McHugh (ed.), *Dublin 1916*, pp. 122 f. See also J. Van Voris, *Constance de Markievicz* (1967), p. 173.

The Making of 1916

5. Chalmers in *Royal Commission Evidence*, p. 39. Lieut.-Col. W. Edgeworth Johnstone, Chief Commissioner, Dublin Metropolitan Police agreed with Chalmers; he thought the Rising was 'all done very well' and praised the articles on military matters which had appeared before the Rising in *The Irish Volunteer*—*Ibid.*, p. 55. Sir Matthew Nathan, Under Secretary for Ireland (who had been a Lieut.-Col. in the Royal Engineers) thought that 'the conduct of the insurrection showed greater organising power and more military skill than had been attributed to the Volunteers' —*Ibid.*, p. 10. For modern military appreciations of the Rising see Col. P. J. Hally, 'The Easter 1916 Rising in Dublin: the Military Aspects' in *The Irish Sword*, VII, pp. 313 ff and VIII, pp. 48 ff; and Col. E. O'Neill, 'The Battle of Dublin, 1916' in *An Cosantoir*, XXVI, pp. 211 ff and report of lecture, *Irish Times*, 3 January 1966.

6. Nathan was aware of the claim of history when he said after the Rising 'I hope some effort is being made by the military authorities to discover exactly what were the places and orders for the insurrection and that they have not disposed of all of the prisoners who could give information as to this'—L. Ó Broin, *Dublin Castle and the 1916 Rising* (1966), p. 162, quoting Nathan to Birrell, the Irish Chief Secretary, 11 May 1916.

7. Commandant Ceannt, for example, told his wife on Saturday evening that the Rising would begin next day and that he would occupy the South Dublin Union with the 4th Battalion—Aine Ceannt, 'Looking Back to 1916' in *The Leader*, 20 April 1946. Ceannt occupied that position on Easter Monday. Commandant Daly knew as early as February 1916 that the 1st Battalion would fight in the Four Courts area. Commandant de Valera also knew in advance that his 3rd Battalion would occupy the positions which it did—see the statement of one of his Company Captains quoted in *Irish Press*, supplement, 9 April 1966, p. 11.

8. County Inspector Sharpe (see Note 1 above) was asked at the Royal Commission enquiry if the plan which was found in Wexford had listed any places in Dublin which were not seized—a natural question of men who were impressed by the insurgent behaviour and wanted to know if the insurgents had hoped to do even more. Sharpe said no—*Royal Commission. Evidence*, p. 83.

9. *Cf.* M. Ó Dubhghaill, *Insurrection Fires at Eastertide*, pp. 236 ff on the question of leadership. He is concerned to quote the views of D. Lynch, *I.R.B.* on this matter against those of P. S. O'Hegarty, *History of Ireland under the Union* (1952) and R. M. Fox, *op. cit.*, but much regarding the insurgent leadership still remains obscure. It is hard to believe that the 1916 Rising was the work of a committee.

10. *Royal Commission. Evidence*, pp. 39, 55. Wimborne's answer was 'I do not know', Edgeworth Johnstone's 'I am sure there were. I know one soldier amongst them who was in the [British] Army'.

11. Major John McBride, who fought with the Boers and was executed for his part in the Rising, was not in the counsels of the leaders.

12. P. Béaslaí, *Michael Collins and the Making of a New Ireland* (1926), I, pp. 74 ff has an interesting statement on MacDiarmada. For a fine biographical account see Rev. C. J. Travers, 'Sean MacDiarmada, 1883–1916' in *Breifne*, III, pp. 1 ff—see in particular p. 34, in which Fr. Travers agrees with the author that 'MacDiarmada was not a military man'.

13. It has often been said that Connolly was a soldier in his youth. *Cf.* C. Duff, *Six Days to Shake an Empire* (1966), p. 120; *Irish Times*, supplement, 7 April 1966, p. 7 (where it is claimed that he was a corporal). C. D. Greaves, *Life and Times of James Connolly* (1961), pp. 16, 20, 21 f, claims that Connolly joined the 1st Battalion King's Liverpool Regiment at a very early age in 1882 and served in garrison in Ireland until 1889. There is no direct evidence of this. Greaves makes odd and incorrect statements: that the regiment's uniform was green and the badge a crowned harp and that Connolly was 'a raw militiaman' while he served in the regiment. D. Ryan, *James Connolly* (1924) makes no mention of Connolly's army service.

14. George Russell (Æ) said of the insurgent leaders, after the Rising, that 'they had no intellect. Connolly was the only one with a real grip in his mind. They were rather featherbrained idealists'—quoted in L. Ó Broin, *op. cit.*, p. 182. For an estimate of Connolly as a leader see D. Lynch, *op. cit.*, pp. 84 f and *cf.* D. MacDonagh, *An Cosantoir*, XXVI, pp. 398 ff. Connolly appears to have been the author of the notes on military matters in *The Workers' Republic* in 1915 and 1916. He lectured on street fighting in Cork in January 1916, on which occasion he advocated an urban rather than a rural rising—F. O'Donoghue, *Tomás MacCurtain* (1958), p. 61. D. Ryan, *The Rising*, p. 58, says that some I.R.B. men regarded Connolly's views on military matters as 'hopelessly amateur, short-sighted and reckless'. M. Ó Dubhghaill, *op. cit.*, pp. 229 f quotes Cathal Brugha's attribution of the Dublin plan of operations to Connolly; Brugha, in making this statement, gave an account of the plan which is in part incomprehensible. We must remember that Connolly could not have played a leading part—Diarmuid Lynch would have said any part—in planning the Rising until after 21/22 January 1916, when he became a member of the military committee of the I.R.B.—D. Lynch, *I.R.B.*, p. 112. According to Lynch (pp. 30, 99, 114, 134, 152), Pearse outlined 'early in

The Making of 1916

January 1916 'the plan of insurrection for the south-west and west. Connolly could not have had anything to do with this.

15. F. X. Martin, 'Eoin MacNeill on the 1916 Rising' in *Irish Historical Studies*, XII, pp. 247, 255. D. Lynch, *op. cit.*, p. 131 says that Pearse, Ceannt and Plunkett were appointed as a military committee because, having 'devoted special attention to military study', they were 'deemed the best fitted to formulate plans for an insurrection'.

16. J. Stephens on the other hand said of Plunkett that he 'would never strike one as a militant person'—J. Stephens, *The Insurrection in Dublin* (3rd edn., 1965), p. 78. *Cf.* L. Ó Briain, *Cuimhní Cinn* (1951), pp. 162 f (to whom Plunkett said, speaking of the plan of the Rising, 'Nothing was overlooked; nothing was forgotten').

17. P. S. O'Hegarty, *op. cit.*, pp. 700 f.

18. D. Ryan, *The Rising*, pp. 11 f, 268. W. O'Brien, *Fifty Years of Liberty Hall* (1959), p. 67 agrees. D. Lynch, *op. cit.*, p. 113, is on his guard against giving Connolly too great a share in the planning of the Rising; he agrees with O'Hegarty that there were 'insurrectionary plans' before May 1915.

19. J. M. Heuston, *Headquarters Battalion, Army of the Irish Republic, Easter Week 1916* (1966), p. 16.

20. P. Béaslaí (who was Daly's second-in-command), *op. cit.*, I, p. 98. *Dublin Brigade Review* (National Association of the Old I.R.A., 1939), pp. 13 f.

21. D. Ryan, *op. cit.*, pp. 187 ff. *Dublin Brigade Review*, p. 27.

22. *Ibid.*, p. 36. *The Catholic Bulletin*, VIII (1918), pp. 153 ff, 205 ff, 257 ff, 309 ff, and for the Marrowbone Lane post pp. 359 f.

23. R. M. Fox, *History of the Irish Citizen Army*, pp. 144 ff.

24. So commissioned on Saturday, 22 April—*Ibid.*, p. 136; *Fifty Years of Liberty Hall*, p. 68.

25. One near the College of Surgeons (L. Ó Broin, *Dublin Castle and the 1916 Rising*, quoting A. H. Norway, p. 99), another near the Shelbourne Hotel (J. Stephens, *op. cit.*, p. 18; L. Stokes's account in R. McHugh, *Dublin 1916*, p. 65), a third near the Hotel Russell (L. Ó Briain, *op. cit.*, p. 84), and a fourth near Hume Street (*Catholic Bulletin*, VIII, p. 503).

26. D. Ryan, *op. cit.*, p. 77 says that Connolly outlined to an unnamed Citizen Army officer the plan for St. Stephen's Green, which 'had been selected [for occupation] because it commanded so many points for rifle fire'. It is difficult to understand this, but Ryan apparently means that it was thought that it would be possible—and effective—to fire along the streets entering the Green. The Green seems to have been one of Connolly's blind spots. Was its occupation due to the fact that military men were at that time preoccupied with entrenchment and that it was a good place for digging trenches?

27. For what happened at the Castle see pp. 263–6.

28. *Fifty Years of Liberty Hall*, p. 69. Clarke and MacDiarmada, the two 'civilians'—there seems to be no record of their ever having worn uniform —met them at the G.P.O.

29. So called in Pearse's manifesto dated Thursday, 28 April 1916 (*sic*) printed in *Rebellion Handbook*, p. 43. (J. J. Bouch, writing in *Irish Press*, 16 April 1936, commented on the mistake in dating—Thursday was the 27th, not the 28th. Bouch believed that this document, which is timed 9.30 a.m., was written in the small hours of Thursday morning. Lynch, *op. cit.*, p. 172, accepts this. Lynch speaks of the document as having been printed during the Rising, but it appears to be known only in the form of a photograph of a manuscript. The photograph was issued to the press by the military authorities after the Rising. The manuscript presumably still exists among the court-martial material). *Irish War News*, No. 1, 24 April 1916 has 'the Army of the Republic' (*Rebellion Handbook*, p. 42). For Pearse's election as President and nomination as Commander-in-Chief see L. N. Le Roux (trs. D. Ryan), *Patrick H. Pearse*, p. 377. For the use of the title Irish Republican Army (I.R.A.) in 1916 the following may be seen—D. Ryan, *The Rising*, pp. 130, 204; account of Elizabeth O'Farrell, Pearse's messenger (who said 'The Irish Republican Army they call themselves') in *The Catholic Bulletin*, VII (1917), p. 268, reprinted in R. McHugh, *Dublin 1916*, p. 208; statement of Countess Markievicz, *Ibid.*, p. 122. The letters I.R.A. were used by the Fenians who raided Canada in 1866—see *The Irish Sword*, III, p. 47 and illustration on p. 16.

30. Pearse calls it 'the Dublin Division' (manifesto dated 28 April quoted above); *Irish War News*, No. 1 refers to the insurgent force in Dublin as 'the Dublin division of the Army of the Republic' and says that Connolly commanded 'the Dublin districts'; Connolly, in orders dated 25 April (*Rebellion Handbook*, p. 42; *Fifty Years of Liberty Hall*, following p. 40), uses 'Army of the Irish Republic (Dublin Command)'.

The Making of 1916

31. The vagaries of Connolly's command show how unsystematized things were. He acted at the surrender as though he had reverted to his pre-insurrection status; he surrendered for 'the men only [he added this word with his own hand] under my own command' (*Rebellion Handbook*, pp. 4, 11)—that is, for the Irish Citizen Army. He told Fr. Aloysius that he spoke only for his own men as to surrender—*Capuchin Annual*, 1942, p. 213. On the other hand, he had not hesitated to give orders for Co. Wexford—see p. 302—nor to declare what the Ulster orders were to be— see p. 299.

32. Miss L. Stokes saw these two barricades on Tuesday (R. McHugh, *op. cit.*, p. 67) and they are mentioned by many others. For the occupation of the G.P.O. see W. J. Brennan-Whitmore in *An tÓglach*, IV, No. 1 (16 January 1926), pp. 3 ff.

33. J. M. Heuston, *op. cit.*, p. 32. Of Captain Heuston's 16 men, 3 were from other units. See also the statement of P. J. Stephenson, one of Heuston's men, written a few years after the Rising and reproduced for private circulation by his family in 1966, p. 13.

34. P. Béaslaí, *op. cit.*, I, p. 99, notes that since MacDonagh was brigadier the 2nd was his 'old battalion'. Commandant T. Hunter had succeeded him in command of the battalion.

35. *Cf.* P. Ó Cearnaigh's account in S. de Burca, *The Soldier's Song*, pp. 113 ff and *The Catholic Bulletin*, VIII, pp. 452 ff.

36. P. Béaslaí *loc. cit.*, says that the occupation of Jacob's factory 'was of no great apparent military value, and no serious attack was made on it during the week', and that it was 'a meaningless waste of men'. P. S. O'Hegarty, *op. cit.*, pp. 701 f, says that Plunkett—to whom he attributes the working out of the plan of operations—believed that 'Unionist' buildings 'like Jacob's Factory' would not be shelled by the government. D. Ryan, *op. cit.*, p. 78 (and see also pp. 164 ff) says that, in the week before the Rising, Connolly and MacDonagh 'made a thorough tour of the Camden Street area and surveyed Jacob's factory'. Commandant Hunter, accompanied by two of his Company Captains, did the same thing on Easter Sunday night—see J. M. Heuston, *op. cit.*, pp. 60 f, who also raises the question if the occupation of Jacob's factory was a last minute arrangement.

37. J. M. Heuston, *op. cit.* gives the arguments to support an intention to constitute a special Headquarters Battalion of the Irish Volunteers on the outbreak of the Rising. It is suggested that this was to have been done

by taking one company from each of the five Dublin Brigade battalions, and that the new battalion, probably with the addition of the Kimmage force and an Irish Citizen Army detachment, was to have occupied the G.P.O. and provided outposts in the headquarters area. D. Lynch, *op. cit.*, pp. 157, 159 calls the force which occupied the G.P.O. the Headquarters Battalion.

38. This was noticed by the newspapers at the time (*Cf. Rebellion Handbook*, p. 21) and has been mentioned since by those writers—there have been amazingly few of them—who have deigned to mention the British at all. President de Valera has said (*Sunday Press*, 10 April 1966. p. 13) that he was at a Volunteer conference before the Rising at which the battalion Commandants were told of the positions they were to occupy and that 'the positions were selected because they lay across the routes to the city centre which would be taken by the principal British garrisons surrounding the city'. He was accompanied to Grand Canal Street bridge by Connolly before the Rising and they both looked over the position which de Valera later occupied.

39. A contemporary observer, among the non-combatants, of some of these possibilities was F. A. McKenzie. See his *The Irish Rebellion* (1916), pp. 56 f.

40. P. Béaslaí, *op. cit.*, I, pp. 100 f, says that 'the greatest blunder of all' was the locating of headquarters in the G.P.O. The leaders should have been 'in a small obscure building in some side street. By concentrating the heart and brains of the movement in one large central building that could easily be surrounded and isolated they made the task of the English troops a much simpler one'. It is of course hard to gainsay that, although retrospection may place a high emotional value on the blazing G.P.O. Michael Staines, who served in the G.P.O., has said that Pearse told him that the original hope was to remove headquarters from the G.P.O. to Dublin Castle (Quoted by J. M. Heuston, *op. cit.*, p. 36). The insurgent intentions regarding the Castle are referred to at pp. 263–6.

41. See below, p. 303.

42. D. Lynch, *op. cit.*, p. 157.

43. W. O'Brien in Introduction to D. Ryan, *Labour and Easter Week*, p. 21.

44. For the conception of the insurrection as 'a blood sacrifice for a principle' see P. S. O'Hegarty, *History of Ireland under the Union*, pp. 700 f.

The Making of 1916

P. Béaslaí, *op. cit.*, I, p. 101 says there was 'no hope of military success'. This meant (J. Stephens, *The Insurrection in Dublin*, p. 70) that 'they seized certain central and strategical districts, garrisoned those and held them until they were put out of them'. For how long, in these conditions, did they hope to hold out? W. J. Brennan-Whitmore (*Irish Independent*, 11 April 1966) says that MacDiarmada declared shortly before the Rising 'that they would seize Dublin and hold it for a week'. (Col. E. O'Neill, *An Cosantóir*, XXVI, p. 215, explains the wide flung insurgent perimeter as a necessary consequence of an insurgent effort to 'hold Dublin'). D. FitzGerald records (*Irish Times*, supplement, 7 April 1966, p. 1) that The O'Rahilly said on Easter Monday 'By a miracle we might last for twenty-four hours, but I don't think we'll go for that long'. On the other hand, D. Ryan (*The Rising*, p. 98) quotes Ceannt as having told his wife 'If we last a month, the British will come to terms', and in the G.P.O., where they had brought in provisions for six weeks, they 'talked confidently of holding out for two or three weeks'—J. Ryan, 'The G.P.O.' in *Capuchin Annual*, 1942, p. 223.

45. Nathan noted that the insurgents had, by occupying buildings, 'avoided any attack involving concentration or movements under fire'— *Royal Commission. Evidence*, p. 10. This, we observe, was a new tactic in Irish insurgency, and its employment made it possible for the insurgents of 1916 to launch their revolt. Wimborne commented: 'There was no conflict in the streets. The ordinary tactics of revolutionists, which I imagine to be barricades, and so on, were not resorted to . . . at the very start they took to the houses and house-tops'—*Ibid.*, p. 39. These were observations of fundamental importance.

46. Evidence of Colonel H. V. Cowan, Assistant Adjutant-General, Irish Command, *Royal Commission. Evidence*, p. 69. General Maxwell's report to F. M. Sir John French, C.-in-C. Home Forces, 25 May 1916 printed in *Rebellion Handbook*, pp. 160 ff (Hereafter quoted as Maxwell, *Report*) gives the time as 12.15.

47. *Irish War News*, No. 1 (*Rebellion Handbook*, p. 42) says 'the Castle [was] attacked'.

48. Evidence of Colonel Cowan, *loc. cit.*

49. Article by James Connolly in *The Workers' Republic*, 11 March 1916. D. Ryan and W. O'Brien, who quote and comment on this article in *Labour and Easter Week* (ed. by the former), pp. 18 f, 152 ff, omit the possibility of Connolly's having had his tongue in his cheek when he wrote it—that is, of his intention of disarming his readers among the G Branch as to *his own* intentions respecting the Castle.

50. Sir Mackenzie Chalmers, referring to the contents of the Wexford pass-book (see Note 1 above) at the Royal Commission enquiry, asked County Inspector Sharpe—'It has been said they never intended to seize the Castle. Was that mentioned?'—that is, was it mentioned in the pass-book. Sharpe answered—'No, it was not'.—*Royal Commission. Evidence*, p. 83.

51. Introduction to D. Ryan, *op. cit.*, pp. 18 f.

52. After the Rising, Dublin was full of 'reasons' to explain insurgent failures to act differently. R. M. Fox, for example (*History of the Irish Citizen Army*, p. 146) quotes a report that Connolly wanted to use the Bank of Ireland as insurgent headquarters, but that Pearse opposed this becaust he feared that the old Irish Houses of Parliament might be injured by fire. Statements regarding the consequences of the insurgent 'failure' to occupy Trinity College, Dublin are commonplace. Fox (*op. cit.*, p. 149) agrees with William O'Brien that 'there was never any question of taking the Castle'. On the other hand, Miss Helena Molony, who was with the force in the City Hall, has said that Connolly told her that the attack on the Castle was to have taken place a little before the occupation of the other positions and that news that it had been taken, or even attacked, would draw support. And Fox (p. 147) records an alleged statement made by Connolly on Monday morning to the Citizen Army detachment which went to the Castle—'The Citizen Army will have the post of honour. Your detachment will attack. The others will be taking up defensive positions'. As suggested in Note 49 however, it would be unwise to take all the statements of their intentions made beforehand by the leaders of the revolt at their face value.

53. P. Béaslaí, *Michael Collins and the Making of a New Ireland*, I, p. 97.

54. In S. de Burca, *The Soldier's Song*, p. 116.

55. L. N. Le Roux (trs. D. Ryan), *Patrick H. Pearse*, p. 384.

56. D. Macardle, *The Irish Republic* (4th edn., 1951), pp. 169 f.

57. D. Ryan, *The Rising*, pp. 117 f.

58. He alleges that the 'original plan' was to take the City Hall first and *then* to seize the guardroom.

59. D. Lynch, *I.R.B.*, pp. 77 f, 105 f.

60. A Citizen Army man at the Green told James Stephens (*The Insurrection in Dublin*, p. 20) that the Castle was theirs. Countess Markievicz told Margaret Skinnider on Monday evening that an attempt had been made 'to enter Dublin Castle and plant the flag of the Republic on the roof', but that it had failed because Seán Connolly was shot (Miss Skinnider's account in *Irish Press*, supplement, 9 April 1966, p. 12). News that the Castle had been taken was brought by the guard of a train to Wexford at 2.0 o'clock on Tuesday morning—R. Brennan, *Allegiance*, p. 56.

61. D. FitzGerald's account in *Irish Times*, supplement, 7 April 1966, p. 1.

62. Nathan to Birrell, 24 April 1916, quoted in L. Ó Broin, *Dublin Castle and the 1916 Rising*, p. 93. One of the Viceregal aides said on Monday 'They tried to rush the Castle'. (*Ibid.*, p. 108). Later, when giving evidence before the Royal Commission, Nathan recollected the warnings which had been received that the insurgents had designs on the Castle—the statement made by Bailey on his arrest in Kerry (*Royal Commission. Evidence*, p. 8) and what he called a 'sham attack' that had been made by the Irish Citizen Army on the Castle in October 1915 (*Ibid.*, p. 13. Edgeworth Johnstone of the D.M.P. held that this 'attack' was 'a fairy tale' and that the Castle did not form the 'special idea' of the October manoeuvres—*Ibid.*, p. 51).

63. L. Ó Briain in D. Lynch, *op. cit.*, p. 105. There is no question, of course, of a reflection on Captain Seán Connolly, who was killed on the roof of the City Hall early in the afternoon.

64. Account of a V.A.D. nurse, first published in *Blackwood's Magazine*, December 1916, reprinted in R. McHugh, *Dublin 1916*, p. 90.

65. The Beggar's Bush garrison consisted of 'not more than 10 men'— statement of one 'who was present at the Mount Street action' in *Irish Times*, 4 July 1966. There were also (after Monday) the members of the Volunteer Training Corps and (after Wednesday) a platoon of A Company, 2/7th Sherwood Foresters who 'knew nothing of the district, much less of the existence of the barracks' until they were called in by the Training Corps sentries—*Rebellion Handbook*, pp. 19 f. As to the insurgent intelligence, F. Robbins, who was present, says that scouts reported to Liberty Hall during the night of 23/24 April on the disposition of government troops in the city—*Sunday Press*, 10 April 1966, p. 14. Miss M. Skinnider (*loc. cit.*) says that Connolly sent her by bicycle on Monday morning 'to scout about the city and report if troops from any of the barracks were stirring'. She went to scout at St. Stephen's Green before

Mallin's arrival there, to see if any soldiers were in sight; after his arrival she was sent up Leeson Street to see if soldiers were leaving Beggar's Bush or Portobello barracks.

66. The best statement of strength is in D. Lynch, *op. cit.*, pp. 143 f, but note that J. M. Heuston, *Headquarters Battalion, Army of the Irish Republic, Easter Week 1916*, p. 8 suggests that the G.P.O. garrison may have been a little bigger than Lynch allows. The total was perhaps a little bigger than 1,600.

67. Sir John Maxwell's figure is 2,427 of all ranks (Maxwell, *Report*, p. 160). Col. Cowan, giving evidence before the Royal Commission (*Royal Commission. Evidence*, p. 68) says 2,385. The total force in Ireland then was about 3,000 cavalry, 17,000 infantry and 1,000 artillery, all draft-finding units and third line troops—Maxwell to the Prime Minister, 12 May 1916, quoted in L. Ó Broin, *op. cit.*, p. 117. Some 150,000 Irishmen had volunteered for service in the British Army since the outbreak of war in 1914—Birrell to the Royal Commission (*op. cit.*, p. 24).

68. Available strengths of the units from Maxwell, *Report, loc. cit.* The *General Monthly Return of Regimental Strengths of the British Army*, May 1916 (Hereafter quoted as *Monthly Return*), pp. 4 f gives the effective strength of the 6th Reserve Cavalry Regiment as 1,187 all ranks. The *Weekly Return of the British Army*, 1 May 1916 (Hereafter quoted as *Weekly Return*), p. 16 gives an establishment strength of 1,059, a total strength of 1,171 and an effective strength of 885. No. 2 Cavalry Depot, which supplied drafts for the 4th, 8th, 11th and 13th Hussars, was also in Dublin.

69. S. Geoghegan, *The Campaigns and History of the Royal Irish Regiment*, II, p. 102. *Monthly Return*, pp. 216 f, gives effective strength as 1,252; *Weekly Return*, p. 23 gives establishment strength 2,086, total strength 1,188 and effective strength 825.

70. The 10th was a 2nd Unit Reserve battalion with (*Monthly Return*, pp. 266 f) an effective strength of 1,016. *Weekly Return* (p. 32) gives strengths—establishment 1,017, total 992, and effective 939. There is no complete history of the Royal Dublin Fusiliers for 1914–18.

71. The 3rd was a Reserve battalion with (*Monthly Return*, pp. 260 f) an effective strength of 1,308. *Weekly Return* (p. 26) gives strengths—establishment 2,086, total 1,361, and effective 900. It was made up largely of recruits in training. See C. Falls, *History of the first seven battalions, The Royal Irish Rifles in the Great War*, II (1925), pp. 87 ff. The fact that all the

The Making of 1916

infantry in Dublin was Irish was commented on by the Royal Commission (*Royal Commission. Evidence*, pp. 15 f. Wimborne said 'The Dublins behaved magnificently . . . They were called upon to fire on their own fellow-citizens, and, possibly, their own relatives'—*Ibid.*, p. 38) and of course by the journalistic world (Cf. F. A. McKenzie, *The Irish Rebellion*, pp. 37, 38). *The Freemanés Journal*, 5 May 1916, noted that 'the 4th and 10th Dublins kept the glorious anniversary of their regiment's heroic landing at Sed-el-Barr by defending their own city against the blind, self-devoted victims of the hun'—which was rather hard on the insurgents. The Royal Dublin Fusiliers were in the famous *River Clyde* landing at Gallipoli on 25 April 1915. Pearse's statement 'Irish regiments in the British Army have refused to act against their fellow countrymen' (Manifesto of the Provisional Government to the citizens of Dublin, *Rebellion Handbook*, p. 41) was incorrect.

72. *Royal Commission. Evidence*, pp. 65, 68.

73. Colonel Cowan was asked by the Royal Commission 'Candidly, you were not expecting this?' He replied 'No, not in the least'—*Ibid.*, p. 69. Cf. L. Ó Broin, *op. cit.*, pp. 63, 65, 73.

74. Asked by the Royal Commission (*Royal Commission. Evidence*, p. 38) who technically was in command in Ireland when Friend was away, and if there was another General, Wimborne said that Brigadier-General Lowe was at the Curragh, but that Friend 'gave me to understand that Colonel Cowan and Major Owen Lewis would be responsible for everything'. Friend told the Commission (*Ibid.*, p. 67) that he had told Wimborne before his departure for London that Cowan and Lowe would be his substitutes and that the former would be in control of the administration. Lowe was next in seniority to Friend. Lewis was an officer on Friend's staff. Cowan told the Commission that he was in command in Friend's absence (*Ibid.*, p. 69). M. Caulfield, *The Easter Rebellion*, p. 96, is in error in saying that Cowan was Colonel Kennard's—the Dublin garrison commander's—deputy. L. Ó Broin, *op. cit.*, p. 93, says that it was Nathan and Major Price, a military intelligence officer, who called the troops from Ship Street barracks into the Castle and alerted Command headquarters. Nathan gave details to the Royal Commission (*Evidence*, p. 8) of the police reports as to the insurgents' occupation of the various positions.

75. Maxwell says he ordered out 'all available troops'—Maxwell, *Report, Rebellion Handbook*, p. 160.

76. For the messages to Richmond barracks see S. Geoghegan, *loc. cit.* This seems to be the only reference to the G.P.O. message.

77. Or to the Magazine Fort.

78. P. Holahan in *Capuchin Annual*, 1942, p. 233. Maxwell's *Report, loc. cit.* The carters whom the lancers were escorting stayed with them and were twice relieved by others, who brought forage for the horses—*Rebellion Handbook*, p. 166. Connolly proposed attacking the lancers in Charles Street on Wednesday, using a party from the G.P.O. and another from Daly's command. He hoped particularly to capture the ammunition. The attack was prevented by the movement of the troops into Capel Street on Wednesday evening—I. Callender, 'A Diary of Easter Week, 1916' in *Dublin Brigade Review*, pp. 93 f.

79. For Connolly's ideas on street warfare see *The Workers' Republic*, 1915–16 and *cf. Fifty Years of Liberty Hall*, pp. 26, 64. For Wimborne see Note 45 above.

80. G. F. R. Henderson, *The Science of War* (ed. N. Malcolm, 1905), p. 53.

81. Nathan noted that the attempt to use mounted cavalry was unsuccessful—*Royal Commission. Evidence*, p. 16. James Stephens soliloquized 'It is foolish to send cavalry into street war'—J. Stephens, *The Insurrection in Dublin*, p. 29. The Volunteers thought during the week that cavalry would be used against them. Tin can grenades were being prepared to throw from the roofs at cavalry in O'Connell Street on Monday afternoon. Nails were scattered in Church Street on Wednesday to prevent a cavalry charge if the barricade at Church Street bridge was carried—I. Callender, *op. cit.*, pp. 88, 94. Mounted cavalry was used outside Dublin: at 3 p.m. on Sunday, 30 April 700 lancers and hussars passed northward along Ballymun Road—*Irish Independent*, 26–29 April, 1–4 May 1916. This was part of the force to which Ashe's 5th Battalion surrendered—D. Ryan, *The Rising*, p. 226. Mounted cavalry also patrolled the southern suburbs—I.O., *The Administration of Ireland, 1920* (1921), p. 25.

82. S. Geoghegan, *op. cit.*, II, p. 103. M. Caulfield, *op. cit.*, pp. 102 ff, quotes the evidence of Lieut. (later Major) Malone and of a survivor of the 4th Battalion and gives a spirited account of the attack on the South Dublin Union.

83. Maxwell, *Report, Rebellion Handbook*, loc. cit. For Kennard see C. Falls, *op. cit.*, II, p. 88.

84. For the advance of these troops see the account of Miss L. Stokes in R. McHugh, *Dublin 1916*, p. 64 and the statement of P. J. Stephenson

already quoted, pp. 17–20. D. Ryan, *op. cit.*, p. 159 looks upon the military movements by the quays on Monday and Tuesday as a 'siege' of the Mendicity Institution.

85. Miss Stokes (R. McHugh, *op. cit.*, p. 66) saw the troops in Ship Street barracks late in the afternoon. They were 'standing ready, with bayonets fixed'.

86. L. Ó Briain, *Cuimhní Cinn*, pp. 72 f. *Rebellion Handbook*, p. 23.

87. D. Ryan, *op. cit.*, p. 166, who considers the advance down Camden Street as an attack on MacDonagh's position. C. Falls, *op. cit.*, pp. 88 f for the troops, and *cf. The Catholic Bulletin*, VIII, pp. 452 f.

88. Telephone communication between the military Railway Transport Office in the station and G.H.Q., Parkgate remained intact throughout—statement of P. A. Foley, who was on duty at Amiens Street Station in 1916, in *Sunday Independent Easter Rising Commemorative Supplement*, 1966, p. 2. A sniper in the station fired on the insurgent positions in O'Connell Street during Monday night—D. Ryan, *op. cit.*, p. 135. The station was occupied by troops moving westward from the dock area.

89. *Rebellion Handbook*, p. 221. For the insurgent failure to seize the telephone exchange see R. M. Fox, *History of the Irish Citizen Army*, pp. 172 ff. The exchange was occupied by 2nd Lieut. Kearns and 25 Royal Irish Riflemen, who left Portobello barracks at 1.45 p.m. on Monday —C. Falls, *op. cit.*, II, p. 89. I. Callender (*op. cit.*, p. 90) saw them in the exchange, behind sandbags, on Wednesday.

90. Maxwell, *Report, Rebellion Handbook*, pp. 160 f.

91. For the effect of these and later movements in this area see F. O'Donoghue, 'Easter Week, 1916' in G. A. Hayes-McCoy (ed.), *The Irish at War*, p. 91.

92. *Rebellion Handbook*, p. 17. R. McHugh, *op. cit.*, p. 66 and (an account by a member of the T.C.D. 'garrison'), pp. 160 ff. M. Taaffe, *Those Days are Gone Away* (1959), pp. 173 ff.

93. D. Lynch, *I.R.B.*, p. 160 says that communication with England was disrupted by the cutting of the wires between Dublin and Kingstown (Dun Laoghaire), but the cross-channel cable from the G.P.O. passed through the telegraph office in Amiens Street Railway Station and the military were soon able to reestablish telegraphic communication with London—

statement of P. A. Foley, as quoted in Note 88 above. The wireless message may have been sent by the cruiser *Adventure* (See J. de Courcy Ireland, *The Sea and the Easter Rising*, pp. 40, 46), but it is probable that the *Adventure* did not arrive in Kingstown Harbour until Monday night (See letter of A. N. Bonaparte-Wyse, 3 May 1916, printed in *Irish Times*, 24 April 1965).

94. G. French, *Life of F.M. Sir J. French*, p. 338.

95. Statement of G. C. Duggan, who was employed in the Transport Department of the Admiralty in 1916, in *Sunday Press*, 29 March 1964.

96. '*The Robin Hoods*' 1/7th, 2/7th & 3/7th *Battns. Sherwood Foresters.* Written by Officers of the Battalions (1921), p. 281.

97. Maxwell, *Report, loc. cit.*

98. Major-General Friend, at the Royal Commission's enquiry—*Royal Commission. Evidence*, p. 65. The function explains the use of a cavalry formation to make up the column.

99. Maxwell, *Report, loc. cit.*, who says that just after the call was made 'telephonic communication in Dublin became very interrupted'. The brigade consisted of the 8th and 10th Reserve Cavalry Regiments and the 1st and 2nd Reserve Squadrons, King Edward's Horse (Special Reserve).

100. Original document in National Museum, Dublin, reproduced in L. Ó Briain, *op. cit.*, facing p. 57. For a defence of Cowan against the contemporary allegation that he was 'unduly nervous' in summoning reinforcements see C. Duff, *Six Days to Shake an Empire*, p. 117.

101. Maxwell, *Report, loc. cit.*, gives 4.45 p.m. as the arrival time of the first train, but Cowan (*Royal Commission. Evidence*, p. 69) says 4.15, and he says that the remaining trains came in at twenty minute intervals. Nathan, on the other hand, told the Commission that the first train came at 1.35 p.m. and the second at 2.45 (*Ibid.*, p. 10).

102. E. O'Malley, *On Another Man's Wound* (1936), p. 36, 'found Lancers firing at snipers in a very unmeaningly impressive way' near the North Wall on Tuesday.

103. Statement of P. A. Foley, as quoted in Note 88 above.

104. Edgeworth Johnstone told the Royal Commission (*Evidence*, p. 55)

The Making of 1916

that the special branch men were sent out scouting in plain clothes after the uniformed policemen were withdrawn. 'They sent in a stream of information about the movements of the rebels, the houses they were occupying and so on, and that was passed on to the military'. *Cf.* L. Ó Broin, *op. cit.*, p. 105; L. N. Le Roux, *Patrick H. Pearse*, p. 379.

105. General Lowe said in a report to Home Forces at 11.20 a.m. on Tuesday—'am not attacking their main strength in Sackville Street about G.P.O. till reinforcements arrive.' He said that there were then about 3,500 men available in Dublin; obviously he meant available for immediate use, since there must have been about 5,000 in all. Lowe's report is in the statement of P. A. Foley, as quoted in Note 88 above. Maxwell (*Report, Rebellion Handbook*, p. 161) said: 'The main forces of the rebels now [Tuesday] having been located in and around Sackville Street, the Four Courts and adjoining buildings, it was decided to try to enclose that area north of the Liffey by a cordon of troops so as to localise as far as possible the efforts of the rebels.'

106. Maxwell, *Report, loc. cit.* Cowan (*Royal Commission. Evidence*, p. 69) said that only 600 men were sent to Dublin by the 25th Infantry Brigade.

107. J. Stephens, *The Insurrection in Dublin*, p. 20. An attack in force was expected in the G.P.O. from Tuesday—B. O'Higgins's account, *Wolfe Tone Annual*, 1935, p. 68.

108. *Irish War News*, I, No. 1, 25 April 1916.

109. R. M. Fox, *op. cit.*, pp. 152 f. L. Ó Broin, *op. cit.*, p. 97. The wounded from the attack were of King Edward's Horse (from the Curragh?) and the 4th Hussars (from No. 2 Cavalry Depot?)—account of a V.A.D. nurse in R. McHugh, *Dublin 1916*, pp. 96, 102 f, 119. A report sent through Amiens Street Station Telegraph to G.H.Q. Home Forces at 2.50 a.m. ('We have occupied Municipal Buildings') seems rather to have anticipated the capture of the City Hall—quoted in statement of P. A. Foley; see Note 88 above.

110. Statement of E. Norgrove Hanratty, who was present and who describes the fighting, in *Irish Press*, supplement, 9 April 1966, p. 13.

111. D. Lynch, *I.R.B.*, p. 163. They reached Parliament Street after the City Hall had fallen.

112. F. A. McKenzie, *The Irish Rebellion*, p. 67.

113. M. Caulfield, *The Easter Rebellion*, pp. 160, 166 ff gives details. *Cf.*
Irish Times, supplement, 7 April 1966, p. 16; R. McHugh, *op. cit.*, p. 101;
J. Stephens, *op. cit.*, p. 31. D. Ryan, *The Rising*, p. 121, says that Mallin
had found it impossible to occupy the Shelbourne Hotel because 'fifty
Volunteers and Citizen Army men who should have taken it were simply
not there'. Many such explanations of apparent insurgent neglect are
given. The most recent in this regard appears in J. Van Voris, *Constance de
Markievicz* (1967), pp. 189 ff, where it is said that the Citizen Army
man George Norgrove was to have occupied the Shelbourne Hotel with
fifty men, but that Norgrove was detailed to the G.P.O. and later to
the City Hall (on Monday evening, with eight men—see Note 110)
instead; Mrs. Van Voris says that it was never intended that Mallin
should occupy the Shelbourne with the men he had with him in St.
Stephen's Green. It is impossible to check these assertions; we suffer
from a distinct lack of information regarding the orders of the various
insurgent commanders. Note that Mallin's failure to occupy the Shelbourne is commented on by P. J. Hally (*op. cit.*, VII, p. 321), whose work
is a valuable commentary on the fighting from the modern military
viewpoint.

114. L. Ó Briain, *Cuimhní Cinn*, pp. 88 ff.

115. *Rebellion Handbook*, p. 17.

116. Account of a member of the T.C.D. 'garrison' in R. McHugh,
Dublin 1916, pp. 163 f. M. Taaffe, *Those Days are Gone Away*, p. 175.
The front of the College was being fired on from an insurgent post in
Westmoreland Street, between Fleet Street and the College Restaurant,
from Monday evening until 4 p.m. on Tuesday, when the occupants were
withdrawn and placed in the Imperial Hotel in O'Connell Street—D.
Lynch, *I.R.B.*, pp. 161, 165.

117. *Rebellion Handbook*, pp. 18, 21. Nathan (*Royal Commission. Evidence*,
p. 9) said that only three guns came from Athlone. The artillery establishment in Ireland in 1916 was as follows:—In Athlone—No. 5 Depot, Royal
Field Artillery. 5A Reserve Artillery Brigade (25, 26, 27 Batteries, with an
establishment strength of 573 all ranks in each battery). In Ballincollig—
three batteries. There were also of the Royal Garrison Artillery—in
Derry—one company (with a Special Reserve company in Carrickfergus);
in Cork—three companies (with a Special Reserve company in Spike
Island)—*Monthly Return*, pp. 102, 106, 108, 116, 122; *Weekly Return*, pp. 8,
19. Friend (*Royal Commission. Evidence*, p. 67) said there were no guns in
Dublin before Tuesday. There were no guns in the Curragh. There was
in Athlone 'about the equivalent' of one battery—six 18-pounders; he

*22

The Making of 1916

must have meant that this was the number of guns available. P. J. Stephenson (statement, p. 23) says that the insurgents in the Mendicity Institution heard 'the unmistakable sound of horse drawn artillery' coming from the direction of Kingsbridge after nightfall on Monday (*sic*). The guns—as they believed them to be—and their teams passed along the south quays in front of the Institution and turned southward into Bridgefoot Street. Either Stephenson and his comrades were mistaken in believing that the sounds which they heard betokened the movement of artillery or his memory was at fault and he confused Monday with Tuesday night. The noises may have been caused by the movement of the two guns to Trinity College on Tuesday evening. According to Stephenson, Heuston ordered his men not to attempt to stop the passing party.

118. R. McHugh, *op. cit.*, p. 165.

119. Maxwell, *Report, Rebellion Handbook*, p. 161.

120. There were troops on the roof of University Church on Wednesday —M. Skinnider's account in *Irish Press*, supplement, 9 April 1966, p. 12. These and the troops evident then in Harcourt Street appear to have come from Portobello barracks.

121. *Rebellion Handbook*, p. 217. D. Lynch, *I.R.B.*, p. 163.

122. *Rebellion Handbook*, p. 216. I. Callender (*Dublin Brigade Review*, pp. 88 f) saw a large party of artillerymen at Castleknock on Tuesday. They told him that they had been ordered to go to the Phoenix Park.

123. Only one gun may have been used for this work.

124. The shell fire—about a dozen rounds—did little damage to surrounding buildings. *Rebellion Handbook, loc. cit.* I. Callender, *loc. cit. Irish Independent.* 26–29 April, 1–4 May 1916. Unsuccessful attempts had been made by Daly on Monday night to blow up the two bridges—*Royal Commission. Evidence*, p. 8. In the end, there were 57 1st Battalion men in the G.P.O.—J. M. Heuston, *Headquarters Battalion*, p. 6.

125. D. Lynch, *op. cit.*, pp. 165 f.

126. *Rebellion Handbook*, p. 217. The guns (or gun) were brought down to this area. Three shells were fired from the railway embankment into the grounds of the Christian Brothers' novitiate, Marino, and one into the grounds of the O'Brien Institute on one evening during the week—*Irish Independent, loc. cit.*

Studies in the History of the Rising

127. *Rebellion Handbook*, pp. 10, 39.

128. S. Geoghegan, *The Campaigns and History of the Royal Irish Regiment*, II, p. 103.

129. Ceannt's outpost in Roe's distillery, not far from the British position in the Royal Hospital and on the Kingsbridge-T.C.D. line, was abandoned by the Volunteers on Tuesday. The Ardee Street outpost to the south-east of the Union was withdrawn on Wednesday, Colbert's men from that position joining the Marrowbone Lane post, the garrison of which at the end of the week was over a hundred strong, although it was only twenty at the start—D. Ryan, *op. cit.*, p. 175. The insurgents at the G.P.O., the South Dublin Union, Jacob's factory and St. Stephen's Green all contracted as the week went on. For the retirement into Jacob's factory on Wednesday—following attacks by troops from Portobello barracks—of men from outposts which had been occupied in Camden Street on Tuesday see *The Catholic Bulletin*, VIII, pp. 454 f. D. Ryan (*op. cit.*, pp. 172 ff) fails to see the reason for the British retirement from the South Dublin Union and makes it take place on Wednesday instead of Tuesday; indeed he speaks of the fighting at the Union as having been continuous up to Thursday, which of course it was not.

130. Heuston was ordered to hold the Mendicity Institution for three or four hours so as to delay the approach of troops from the Royal barracks towards the centre of the city—P. Holahan in *Capuchin Annual*, 1942, p. 232. See J. M. Heuston, *op. cit.*, particularly pp. 34 ff, who argues that Ceannt, because of the failure of his full battalion to turn out, was unable to occupy Guinness's brewery and Kingsbridge Station, and that Connolly, realising this, sent Heuston to hold the Institution as the best alternative to Kingsbridge. P. J. Stephenson (statement already quoted, p. 15) says that Heuston explained to his men that their purpose was to engage any troops who might come eastward from the Royal barracks 'until such time as the 1st Battalion had taken over the Four Courts and had established itself there'. When this last had been done, the Institution was to be vacated and Heuston was to take over 'the Waiting Room of Guinness's Brewery at the corner of Watling Street in James's Street' and to establish contact with Ceannt in the South Dublin Union.

131. D. Ryan, *op. cit.*, p. 155. Note that P. J. Stephenson (*op. cit.*, pp. 21 f) says that on Monday evening Heuston questioned him about the streets leading from the Institution towards Thomas Street, that he appeared to be considering the possibility of moving southward from the Institution, and that he began preparations to evacuate the building—he went so far as to order his men to 'make for home'. The return of a messenger (Sean

22

MacLoughlin) who had earlier been sent to the G.P.O. and who brought the news that 'we had won hands down [and that] the whole city was in our hands' altered matters and Heuston ordered his men to go back to their posts.

132. Connolly's statement of 28 April, a copy of which was found on The O'Rahilly, and which was communicated by the military to the press—*Rebellion Handbook*, p. 43.

133. *Cf.* J. M. Heuston, *op. cit.*, p. 49 on this.

134. Communication between the insurgent posts was not very difficult up to Wednesday. The best accounts of how it was carried on are given by I. Callender (*Dublin Brigade Review*, pp. 88 ff—He acted as a messenger between Daly and Connolly and scouted for Daly. He went as far to the east as Westmoreland and D'Olier Streets, to the west as the South Dublin Union, and to the north as Broadstone Railway Station—to see if there was artillery there—on Wednesday) and Miss J. Grennan (The author is indebted for this information to Miss M. Comerford)—She bought food and brought it on Connolly's orders to the College of Surgeons on Tuesday. She carried a despatch from Connolly to Daly on Wednesday ordering the burning of Linenhall barracks, and she carried a message from Pearse for Friend on the same day protesting at alleged firing on the Red Cross). Miss M. Skinnider carried despatches between Mallin and Connolly. Another courier sent by Mallin to the G.P.O. at 3.0 p.m. on Wednesday failed to get beyond T.C.D.—R. M. Fox, *op. cit.*, p. 163. According to M. Caulfield, *The Easter Rebellion*, p. 223, Connolly sent a typed message to Lieut. Malone to 25 Northumberland Road (See p. 287) on Wednesday forenoon warning him that troops had landed at Kingstown during the night and ordering every effort to be made to deny them passage, should they try to come through Northumberland Road. See D. Lynch, *I.R.B.*, p. 167 for the departure of a car from the G.P.O. at 6.0 a.m. on Wednesday to collect fuses, etc. from Bride Street. After Wednesday, de Valera found communication with the G.P.O. unsatisfactory and was unable to assess the general situation—*Sunday Press*, 10 April 1966, p. 13.

135. D. Ryan, *op. cit.*, pp. 161 f.

136. R. M. Fox, *op. cit.*, pp. 169 f; *Fifty Years of Liberty Hall*, p. 70. But note the statement in R. McHugh, *op. cit.*, p. 164 regarding the scout who was sent from T.C.D. on Tuesday afternoon to see if Butt Bridge was occupied by the insurgents. He walked through Beresford Place, turned and walked back; he claimed that two shots were fired at him from Liberty Hall.

Studies in the History of the Rising

137. See *Rebellion Handbook*, p. 21 for the official, and probably the popular, attitude to Liberty Hall. When Birrell came to Ireland on Thursday he informed the government in London that it would be necessary—because of the stubborn resistance of the insurgents and to avoid heavy casualties among the troops—to employ artillery fire to demolish some houses so as to enable the troops to assault the main insurgent positions in O'Connell Street—L. Ó Broin, *Dublin Castle and the 1916 Rising*, pp. 116 f. In fact, this was not necessary.

138. Details in *Rebellion Handbook*, p. 22. D. Ryan, *op. cit.*, p. 140. Fr. J. Flanagan (R. McHugh, *op. cit.*, p. 190 and *Catholic Bulletin*, VIII, p. 405) records that the firing began at 8.0 a.m., when he claims to have heard the passage of shells over the Cathedral as he said Mass.

139. J. de Courcy Ireland, *The Sea and the Easter Rising*, pp. 38 ff, 45 f. There is nothing in the *Helga's* log (which Dr. de Courcy Ireland prints) to indicate any difficulty in laying the gun. The story of the lobbing of the shells over the Loop Line railway bridge seems to have originated with the newspapers—*Rebellion Handbook*, p. 22, where it is said that the gunners adopted 'a plan of dropping fire'; on the other hand, *The Daily Mirror*, 1 May 1916 says 'the gunner [of the *Helga*] had to lay his gun to fire under a river bridge and between some other buildings'. The gun seems to have fired under rather than over the bridge; its flat trajectory would almost certainly have made the lobbing of shells over the bridge and into Liberty Hall impossible.

140. Photographs of the damaged building in *Fifty Years of Liberty Hall*, following p. 40.

141. A. N. Bonaparte-Wyse found a military guard on the bridge later in the morning—*Irish Times*, 24 April 1965.

142. The Versailles government proclamation, of 28 May 1871, quoted in W. Gibson, *Paris during the Commune* (1871), p. 171.

143. It was strange that Plunkett did not, apparently, think of the Paris of 1871 when O'Connell Street was on fire. It was remembered that he said in the G.P.O. on Friday 'It is the first time it has happened since Moscow, the first time that a capital has been burnt since then'—D. Ryan, *op. cit.*, p. 151. There was also, of course, the parallel of the revolt in Prague in 1848.

144. For 'the final charge', the expected general assault with fixed bayonets in which, as Tom Clarke said, 'most of us will die', but which

never materialised, see J. Ryan, 'The G.P.O.' in *Capuchin Annual*, 1942, pp. 222 f and *Sunday Press*, 10 April 1966, p. 11. *Cf.* D. Ryan, *The Rising*, p. 139, who records that preparations were made in the G.P.O. to resist a gas attack. Each of the insurgent positions expected a general assault. S. O'Duffy of Daly's command says 'we could not understand why no enemy attack was made on our positions from the Royal military barracks' on Tuesday—*Sunday Press*, as quoted, p. 22. One of MacDonagh's first actions at Jacob's was to build a heavy barricade inside the main entrance—W. Stapleton in *Irish Independent, Golden Jubilee Supplement*, 1966, p. 10.

145. Statement of E. McDermott, *Daily Chronicle*, 29 April 1916. R. McHugh, *op. cit.* (L. Stokes's account), p. 69. The curve in Westmoreland and O'Connell Streets prevented the Trinity College gunners from firing on the G.P.O.

146. Abbey Street was swept from the Custom House, Marlborough Street from the Theatre Royal. See *Rebellion Handbook*, pp. 10, 13, 18. For O'Connell Street see S. MacEntee, *Episode at Easter* (1966), pp. 133 ff.

147. *Rebellion Handbook*, p. 10. R. Humphreys, 'A Rebel's Diary' in *The Belvederian*, XXI, No. 2 (Belvedere College Annual, 1966), p. 161. J. Stephens, *The Insurrection in Dublin*, pp. 40 ff. I. Callender, 'A Diary of Easter Week, 1916' in *Dublin Brigade Review*, p. 90.

148. The Irish Citizen Army starry plough flag (which is now in the National Museum, Dublin—as is the 'Irish Republic' flag from the G.P.O.) was hoisted over the Imperial Hotel at 7.0 a.m. on Wednesday, or perhaps the tricolour was hoisted there then and the I.C.A. flag later—D. Lynch, *I.R.B.*, pp. 89, 158, 167. For happenings in the G.P.O. on Wednesday see also *An tOglach*, IV, No. 2, pp. 3 ff (23 January 1926).

149. There was a military barricade across Lower Merrion Street at the corner of Clare Street, manned to face south—see contemporary photograph in National Museum, Dublin.

150. S. Geoghegan, *The Campaigns and History of the Royal Irish Regiment*, II, p. 103.

151. The armoured lorries which made their appearance 'by the score' (*Irish Independent*, 26-29 April, 1-4 May 1916—a very considerable exaggeration) in the streets on Wednesday (P. Holahan—*Capuchin Annual*, 1942, p. 234—saw one in Bolton Street on Wednesday) were designed by Colonel H. T. W. Allatt (C. Falls, *History of the First Seven Battalions The Royal Irish Rifles in the Great War*, II, p. 89), who was killed during the

Studies in the History of the Rising

week (*Rebellion Handbook*, p. 45). They were of two kinds, those made up from locomotive boilers and straight sided, box like structures; they were mounted on motor lorries supplied by Guinness's brewery and were constructed at Inchicore Railway Works. They were loopholed for rifle fire, many false 'holes' being painted on to confuse insurgent snipers.

152. D. Lynch, *op. cit.*, p. 169.

153. I. Callender (*op. cit.*, p. 94) found troops at the Capel Street end of Abbey Street on Wednesday evening, but he brought despatches from Daly into the G.P.O. by Cole's Lane and Moore Street, and came out again.

154. D. Lynch, *op. cit.*, p. 170.

155. Manifesto dated 28 April 1916 (*Rebellion Handbook*, pp. 43 f; for the mistake in the dating of this document see Note 29 above). D. Ryan, *op. cit.*, p. 144, believed that the manifesto was issued on Friday.

156. Maxwell, *Report, Rebellion Handbook*, p. 161. G. French, *Life of F.M. Sir John French*, p. 339. The remainder of the 59th Division, a battery of Stokes' mortars and 10,000 hand grenades were sent to Ireland on Wednesday afternoon and the 60th Division was held in readiness. For the shipping arrangements see the article by G. C. Duggan referred to in Note 95.

157. D. Ryan, *op. cit.*, p. 193 mistakenly speaks of three columns instead of two. M. Caulfield, *op. cit.*, p. 219 is in error in saying that both columns were marching to the Royal Hospital.

158. '*The Robin Hoods*' *1/7th, 2/7th & 3/7th Battns. Sherwood Foresters*, p. 282.

159. *Ibid.*, p. 283. But note that the regimental history is at pains to disprove a contemporary newspaper statement that the column was ambushed.

160. For the action see *An Cosantoir*, XXVI, pp. 241 ff; J. McCann, *War by the Irish* (1946), pp. 46 ff; M. Caulfield, *op. cit.*, pp. 208, 219–228, 243–267; D. Ryan, *op. cit.*, pp. 196 ff; and (the most detailed account) *The Catholic Bulletin*, VII (1917), pp. 639 ff, 695 ff, 767 ff. A. N. Bonaparte-Wyse (*Irish Times*, 24 April 1965), who witnessed the struggle, says that when the insurgents first opened fire 'the whole regiment fell back to Ballsbridge in a fearful stampede' and 'I must say this first attack was badly bungled'.

161. Miss L. Stokes in R. McHugh, *op. cit.*, pp. 69 f.

162. Regimental history as quoted in Note 158. The battalion later claimed (p. 290) that they were, when passing through the Dublin streets, under fire from air guns; bullets came soundlessly through the air. This was perhaps the worst case of the ubiquitous-sniper complex, a complex displayed by all the troops.

163. It is sometimes said (See, for example, the popular account in A. V. Sellwood, *The Red-Gold Flame*, pp. 102 ff) that all Fane's difficulties were due to his having been misinformed regarding the school. The 7th Battalion regimental history makes it clear that Fane believed that the school was occupied by the insurgents, but certainly does not indicate that the school was all-important.

164. Maxwell, *Report, Rebellion Handbook*, p. 162.

165. See a reply to the most recent of these suggestions, *Irish Times*, 7 May 1966.

166. The 2/4th and 2/5th Lincolnshire Regiment (177th Brigade) and the 2/5th North Staffordshire Regiment (176th Brigade) were also in Lower Mount Street on the night of Wednesday-Thursday—W. Meakin, *The 5th North Staffords and the North Midland Territorials* (1920), p. 72. The Staffords, according to Meakin, had 'instructions to advance as best they could to Dublin Castle', but it took them two days—due entirely to an excess of caution, for there was nothing but perhaps a few snipers in their way to reach Trinity College. The fact that the insurgents held the College of Surgeons, remote though it was from the streets between Mount Street Bridge and the city centre, seems to have accounted for much of this caution.

167. C. Falls, *op. cit.*, p. 89, mistakes it for 'a supply column from the Curragh'.

168. F. Vane, *Agin the Governments*, p. 270. Two R.I.C. constables who were attending an N.C.O. instruction school in Portobello barracks were with Vane. One was killed, the other wounded—*Rebellion Handbook*, p. 50.

169. M. Caulfield, *op. cit.*, pp. 282 ff, draws on information supplied by the two officers of the 2/8th Battalion who were involved. See also *The Catholic Bulletin*, VIII, pp. 309 f.

170. Described by Miss L. O'Brennan, who was present, in *An Cosantoir*,

Studies in the History of the Rising

XXVI, pp. 340 ff. C. Duff, *Six Days to Shake an Empire*, pp. 135, 154 f, 160 (who is guilty of many military errors) is under the impression that the South Dublin Union was 'a centre of fighting' throughout the week.

171. Memorandum by E. MacNeill, February 1916, in F.X. Martin, 'Eoin MacNeill on the 1916 Rising', *Irish Historical Studies*, XII, p. 236. See L. Ó Briain, *Cuimhní Cinn*, p. 163 for Mallin's criticism of the plan for the Rising on the ground that there was no alternative plan.

172. Miss Skinnider's statement—*Irish Press*, supplement, 9 April 1966, p. 12. Statement of Countess Markievicz—R. McHugh, *op. cit.*, p. 124. See R. M. Fox, *op. cit.*, pp. 159 ff and *Catholic Bulletin*, VIII, p. 504, 551 f for sorties and proposed sorties from the College of Surgeons.

173. P. Béaslaí, *Michael Collins and the Making of a New Ireland*, I, p. 101, regards it as a defect that the Volunteers had not occupied Capel Street from the start so that headquarters might have fallen back on 1st Battalion.

174. Brought there from Kingstown (Dun Laoghaire) on Wednesday evening and taken by the Sherwood Foresters to the Royal Hospital on Thursday.

175. J. de Courcy Ireland, *op. cit.*, p. 46. The *Helga* fired between 12.15 p.m. and 12.30. For de Valera's having drawn fire to an unoccupied distillery by hoisting a flag there see Earl of Longford and T. P. O'Neill, 'De Valera in the Easter Rising', *Sunday Telegraph*, 27 March 1966, p. 6.

176. Information of B. Stapleton, one of the cyclists—*Irish Independent Golden Jubilee Supplement, 1966*, p. 10. *The Catholic Bulletin*, VIII, pp. 455 f, says that this party (said to have gone on Saturday) was sent out in response to a message from de Valera requesting ammunition, and that its purpose was to reconnoitre. MacDonagh had earlier sent food to the College of Surgeons, whence his men returned with O.T.C. rifles—P. Ó Cearnaigh in S. de Burca, *The Soldier's Song*, p. 122. For other local movements of men from Jacob's see D. Ryan, *The Rising*, p. 167. The troops were very nervous in Merrion Square on Friday—J. Stephens, *The Insurrection in Dublin*, p. 53.

177. The time is fixed by an entry in the diary of Joseph Holloway, who was close by in Cavendish Row—excerpt from the original, which is in the National Library of Ireland, in *Irish Press*, supplement, 9 April 1966, p. 7. *An tÓglach*, IV, No. 2, p. 4 (23 January 1926), agrees, and notes that no direct hit was scored on the G.P.O. on Thursday. S. MacEntee, *Episode at Easter*, pp. 138 f, says however: 'About three o'clock the big guns scored

The Making of 1916

their first notable hit when shrapnel fire carried away the flagstaff from which the Republican flag [that is, the tricolour—B. Lynch, *I.R.B.*, p. 158] flew over the Henry Street corner of the G.P.O. A little later a shell struck the corner of the Metropole Hotel, and a minute after that another struck the balustrade of the G.P.O., and carried a large part of it away. After this there were a few more close shots but no more hits.' J. Stephens, *op. cit.*, p. 47, heard heavy gunfire in the O'Connell Street direction at 11.30 a.m. S. Geoghegan, *Campaigns and History of the Royal Irish Regiment*, II, p. 103, mentions the positioning of an 18-pounder at the Parnell Monument. D. Lynch, *op. cit.*, p. 173, says that the erection of a barricade in Middle Abbey Street was prevented by artillery fire—apparently from a second gun, probably the gun that shelled the Lower Abbey Street (Wynne's Hotel) barricade—*Irish Independent*, 26–29 April, 1–4 May 1916. It seems to be incorrect to say that buildings were blasted or burnt to give a field for gunfire—Pearse made this statement in the bulletin dated 28 April 1916 (*Rebellion Handbook*, pp. 43 f). The difficulty of the gunners in using their 18-pounders against the insurgents in the narrow confines of O'Connell Street and the surrounding streets was certainly very great and if the struggle had been continued they might have been forced to clear a field for their fire. Any obstruction of a greater height than twelve or so feet between gun and target would have made a hit impossible. The 18-pounder field guns could not have fired *over* intervening buildings. The ammunition used appears to have been largely high explosive shell, which, on bursting, would have had an incendiary effect; but shrapnel, which was an anti-personnel charge, was used to clear the roof of the G.P.O., and smoke shell, which was an incendiary projectile with a phosphorus charge, may also have been used and may have been the shell referred to in Note 196.

178. Pearse claimed on Thursday afternoon 'that K. has succeeded in overturning the armoured car [the one in Henry Street] with a bomb'— R. Humphreys in *The Belvederian*, XXI, p. 162. There seems to be no other reference to this. Humphreys also says that 'two howitzers' were mounted near Findlater's Church.

179. D. Lynch, *op. cit.*, p. 174. N. Connolly O'Brien, *Portrait of a Rebel Father* (1935), p. 318. D. Ryan, *op. cit.*, p. 146. Dr. J. Ryan in *Capuchin Annual*, 1942, p. 223. Connolly claimed to have been shot by a sniper. The British were in Upper Abbey Street, where they had built a barricade near the entrance to Jervis Street Hospital by Friday—Fr. J. Flanagan in R. McHugh, *op. cit.*, p. 193.

180. D. Lynch, *op. cit.*, pp. 173, 175.

Studies in the History of the Rising

181. Maxwell, *Report, Rebellion Handbook*, p. 162. The area between the line Kingsbridge-T.C.D. and the river was full of troops on Thursday— P. Holahan in *Capuchin Annual*, 1942, pp. 234 f (a party fired on at Usher's Quay); I. Callender in *Dublin Brigade Review*, p. 94 (troops sandbagged at the ends of Watling and Bridgefoot Streets); *Rebellion Handbook*, p. 220 (no longer possible for civilians to move about in Westmoreland Street area).

182. The lancers and the ammunition convoy were rescued from Charles Street at this time.

183. *Cf.* W. Meakin, *op. cit.*, p. 72, who, in describing the use of the armoured lorries, says 'the way of fighting was peculiar'.

184. Report of Captain Purcell, Dublin fire chief, given to the press— *Rebellion Handbook*, pp. 27 ff. R. Humphreys, *op. cit.*, p. 163. S. MacEntee, *op. cit.*, pp. 139 ff. *An tÓglach*, IV, No. 2 (23 January 1926), p. 5. It is widely accepted, following Pearse's statement (See Note 177 above), that the British 'burnt down whole blocks of houses' so as to gain 'a clear field' for artillery fire, but there is no evidence that the fires were started with this intention, and the clear field was not gained. In fact, the shells of the burnt bnildings, which were in themselves obstructions, stood until after the surrender, and there is no reference to the guns having been placed anywhere save in the streets. The damage caused to buildings by gunfire (other than that from incendiary shells or high explosive shells which had an incendiary effect) was not great; the external walls of the G.P.O. as seen in the post-surrender photographs appear almost untouched. L. N. Le Roux, *Patrick H. Pearse*, p. 386 (The British did not hesitate 'to burn down the buildings facing and adjacent' to the G.P.O. so as 'to expose the edifice to artillery fire') is far more guilty of exaggeration than G. Arthur, *General Sir John Maxwell*, p. 250 ('Except for the bombardment of Liberty Hall . . . guns were scarcely used, and only when sniping could not be mastered by machine-guns or rifle fire was a round of shell called into requisition'). For Connolly's belief that capitalist property would not be shelled see Le Roux, *op. cit.*, p. 385 and D. Ryan, *James Connolly*, p. 126. The fires were clearly a result of the activities of the military, but it has not been proven that they were all deliberately caused.

185. On Thursday about 6.50 p.m. there was 'a loud explosion, which we believe was a shell' and Clery's and the Imperial Hotel went on fire. The Volunteers who held this building crossed to the G.P.O. 'under a rain of machine-gun and rifle fire'—Report of a tramway man who was in his office in O'Connell Street then—*Irish Independent*, 26–29 April, 1–4 May 1916. *Cf.* B. O'Higgins in *Wolfe Tone Annual*, 1935, pp. 70 f and S. MacEntee, *op. cit.*, pp. 140 ff.

186. See *An tOglach, loc. cit.* for Connolly's efforts to extend his posts along Henry Street; he was aware that the troops in Parnell and Capel Streets were threatening his flank.

187. It was announced on Thursday night that there were 10,000 (F. A. McKenzie, *op. cit.*, p. 81), but the total seems to have been somewhat greater.

188. C. Falls, *The First World War*, p. 143.

189. G. Arthur, *op. cit.*, p. 247. G. French, *Life of F.M. Sir John French*, p. 339.

190. Maxwell, *Report, Rebellion Handbook*, p. 162.

191. C. Falls (report of lecture, *Irish Times*, 2 May 1966) speaks of Maxwell as the author of the plan which suppressed the Rising. G. Arthur (*op. cit.*, pp. 249, 252) makes the same claim. He was not; he merely followed the existing plan. They were aware of Maxwell's arrival in the G.P.O. on Friday morning—R. Humphreys in *The Belvederian*, 1966, p. 164.

192. D. Lynch, *I.R.B.*, p. 175.

193. The document which was found in the O'Rahilly's pocket after his death—*Rebellion Handbook*, p. 42. It was communicated to the press at the time; the original is not forthcoming. The 'files' were not, apparently, brought out from the G.P.O. and the recorded insurgent documents are merely strays. An anonymous British officer whose account of the courts martial is in *Irish Press*, supplement, 9 April 1966, p. 15 says that the insurgent documents used there were very few.

194. D. Lynch, *op. cit.*, p. 176.

195. *Ibid., op cit.*, p. 178.

196. It seems impossible to fix the time of the commencement of the fire. R. Humphreys (*loc. cit.*) says that about 3.30 p.m. 'a differently-noted fusillade rings out from the Gresham hotel direction'—these were the smoke or incendiary shells—and that 'the side of the walls where the bullets lodge seem to flash into flame'; the roof is soon on fire; the flames are for a time controlled, but later they spread. S. MacEntee (*Episode at Easter*, pp. 155 ff) seems to time the commencement as about 3.0 p.m. *An tOglach* (23 January 1926) says that the fire followed the explosion of a

shell over the portico about 3.0 p.m. D. Ryan (*The Rising*, p. 152) says that the first fire broke out at 1.0 p.m. and was mastered; another followed the bursting of an incendiary over the portico at 3.0. Fr. J. Flanagan (*Catholic Bulletin*, VIII, p. 407) says that the first incendiary shell fell on 'the roof of the parapet' about 4.0. The tramway official (*Irish Independent*, 26–29 April, 1–4 May 1916) says 'First a shell struck the northern corner parapet and started a fire, which the Volunteers put out. Then another shell at about 5.30 p.m. struck the Prince's Street corner and started the fire which burned the place.' Joseph Holloway (*Irish Press*, supplement, 9 April 1966, p. 7) says 'About 5 o'clock the roof of the G.P.O. took fire.'

197. S. MacEntee, who formed one of the advance guard, says (*op. cit.*, p. 160) that Pearse told them that their task was 'to secure possession of the factory belonging to Williams and Woods in Parnell Street and to hold that position until the main body came up.' Corroboration in D. Ryan, *op. cit.*, p. 153. See also R. Humphreys, *op. cit.*, p. 165; D. Lynch, *op. cit.*, p. 180; and S. F. Lemass in *Studies*, LV, p. 8 (Spring, 1966).

198. D. Ryan, *loc. cit.* B. O'Higgins in *Wolfe Tone Annual*, 1935, p. 73.

199. J. Ryan in *Capuchin Annual*, 1942, p. 225. B. O'Higgins, *loc. cit.*

200. Of contemporary documentary information there appears to be nothing later than the entry of Friday in Plunkett's message book: 'Signal to Imperial . . . Cut way to Liffey Street . . . Order to remain at posts unless summoned. Barricades in front.'

201. S. MacEntee (*loc. cit.*) says 25 files (of two ranks). D. Ryan (*loc. cit.*) says 40 men. J. Ryan (*op. cit.*, p. 224) says half a company.

202. Maxwell, *Report, Rebellion Handbook*, p. 162. P. Holahan's statement (*Capuchin Annual*, 1942, p. 235) that the plan to cordon the Four Courts area 'took shape' on Wednesday is probably derived from the fact that the troops occupied Capel Street then. Maxwell told *The Daily Mail* on 18 May 1916 (*Rebellion Handbook*, p. 212) that it was discovered when the G.P.O. had been cordoned that 'there was another centre of importance at the Four Courts,' and that it was determined to encircle that also. But the general disposition of the insurgents on the north side was known earlier in the week. Maxwell was being cautious in his statements, following the happenings in North King Street.

203. '*The Robin Hoods*' 1/7th, 2/7th & 3/7th Battns. *Sherwood Foresters*, p. 290. See p. 300.

204. See the reports of the coroner's inquests of 12 and 16 May 1916 in *Rebellion Handbook*, pp. 210 ff. Note the exaggeration of the military difficulties. Maxwell's explanation is given *Ibid.*, p. 212. Statements of relatives of deceased men are in R. McHugh, *Dublin 1916*, pp. 220 ff. There is much evidence of the nervousness shown by the troops throughout the week—see D. Ryan, *op. cit.*, p. 162; L. Ó Broin, *Dublin Castle and the 1916 Rising*, pp. 110, 116 (shrapnel shell bursting in Phoenix Park 'where it was not meant to do' and causing 'excited young soldiers' to open fire; Birrell being told on his arrival in Dublih that there were snipers in civilian clothes all over the city); and the comments of Professor G. O'Neill, S.J. in R. McHugh, *op. cit.*, pp. 187, 189 ('The soldiers were badly led, and extremely "jumpy" ').

205. Maxwell, *Report, Rebellion Handbook*, p. 162. S. Geoghegan, *op. cit.*, II, p. 104. J. Ryan (*Sunday Press*, 10 April 1966, p. 11) speaks of the fire at this time of 'a big gun, a much bigger one than those we had become accustomed to'—perhaps it sounded bigger because it was nearer.

206. E. O'Farrell in *The Catholic Bulletin*, VII, pp. 265 ff, 329 ff. Maxwell, *loc. cit.*, times Pearse's surrender as 2.0 p.m. E. O'Farrell says about 3.30, but this must be too late, since Pearse signed the surrender order at Irish Command headquarters at 3.45. See also J. Grennan in *Catholic Bulletin*, VII, pp. 396 ff and *Wolfe Tone Annual*, 1935, pp. 18 ff. For letters written by Lowe to Pearse prior to the surrender see *Irish Independent*, 21 April 1965, reprinted in M. Ó Dubhghaill, *Insurrection Fires at Eastertide*, pp. 266 ff.

207. G. Arthur, *op. cit.*, p. 248.

208. P. S. O'Hegarty, *Ireland under the Union*, pp. 170 f. When MacNeill and Connolly spoke of insurrection in January 1916 Connolly spoke of a plan of revolt in which 'the main blow was to be struck in Dublin by the seizure of certain large buildings' and said that he believed 'this would galvanize the country to a general uprising against the government'. MacNeill replied 'You simply cannot see over the tops of the houses'— F. X. Martin, 'Eoin MacNeill on the 1916 Rising' in *Irish Historical Studies*, XII, p. 252.

209. F. O'Donoghue, *Tomás MacCurtain*, p. 65, says that the Cork Brigade was to occupy positions from Newmarket to the Boggeragh mountains, linking with the Limerick Volunteers to the north and the Kerry Volunteers to the west. One notices that the Corkmen would, in this position, have been astride the main Kerry railway line.

210. D. Ryan, *op. cit.*, pp. 79 ff.

211. J. A. Gubbins and A. J. O'Halloran, 'Limerick's projected role in Easter Week, 1916' in J. M. MacCarthy (*ed.*), *Limerick's Fighting Story*, pp. 31 ff, give details.

212. *Irish Independent*, 21 February 1966; 18 March 1966; and *Golden Jubilee Supplement*, 1966, p. 23. McCullough brought 132 men to Tyrone, but, finding 'complete confusion' there, sent them back to Belfast on Easter Sunday.

213. R. Brennan, *Allegiance*, p. 51.

214. *Clonmel Easter Monday, 1966 Commemoration* programme, pp. 10 f, 20.

215. S. MacEntee, *op. cit.*, pp. 69 f, 117.

216. D. Ryan, *The Rising*, pp. 85 ff, and *cf.* p. 79, where he refers to a more widespread movement by country Volunteers towards Dublin. Note however the statement (J. A. Gubbins and A. J. O'Halloran, *op. cit.*, p. 37) in regard to Limerick that 'no plans existed other than for [German] arms reception, transport and distribution'. Note too that MacNeill mentions (F. X. Martin, *op. cit.*, p. 266) as places to which he sent countermanding orders Cork, Limerick, Galway, Waterford, Wexford, Tralee and Tyrone, and that all these save Waterford are either places mentioned for proposed operations or places where, in fact, operations took place; but he sent countermanding orders elsewhere as well.

217. D. Ryan, *op. cit.*, pp. 79, 229.

218. *Ibid.*, p. 80.

219. The activities of the 5th Dublin Battalion, to be mentioned in a moment, form—perhaps because its strength was so small—an exception to this. See an interesting commentary by the flying column leader of 1920–21, Comdt.-General T. Barry, in *Irish Press*, 11 April, 1966. Barry holds that the absence of a known plan for a general rising suggests that the insurgent leaders accepted the fact that action was unlikely outside Dublin. He criticises the arrangements for the landing and distribution of the arms cargo.

220. *Sunday Press*, 10 April 1966, p. 13.

The Making of 1916

221. P. Ó Cearnaigh in S. de Burca, *The Soldier's Song*, p. 129. *Cf.* W. Stapleton in *Irish Independent Golden Jubilee Supplement, 1966*, p. 11.

222. 200 men of the North Staffordshire Regiment were sent by destroyer from Kingstown (Dun Laoghaire) on Wednesday (Maxwell, *Report*, p. 163 says Thursday) to Skerries to reinforce the guard on the Marconi station there—*Rebellion Handbook*, p. 33. Cavalry (6th Reserve Regiment from Marlborough barracks?) were in Dunboyne on Tuesday (S. MacEntee, *op. cit.*, p. 118). Cathal Brugha said in 1922 (as interpreted by D. Ryan, *op. cit.*, p. 229) that it was intended that a line should be left open for the retreat of the Dublin insurgents through Cabra and Phibsboro to the country. There is no indication of this in the north side dispositions, nor do the 5th Battalion movements conform.

223. Colonel J. V. Lawless, who was present at Ashbourne, in *An Cosantoir*, I, Nos. 24 and 25 (1941), and VI, No. 11 (1946). *An tÓglach*, V, No. 4, 31 July 1926. D. Ryan, *op. cit.*, pp. 218 ff.

224. Recorded in the *Laburnum's* log—J. de Courcy Ireland, *op. cit.*, pp. 44, 47. It seems extraordinary—and must be evidence of panic—that the sloop fired blindly into an inhabited area. The log does not indicate that the rounds were blanks. The author recollects that, during the fire, a signaller transmitted a message—apparently to the sloop—from the roof of the Railway Hotel; he could not have been spotting for the fall of shell, since there was nothing to fire at—the Volunteers who were engaged at Carnmore had long since gone to Athenry to join Mellows.

225. For the Rising in Co. Galway see M. Dolan, 'The 1916 Rising in Co. Galway' in *Connacht Tribune*, 2 March to 7 May 1966; Gaillimheach, 'Galway and the 1916 Rising' in *An tÓglach*, V, No. 2 (new series, February 1933), pp. 1 ff; A. Monaghan's account in *Irish Independent Golden Jubilee Supplement, 1966*, p. 13; D. Ryan, *The Rising*, pp. 244 ff, 265 ff; *Rebellion Handbook*, pp. 32, 133 ff; I. O., *The Administration of Ireland, 1920*, p. 29; *Royal Commission. Evidence*, pp. 76, 78; J. de Courcy Ireland, *op. cit.*, p. 46.

226. For the Enniscorthy operations see diary of Captain S. Etchingham published in *Cois na Sláinghe* (Enniscorthy Gaelic League, 1941); statement of Captain S. Ó Dubhghaill in *Irish Independent Golden Jubilee Supplement, 1966*, p. 19; R. Brennan, *Allegiance*, pp. 56 ff, 64; D. Ryan, *op. cit.*, pp. 249 f; *Royal Commission. Evidence*, pp. 82 f (which states that the strength of the troops assembled in Wexford was 1,100 infantry, 70 cavalry, two field guns and a 4.7 inch gun, but that 'not a single shot was fired'); letter from Colonel French, O.C., Wexford, who received the surrender and holograph surrender order from Pearse in National Museum of Ireland;

Studies in the History of the Rising

Dail Debates, LXXXVII, columns 2322 f. For information about the impact of the Rising on the Volunteers in other areas see D. Ryan, *op. cit.*, pp. 228 ff. Cork was reinforced from England on 30 April by a battalion of the 179th Brigade, 60th Division (and later by the remainder of the brigade) and a battalion of Royal Marines—Maxwell, *Report, Rebellion Handbook*, p. 163.

227. The government publication *Oidhreacht* (1966), p. 18 gives 62 killed. John Devoy said on 20 July 1916—with much exaggeration—'Only 1,500 men fought in Dublin and they held up an army of 20,000 or 25,000 Britishers for a whole week . . . our fellows had only 103 killed and wounded. The English had 2,700'—*Documents relative to the Sinn Fein Movement* (H.M.S.O., 1921), p. 20. It has been calculated that 50,000 Irishmen were killed in the first world war.

228. The official totals of combined insurgent and civilian casualties are 318 killed and 2,217 wounded—*Ibid.*, p. 14.

229. *Ibid., loc. cit.*, G. Arthurs, *ob. cit.* p. 252, gives 108 killed and 334 wounded. The British losses in the 21 days fighting which ended in Sir Colin Campbell's capture of Lucknow in 1857 were 735 killed and wounded. The battle of Tel-el-Kebir was won in 1882 with a British casualty list of 469, 57 of them fatal. General Richard O'Connor in the three days' fighting of his first offensive against the Italians in North Africa in 1940 destroyed four divisions and captured 38,000 prisoners for a total British loss, killed, wounded and missing, of 624.

230. *Rebellion Handbook*, pp. 43 f.

231. L. N. Le Roux, *Patrick H. Pearse*, p. 394, quotes a similar statement, said to have been made by Pearse on Friday: the fact that the insurgents had been able to hold out so long with 1,000 men proved that if they had had 2,000 and if there had been a rising in the country which would have threatened the British forces encircling the Dublin positions and would have reinforced the Dublin insurgents 'we would have won'.

232. *Irish Times*, supplement, 7 April 1966, p. 1.

233. D. Ryan, *The Rising*, p. 83.

The author is much indebted for their kind assistance in providing valuable information to Oliver Snoddy, M.A., National Museum of Ireland, Miss Maire Comerford and Major H. E. D. Harris. He also wishes to acknowledge his indebtedness to Captain Kevin Danaher for technical assistance in regard to the artillery practice of the week of the Rising. He has benefited greatly by many conversations with the late Major Florence O'Donoghue, the pioneer of objective studies, not only of the Rising but of the martial events of the years which followed, and he also wishes to thank the General Editor Professor K. B. Nowlan and Mr. Pádraig Ó Murchadha, Department of Defence for many most helpful suggestions. Although the help of others has, the author hopes, reduced the number of errors which his work must—alas—still contain, responsibility for expressions of opinion and for interpretations of evidence remains, of course, entirely his own.

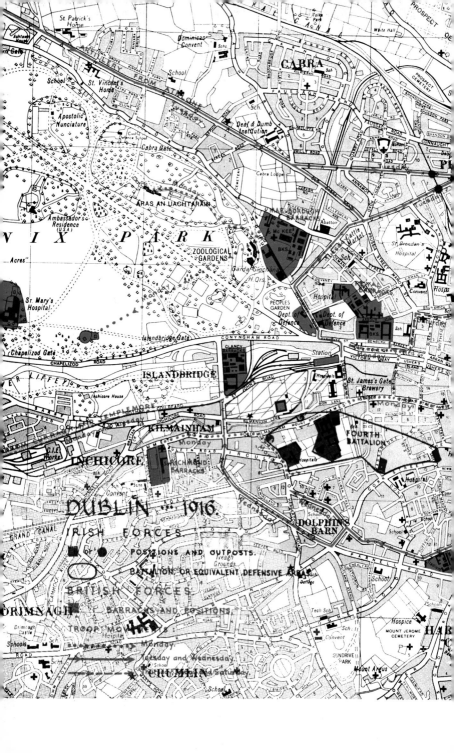

DUBLIN :: 1916.

IRISH FORCES

POSITIONS AND OUTPOSTS.

BATTALION OR EQUIVALENT DEFENSIVE AREA.

BRITISH FORCES

BARRACKS AND POSITIONS.

TROOP MOVEMENTS: Monday.
                 Tuesday and Wednesday.

Based on the Ordnance Survey by permission of the Government (Permit No. 942).

This map is reproduced by kind permission of the Editor of
The Irish Sword, Journal of The Military History Society of Ireland.